No space of their own

NO SPACE OF
THEIR OWN

Young people and social control in Australia

ROB WHITE

Western Australian College of Advanced Education

The right of the
University of Cambridge
to print and sell
all manner of books
was granted by
Henry VIII in 1534.
The University has printed
and published continuously
since 1584.

Cambridge
New York   Port Chester   Melbourne   Sydney

CAMBRIDGE UNIVERSITY PRESS
Cambridge, New York, Melbourne, Madrid, Cape Town,
Singapore, São Paulo, Delhi, Tokyo, Mexico City

Cambridge University Press
The Edinburgh Building, Cambridge CB2 8RU, UK

Published in the United States of America by Cambridge University Press, New York

www.cambridge.org
Information on this title: www.cambridge.org/9780521377782

© Cambridge University Press 1990

First published 1990
Re-issued 2011

A catalogue record for this publication is available from the British Library

Library of Congress Cataloguing in Publication Data:

White, R. D. (Robert Douglas), 1956–
   No space of their own.
   Includes bibliographical references.
   1. Youth – Australia.   I. Title.
HQ799.A8W48 1990   305.23'5'0994   89-71182

ISBN 978-0-521-37423-1 Hardback
ISBN 978-0-521-37778-2 Paperback

For my grandmother
and my parents

Contents

Figures and tables

Acknowledgements

Many people have contributed their ideas and opinions to the writing of this book. From pubs to loungerooms, conference venues to youth centres, lecture halls to personal interviews, I have had the good fortune of discussing and debating all manner of 'youth issues' with teachers, youth workers, academics and young people who are directly involved in youth affairs. The sheer number of individuals and groups who helped shape this project precludes me from attempting to acknowledge each of them. To all of these people I can but offer in a very general way my sincere thanks for the assistance they provided at various stages and at various times over the last couple of years.

As the book began to take a concrete form, three people in particular were especially instrumental in its development and I wish to highlight their contributions to the project. Mike Presdee is a close colleague and friend and his wonderful ability to get to the nub of the issues and eloquently record broad policy trends and the personal feelings and responses of young people has been an inspiration to me. His work and advice has provided an excellent model for critical social science research which attempts to be dynamic, exciting, relevant and useful. I am indebted to Mike for the enthusiasm, creative talent and critical abilities which he consistently shows in his own work and which have contributed so greatly to my own thoughts and ideas in this area.

The many, many conversations with Gill Westhorp, particularly when she was working with the Youth Affairs Council of South

Australia, were a crucial part of gaining first-hand knowledge of what is going on in youth affairs. Gill's advice, criticism and support has had a major impact on my perceptions and evaluations of the current state of youth policy and the major issues affecting young people. I thank her for her willingness to discuss the 'hard' issues at length, her patience and her sense of humour.

Much of this book could not have been written without the continual support of and critical feedback provided by Lisa Macdonald. In addition to commenting on the final draft, Lisa played a critical role in shaping the general outline and argument of the book. Although professing not to know much about the specific issues affecting young people, she was instrumental in helping me make sense of the general trends in Australian society, of which young people are only one part, and for this I am very grateful.

Finally, I wish to acknowledge the support provided by Robin Derricourt and Karen McVicker at Cambridge University Press and the editorial help provided by Janet Mackenzie as the book entered its final production stages.

To these people and others who have assisted me in some way my generous thanks are due. While I have tried to do justice to their contributions and perspectives, the final responsibility for the book is of course mine.

Rob White

Abbreviations

ASWU	Australian Social Welfare Union
ABC	Australian Broadcasting Corporation
ACTU	Australian Council of Trade Unions
AEDP	Aboriginal Employment Development Policy
ALP	Australian Labor Party
ATS	Australian Traineeship Scheme
AUS	Australian Union of Students
BLIPS	Basic Learning in Primary Schools (programme)
CEP	Community Employment Programme
CES	Commonwealth Employment Service
CITY	Community Improvement Through Youth
CPI	Consumer Price Index
CRAFT	Commonwealth Rebate for Apprentice Full-time Training
CTP	Community Training Programme
CVP	Community Volunteer Programme
CYSS	Community Youth Support Scheme
DEET	Department of Employment, Education and Training
ESL	English as a Second Language
EPAC	Economic Planning Advisory Council
EPUY	Education Programme for Unemployed Youth
IYY	International Youth Year

NEAT	National Employment And Training (scheme)
NDP	Nuclear Disarmament Party
NOLS	National Organisation of Labor Students
NUS	National Union of Students
OECD	Organisation for Economic Co-operation and Development
PEP	Participation and Equity Programme
REDS	Regional Employment Development Scheme
SWTP	School to Work Transition Programme
SYETP	Special Youth Employment Training Programme
TAFE	Technical And Further Education
TDC	Trade Development Council
WPP	Wage Pause Programme
YAN	Youth Advocacy Network
YACA	Youth Affairs Council of Australia
YMCA	Young Men's Christian Association
YTP	Youth Training Programme
YWCA	Young Women's Christian Association

Introduction

This book is about young people in Australia. It examines the impact of contemporary social and economic trends and policies on young people, and explores the experiences of different categories of young people (working-class, young women, Aborigines) in the context of greater economic hardship and increasing controls on their behaviour and activities.

The theme of the book is that current attempts to regulate and control the lives of young people, and in particular those who have been most disadvantaged by the economic crisis, are ill-conceived, ad hoc in nature and inappropriate to the needs of Australian young people. Developments in the areas of welfare and employment, education, training, policing and community work are examined in order to show tensions and problems experienced by young people in an era characterised by a collapse of the teenage job market and a further decline in the adult job market.

While the specific content of the book is based upon the situation within which young people find themselves in South Australia and Australia generally, the major concerns addressed are common to most advanced capitalist countries. Whether in Adelaide, London, New York or Montreal, the transition from young person to 'adult' is increasingly a broken one. In societies where wages for labour are a central measure of social value as well as a key means of social participation, young working-class people are systematically being excluded from meaningful paid work. They are also being prevented from claiming their rights as citizens and human beings to income support, freedom of movement, personal security and deciding for themselves where their future lies. This phenomenon of 'exclusion' is one which cuts across national boundaries. While political leaders are anxious to be seen to be doing something about the 'youth problem', in most industrialised nations this has, in practice, been accompanied by an active cutback in resources that directly affect the quality of life for young people and their future life chances.

The broken transitions experienced by young people are many and varied in nature. Excluded from waged work, many are being forced into a new dependency on the parental home or on to the streets to join the growing ranks of the homeless. Those who are persuaded or coerced back to school or into a training programme find that to be a student is to be poor, and this state of affairs is compounded because fewer educational resources are being made available and there is minimal provision in the way of skill training. Out of (paid) work, and reliant on meagre state handouts, many young people are being forced to use their 'spare time' in new ways to escape chronic boredom and persistent money worries. When they attempt to move beyond individual solutions to their circumstances to voice their concerns collectively, young people are finding that here too, in the realm of 'politics', they are relegated to the backbenches of policy development and social change.

The year 1988 was the Australian Bicentennial and was supposed to be the 'celebration of a nation'. Aborigines were not the only people to find little to celebrate, however. Young working-class people of both sexes and from a variety of ethnic backgrounds also had little to cheer about in the midst of the politically constructed, media-driven nationalist sentiment and self-congratulation. Pushed to the margins of Australian society, young people are losing any material or cultural space of their own to express themselves, to develop their own creative talents and to gain a measure of financial and social independence.

Instead, their lives are increasingly marked by new forms of social control being imposed upon them. These range from financial and administrative measures designed to keep them occupied and off the street, to campaigns designed to regulate their behaviour in the 'public sphere' while simultaneously putting pressure on them to conform to certain ways of behaving in the 'private sphere' of the parental home. Training and education programmes are being implemented or manipulated in ways which are directed at maximising the self-discipline of, and discipline over, young people. Part of this process involves narrowing the scope for the development of critical thinking skills in lieu of a greater emphasis on narrow 'practical' skills.

The situation within which young people find themselves is directly related to wider political and economic developments occurring in the advanced capitalist countries. Fundamental changes are taking place in the international economy, and therefore in domestic national economies, and also in the nature of the state in Western liberal democracies. In the context of a transformation in production and consumption relations, a drastic restructuring of the world economic system along new international divisions of labour, and the search for new capital investment outlets by transnational corporations, political relations in the West could not but be significantly affected. Governments facing huge budget deficits are simultaneously confronted by the threat of big capital 'going on strike' and taking their business elsewhere if certain conditions are not met. At the same time, the social fallout from the economic crisis – homelessness, unemployment, poverty, crime – is draining an ever larger proportion of state funds. As the crisis has grown, so too have the needs of those caught without the resources to weather the storm.

The emergence of right-wing pragmatism as a central feature of 'social democractic' governments in Australia and New Zealand, the entrenched position of 'conservatives' in the United States, Britain and Canada, and the rapid rise and high profile of 'New Right' thinktanks and organisations throughout the advanced capitalist countries are inextricably bound up with the economic crisis of the international economic system. During the 1980s, chronic unemployment, low prices for primary industry commodities, the hardships experienced by Third World debtor nations, an accelerated 'technological revolution', enormous trade imbalances, and steadily increasing state deficits became permanent features of the international economic order. In response, mainstream political parties of the traditional 'right' and 'left' have adopted many of the tenets of classical liberalism in the formulation of public policy and in shaping debates over the nature of the welfare state and the role of government. Thus, for example, the main agendas for public discussion and policy development now revolve around essentially the same concerns, although the degree of change and methods of implementation vary depending upon the particular political party in question.

Increasingly, the concern is not with economic redistribution, compassion or social justice, but with deregulation of the labour market; privatisation of public services; profitability rather than social need; traditional values such as authority and obedience, law and order; reduced state intervention in areas pertaining to equal opportunities; and making the 'family' rather than the state responsible for each individual's welfare. In many cases, the actions of government show that there is no fundamental difference in overall approach between supposed political rivals. In youth affairs, for instance, Australian Prime Minister Bob Hawke and several of his Ministers have at times gone out of their way to attack the unemployed, to blame them for their situation, and have forged ahead with plans to introduce a work-for-the-dole scheme. After one such public comment, former Opposition Liberal leader John Howard was to observe: "All the signs are there that Mr. Hawke is coming around to supporting working for the dole. He is laying the groundwork, he is giving the warning and screwing up his courage to do it. We would welcome his Damascus Road conversion." (*Adelaide Advertiser*, 10 April 1987). Bipartisan expressions of support for particular public policies, whether it be further privatisation, curtailing welfare spending or granting more resources to law enforcement, are the norm rather than the exception in Australian political circles today.

The shift to the right in the political sphere, accompanied by the decline in economic fortunes following the end of the long boom of post-war development, have had a major impact on the lifestyles and well-being of young working-class people. The economic crisis has affected the young in a particularly devastating fashion. Meanwhile, the state has been called upon to play a more interventionist and regulatory role in their lives, and the economic crisis has been translated into a 'crisis of authority' as young people search for alternative ways to cope with depressed economic and social conditions.

Contemporary literature and policy documents, as well as recent case studies and newspaper accounts, are drawn upon throughout this book in order to illustrate the economic, political and social contraints on young people. The differential impact of wider economic and social trends is of central importance to the analysis. In a capitalist, male-dominated and ethnically divided society, the present crisis must have considerably different consequences for different categories of young people. For the purposes of this book, particular attention is paid to the circumstances of urban working-class young people, young women as a broad social category, and young Aborigines, although these discussions are set in the context of broader policies and trends affecting young people in general.

The discussion is divided into two parts. The first part – Youth Policy and the New Vocationalism – critically reviews the development of youth policy in the Australian context. The position of training as a key aspect of youth policy is dealt with in some depth, as are changes occurring in education. It is argued that, in order to understand why training and education have come to the fore as strategic government policy developments, we have to acknowledge the interrelationship between formerly discrete areas such as government welfare expenditure, industrial relations, the labour market and the objectives of education institutions. The link to be found between these apparently disparate concerns is that of the position of young people as potential workers or non-workers, and the concerns of the state to regulate their activities in either case.

Part Two – Youth Crime, Moral Panics and Public Order – examines the response of young people to their restricted social and physical space and, in turn, the response of the state in countering youth attempts to cope with the economic crisis. One of the concerns of this part of the book is to show the relational character of youth activities by looking at how particular spatial, gender and economic relations impinge upon the 'choices' open to those young people who commit crimes such as car theft. The other concern is to describe the various ways in which the behaviour and activities of young people are being subjected to increasing regulation. This is occurring on the street, via publicity campaigns, and through the role that youth services have been required to play. Here a crucial factor is the increased visibility of young people and the attempts of the state both to reduce their public presence and to control their activities more closely.

The book concludes with a discussion of the individual and collective reactions of young people to their immediate economic, social and political circumstances. Focusing on the question of social power, the final chapter provides a brief summary of how the question of youth politics has been dealt with by the Hawke Labor Government. This is followed by a review of some of the unorganised and organised responses of young people to their various predicaments and their lack of any real power in Australian society.

Much writing in the area of 'youth studies' has focused on specific areas of analysis, whether it be youth subcultures, education and training, or young people and crime. The intention of this book is to provide a more integrated overview of the processes which centre on young people, and to show the linkages between the different facets of their lives. Such an overview is needed to counterbalance a trend to academic specialisation in the area and the resulting fragmentation of youth issues. The continuities of youth experience can be lost in the maze of specific concepts which are used to interpret and explain social processes in narrowly defined disciplines and topics. One of the objectives of this book, therefore, is to place specific youth issues within a wider general framework, to demonstrate the common ground of analytically distinct social practices. The common thread of social control is further exposed as the broken transitions of home, school, training, work, the street and politics are explored.

A critical evaluation of what is being done for and to young people tells us much about present socio-economic realities. It also provides a clear warning of future problems that, if they are to be adequately dealt with, must be addressed today.

PART ONE

YOUTH POLICY AND THE NEW VOCATIONALISM

The adolescent generation and the state

The category of 'youth' or 'adolescent' is by no means universal in conception, nor are these labels used in a consistent way in specific societies and cultures. For example, the concept of an intermediate stage between 'childhood' and 'adulthood' is a relatively recent one. Until well into the nineteenth century, in Western Europe the majority of children lost their 'infant' status at about the age of seven, at which time they were expected to wear adult dress and leave the family home (Boer and Gleeson, 1982). Indeed, many of the convicts transported to Australia in the early part of the century were young people under the age of twenty-one. Between 1812 and 1817, for instance, 916 young people were sent to this country, and even in 1834 a fourteen-year-old boy was sentenced to transportation for seven years for stealing a silk handkerchief (Muncie, 1984: 33). In the present age, the notion of 'youth' has different connotations depending upon the cultural context. The term 'youth' means something quite different in Latin America, in parts of Africa, and in Australia; these differences involve considerable variations in age-range and life experience.

In addition to the relativistic usage of the term 'youth' in historical and cross-cultural terms, there are other variations in its use. Within the Australian context, for example, there are considerable differences in how it is applied. If it is used in relation to legal status, it could refer to all those people below the age of majority (eighteen years of age), or it could refer to broader definitions utilised by government departments and agencies (usually including those people between twelve and twenty-five years of age). Often in public usage and academic study the word 'youth' has implicitly if not explicitly referred primarily to young men. Much of the concern with youth questions has consistently ignored the experiences of young women, or relegated these to secondary importance because of sexist definitions and conceptions of the 'real world' (see McRobbie and Garber, 1976; Dorn and South, 1983; Brake, 1985).

The terminology itself thus makes it difficult at times to speak in precise terms about young people. This also partly explains why there are often confusions among young people about their status, since it is not unusual for them to be addressed at one moment as a 'young person', and at the next as an 'adult'. Nevertheless, there does exist a clear sense of 'generation' in Australian society, one which includes the idea of transition through the stages of infant, child, adolescent, adult and elder. This notion of an intermediary phase between child and adult arose historically – it is the result of a process in which a new category of people was socially constructed.

The social construction of generation is not a 'natural' or 'neutral' process somehow divorced from wider social, political and economic developments. While it may be part of commonsense thinking to assume that 'adolescence' is a natural part of growing-up and that the experience of adolescence is by and large the same for everyone, the circumstances surrounding adolescence have varied considerably over time and the experience varies depending upon one's social background. Widely held ideas relating to dependency, responsibility and control as these pertain to young people today are the outcome and manifestations of long-term processes involving state and market interventions in their lives.

The first key period in the construction of age-based differences involving young people was from the mid-1800s to the turn of the century. Greater concern over the use of child labour, and heightened worry over working-class delinquency and vagrancy, led to calls for reform. As a result, compulsory schooling was introduced, in order to keep young working-class children off the streets, as well as to inculcate new skills, values and attitudes in the prospective workforce. The state also began to intervene actively in the provision of 'care' for the children of the 'perishing classes' (Gamble, 1985). These two measures were closely interlinked in practice. For example, in the same year that the Public Schools Act was passed in New South Wales (1866), the Reformatory Schools

Act (for young people convicted of criminal offences), and the Industrial Schools Act and Workhouse Act (for vagrant children) were passed.

Initially, such measures met with only limited success. For instance, in South Australia, although the 1875 Education Act compelled children between the ages of seven and thirteen to attend school, many children did not attend regularly. This was because of activities relating to domestic and paid work which children were required to do in order to assist their families. It was also due to the fact that the Act did not stipulate that attendance at school had to be full-time. This was to change with the advent of the 1915 Education Act. Davey (1986: 396) comments on the significance of this piece of legislation:

> The Act systematically extended the period of institutionalised dependency for all children by making full-time schooling compulsory for children between the ages of six and fourteen. As well, it laid the foundations of a mass secondary education system which through its extension of schooling beyond the age of puberty heightened the contradiction between bio-logical adulthood and cultural childhood which is at the centre of the modern adolescent experience.

In the case of 'welfare' measures, during much of the nineteenth century action on such concerns had rested in the hands of (usually middle-class) private individuals and societies. By the turn of the century the state had assumed most of the responsibility for provision and control in this area.

State intervention into the lives of young people in Australia dramatically changed their overall position in society – economic, social, ideological. Urban young people were most affected by these changes. Excluded from factory work, they were forced into another regulatory system, the school. As the school became a credentialling agent for the purposes of paid work, it emerged as an even more potent force in the lives of young people. Lacking an economic base, children were no longer deemed able to assume adult responsibilities. Thus, the new extended condition of 'childhood' meant that adults were in a position to control and direct children in a way which previously had not been considered necessary or desirable. Accordingly, new perceptions of the child as weak and innocent gradually emerged, accompanied by greater emphasis on the need for protection by both the family and the state (Boer and Gleeson, 1982).

By the end of the century the state had also moved to directly intervene in the so-called private sphere of the family, setting out the roles and responsibilities of parents to their children. In 1886, the Guardianship of Infants Act was passed in England, and subsequently in all Australian states. This Act reinforced the guardianship and custody rights a father had over his children, while for the first time legally acknowledging the mother's rights in this respect. With the passing of the Child's Protection Act in 1899 in England, fathers became legally obliged to maintain their children (Summers, 1975). The economic dependence of young people (and, significantly, women and wives) was highlighted in the Harvester Case of 1907. In handing down his judgement, Justice Higgins established that a basic wage – in essence, a family wage – should be sufficient to maintain an unskilled labourer, his wife and three children in frugal comfort.

The second key period in the development of 'youth' as a special category was after World War II. The structural position of young people in relation to home, work and school had by this time been fundamentally altered. However, in the post-war period new forces were set in train which redefined their position and role in society. As Murdock and McCron (1976: 197) succinctly put it: "The post-war period has seen the final institutionalisation of adolescence through the establishment of universal secondary schooling and the emergence of a whole complex of leisure and entertainment facilities aimed specifically at youth." In other words, this period saw the development of 'generation consciousness', a phenomenon which was reinforced through the promotion of what came to be labelled as 'youth culture' – a culture tied specifically to the activities and pursuits of young people.

Explanations for the rise of 'youth culture' vary, but generally speaking several factors are seen to be of particular significance (see Clarke et al., 1976). One of the most important of these was the extension of compulsory secondary schooling. This extended the period of enforced dependence; moreover the structure of such schooling emphasised the common ground shared by young people of the same age. The separation of primary and secondary schooling added further impetus for young people to find a shared identity based upon generation and age groupings.

Another major factor in the development of 'generation consciousness' was the specific targeting of young people in the consumer market. The notion of a youth industry gained momentum as teenagers were discovered to have enormous economic potential as consumers in their own right. The spread of mass communications undoubtedly contributed to the effectiveness of business in wooing young people's, and their parents', money. Music, fashion and leisure facilities offered much in the way of economic reward for the financial entrepreneur. They also offered young people the chance to differentiate themselves from the older generations.

The position of young people in social and economic institutions such as the family, school, legal system and consumer market has engendered, and itself been engendered by, historically contingent ways of thinking about young people in society. By and large the application and operation of laws and practices of youth-oriented institutions in the post-war period have been premised upon the ideas that young people are 'consumers', 'dependent', 'dangerous' and that they have a diminished 'responsibility' for their actions and themselves. Youth is seen as describing a movement between dependence and independence: from less responsibility to full legal and social responsibility (Frith, 1984). It is these characteristics which are seen as common to all young people and as constituting the core of the experiences shared by people of the same age.

In the popular view of 'youth' each person is seen to be going through the same thing, the same process of 'experimentation', 'freedom', 'pop consumerism', and 'adolescent–adult transition'. Such a view, fostered by commercial interests and adopted to a certain extent by many young people themselves, tends to gloss over the more fundamental differences between people and their situations. An analysis of young people on the basis of age alone is sure to obscure the primary determining influences in their lives. In this way, the concept of 'youth' can be mystifying insofar as it "segregates young people and relegates their experience to something that will pass as soon as the complexities and responsibilities of real (adult) life take over" (Otto, 1982: 8). As Otto (1982) further suggests, however, structural factors such as gender, class and ethnicity are not something one can easily 'grow out of' in the process of 'becoming an adult'.

In the same way that specific class, sex and ethnic differences between young people cannot be ignored in analyses of young people, likewise the way in which 'adolescence' has been constructed needs to be analysed as something which is contingent upon specific economic, social and political developments. Many of the social processes affecting young people from the mid-1800s onwards were clearly the result of economic and political expediency. The introduction of new social institutions and the expanded use of social welfare policies last century were closely associated with attempts to deal with the class conflicts of the period, and in many instances were aimed specifically at the control of young working-class people. Now, while the context has changed somewhat due to the existence of the category of 'adolescence', the state is once again actively intervening, in a very particular manner, in the lives of young working-class people.

The notion of 'transition' – from school to work, from parental home to independent living, from being 'single' to being in a partnership, from being a child to being a childbearer and child-rearer – is itself a social construct which has been played out in practice according to specific conventions developed over centuries. Particular expectations, attitudes and forms of behaviour, while varying according to different class, gender and ethnic backgrounds, have nevertheless been premised upon established links between home and school, school and work, work and housing, income and independence or security. The sharp break in these established transitions, because of the economic crisis, has severely altered the experiences and expectations of young working-class men and women.

The sheer scope of the problems created by these broken transitions has created an enormous dilemma for the state in contemporary Australia. Faced with fiscal crisis and the considerable power of transnational corporations on the one hand, and the threat of social unrest and the social costs of economic crisis on the other hand, the maintenance of the capitalist social and economic order has necessitated strong government measures. As in the past, it is the least powerful who are bearing the brunt of the economic and social crisis. Also as in the past, education and training are being touted as ways in which working-class young people can be better controlled and prepared for the new social realities of the day. In effect, the direction of public policy in Australia over recent years has constituted yet another phase in the construction and reconstruction of 'youth' in Australia. The precise nature of this 'reconstruction' is an important subject for critical analysis and is fundamental to any debate on the existing livelihoods and life chances of young people and their prospects for the future.

CHAPTER 1

Young people and policy: Priority One?

Although evidence of a slowing in economic growth dates back to the latter part of the 1960s, the first major shock to the world economic order came in the early 1970s. Rising oil prices, and simultaneous growth in rates of inflation and unemployment, signalled the end of the long boom of post-war development in the Western industrialised nations. The economic problems of the 1970s, however, were only the harbinger of the much deeper crisis facing the international capitalist economy in the 1980s. The emergence of more frequent troughs in the economic development cycle in Australia from the early 1970s, and the growing recognition of massive structural changes occurring on a world scale, provide an essential backdrop to the development of government policies and schemes aimed specifically at young people. From the time of the election of Gough Whitlam's Labor Government in 1972 to the fifth year of office of the Hawke Labor Government in 1988, a veritable potpourri of programmes and schemes were introduced, replaced, modified, expanded and experimented with. These have included employer-oriented job subsidy programmes; education transition and 'equity' schemes; and skill training programmes. Each succeeding government has introduced its own 'initiatives' in youth affairs, each tied to particular understandings of the problems besetting young people, and each responding in its own way to specific contemporary economic and political situations.

The aim of this chapter is to provide an overview of government policies affecting young people over the decade and a half from

1974, with particular attention to the efforts of the Hawke Labor Government in this area. The intention is to show how government policies have changed in focus over time and how the overall trend in the area of youth policy has been toward greater control over many facets of young people's lives. From initial concerns with employment programmes and job creation, there has been a steady swing towards seeing 'employability' as the main problem. This has been accompanied by greater efforts to keep young people 'busy' and 'under control'. Simultaneously, much greater attention has been paid to questions of 'economic efficiency' both at the macro-economic level and in specific programmes.

Broadly speaking, youth policy as constructed by the Hawke Labor Government has consisted of three interrelated elements. The first is a concern to get young people involved in some kind of training or education programme to improve the 'skill base' of Australia's workforce. There is also a concern to reduce government expenditure on welfare and unemployment benefits relating to young people. The third is a concern to regulate the behaviour of young people, either through enforcing compliance via labour-market programmes and manipulation of monetary benefits, or through policing the activities and behaviour of young people via propaganda campaigns and greater control over their 'spare time' activities in the public sphere. It needs to be emphasised that the implementation of policy measures along these lines has received bipartisan political support. While the Opposition Liberal Party has at times conflicted with the Government over specific pro-grammes and initiatives, there has been broad agreement on the overall direction of contemporary youth policy. The precise nature and orientation of recent policies in youth affairs can be discerned by briefly surveying the development of state interventions over the last fifteen years.

EMPLOYMENT PROGRAMMES AND TRANSITION EDUCATION

The National Employment And Training (NEAT) scheme intro-duced by the Whitlam Government in 1974 was the first in a long line of schemes to meet the needs of Australian industry in a period of uncertain economic development. The Whitlam Government based its strategy on an expansion of public spending, which saw increased spending in the areas of welfare, education, health, and urban and regional development. The Regional Employment Development Scheme (REDS) was also introduced in 1974 and was intended to improve employment opportunities in areas of high unemployment.

Large-scale, generalised programmes characteristic of the Whitlam era were to end with the coming to power of the Liberals on 11 November 1974. Led by Malcolm Fraser, the Liberal Party–Country Party Coalition moved quickly to discontinue the REDS initiative, and to target the NEAT scheme more directly at young people.

In the latter part of the 1970s the policies of the Fraser Government were premised upon the notion of a mismatch between what the schools were doing and what employers wanted in the way of young workers. The structural nature of unemployment was thus largely ignored in favour of approaches which stressed the need for improvements in the transition from school to work. Throughout the period 1974 to 1979 the Liberal Government "refused to consider job creation schemes for young people, even in association with training programmes. Its position, based fundamentally on ideological grounds, was that jobs should be created by private industry" (Dwyer, Wilson and Woock, 1984: 113).

In 1976–77, the Government moved to counter mounting criticism of its youth unemployment strategies. The Community Youth Support Scheme (CYSS) was initiated to provide support and employment-oriented activities for young people who were unemployed. At the same time, the Education Programme for Unemployed Youth (EPUY) was initiated, to be administered through the Technical And Further Education (TAFE) sector in each State and territory. Each of these programmes was subject to a range of criticisms – from the length of training they provided, the absence of an integrated strategy for creating jobs, and the creation of a bureaucratic maze, through to unsatisfactory working conditions for employees of the schemes (see Dwyer, Wilson and Woock, 1984). Nevertheless, the 'success' of these programmes – at the level of explicitly recognising the specific needs of the young unemployed – was manifested in the public outcry which accompanied the Fraser Government's proposal in 1981 to discontinue funding for the CYSS programme. As a result of strong public pressure, the Government was forced to maintain the scheme (see Chapter 6).

The 1976–77 period also saw the development of assistance to employers offering apprenticeships, in the form of the Commonwealth Rebate for Apprentice Full-time Training (CRAFT) Scheme. This scheme offered tax rebates to employers for the time spent by apprentices at TAFE colleges and other approved on-the-job training. The provision of wage subsidies to employers hiring young people was institutionalised in the form of the Special Youth Employment Training Programme (SYETP).

In 1979 the Government introduced a major new policy initiative, the School to Work Transition Programme (SWTP), which was subsequently to absorb the EPUY scheme. This programme was aimed primarily at school leavers and potential school-leavers, targeting those young people deemed to be 'at risk' in the transition from school to work. Funding was provided to TAFE colleges and to schools for special programmes to improve the level of skills and work experience of these young people.

Under the Fraser Liberal Government unemployment was accorded little attention; where it was noted, the emphasis was on providing rebates and subsidies to the private sector, as opposed to expanding public-sector programmes. Inflation was seen as the major problem of the day. In the early 1980s, the Government embarked on ruthless cost-cutting in the light of a growing federal budget deficit and economic recession. Inadequate government finances were provided for the burgeoning needs of a rapidly expanding social welfare sector; more monies were allocated to propping up private businesses; capital markets were assisted through a range of administrative and fiscal measures; and attempts were made to restrict the industrial rights of public servants, such as teachers, who were concerned about deteriorating working conditions and wages.

In December 1982 a 'wage freeze' was implemented by the Fraser Government and was complemented by a six-month freeze for State public servants and private-sector workers under State awards. Although the Hawke Government was elected to power in March, it was not until late September 1983 that it finally repealed the wages 'pause' for Commonwealth employees. Part of the 'savings' from the wage pause had been channelled by the Liberal Government into the Wage Pause Programme (WPP), which operated from February 1983 to the end of June 1984. The objectives of the WPP were to provide assistance to target groups of unemployed people, offering them an opportunity to work on 'worthwhile' projects. The objectives and structure of the WPP were to form the framework for the creation of the Community Employment Programme (CEP).

The WPP marked a shift in emphasis from 'transition' programmes toward short-term employment programmes as a focus of labour-market strategy. It was implicitly hoped that such 'work experience' would increase the employability of the programme's participants. The deterioration of the labour market in Australia did not, however, come to a halt with the change in parliamentary power. Indeed, by the second half of 1983, unemployment was at its highest post-war level, with over 700 000 persons unemployed, or some 10 per cent of the total labour force. Furthermore, the average duration of unemployment was increasing sharply, to stand at more than ten months by 1983 (Commonwealth Employment Programme, 1985). In this context the Labor Government was forced to come up with a 'solution' which would fit the needs of both the young unemployed and the older unemployed.

In August 1983, the Community Employment Programme was officially launched. Its purpose was to create additional short-term employment opportunities which would provide appropriate work experience for unemployed persons. Jobs were to be generated through the funding of labour-intensive projects of social and economic benefit to the community, and particular assistance was to be given to the long-term unemployed and unemployed persons from 'disadvantaged' groups (Aborigines, people with disabilities, migrants). Half of the jobs were intended for women.

The CEP was the largest and most ambitious short-term job creation initiative ever undertaken by an Australian government. For young people, however, the benefits of the programme were less than satisfactory. For, while there was a disproportionately high representation of young people in the unemployed population, there was a disproportionately low representation of young people in CEP projects. This was due to a range of factors – such as priority being given to the long-term unemployed, and to members of 'disadvantaged' groups. It was also due to the fact that many of the projects in the programme, by their very nature, required people with experience and skills in areas such as construction, welfare or research. In addition, since employment was to be under award conditions (and thus not take into account differing training needs), many projects sought participants who were 'job-ready'.

In 1984 the Participation and Equity Programme (PEP) was introduced in order to increase participation in education and to create greater equity in educational provisions for young people.

Later absorbing the School to Work Transition Programme, the specific objectives of the PEP were:

> to encourage all young people to participate in education or training at schools or technical and further education institutions, or in other forms of education or training, until they have completed a full secondary education or its equivalent;

and

> to ensure that as far as practicable, the education and training provided in schools and further education institutions offers all young people equal opportunities to develop their individual talents and thereby ensure more equitable outcomes of education.

Neither the PEP or CEP schemes addressed the structural issues of creating more jobs or providing young people with secure employment. Furthermore, the rhetoric of equity surrounding the PEP was countered in practice by the prominence given to private schools in the Government's distribution of resources and funding in the education sector (Wilson and Wyn, 1987). While the PEP was clearly oriented toward increasing school retention rates, and thereby 'reducing' youth unemployment, it also implied that young people were not finding jobs because they were ill-equipped for the labour market. This was a line of reasoning which was to grow in significance in later debates over the most appropriate policy responses to youth unemployment.

In 1983 the Labor Government commissioned two reports relating to youth policy and general labour-market trends. The first report was written by a team from the Organisation for Economic Co-operation and Development (OECD, 1984), focusing on youth unemployment, and youth training and educational provision in Australia. The main recommendations of the report included the reallocation of some existing jobs to young people through schemes for early retirement and subsidised youth employment; the rationalisation of existing income-support measures; and bolstering the existing mechanisms for education and training for work by raising school retention rates, enhancing post-compulsory vocational training opportunities and improving access to higher education.

The central message of the OECD report was picked up and further highlighted in the report of the Committee of Inquiry into Labour Market Programmes (Kirby et al., 1985). The thrust of this report was to emphasise the importance of training and education.

It argued that: "Increased education and training effort not only improves the long term employment prospects of the individual, but also assists the economy by developing the nation's skill base and its ability to adjust to changes in economic conditions and technology." (p. 109). Accordingly, the centrepiece of the report's proposed reforms was the development of a new system of traineeships for young people. The emphasis therefore was on upgrading the personal and vocational skills of individuals so that they could maximise their long-term employment prospects – to focus on the 'employability' of young people.

PRIORITY ONE IS EMPLOYABILITY

The glaring weakness of the Kirby report on labour-market pro-grammes was "its inability to demonstrate how the new provisions for education and training would ensure that a pattern of economic growth would lead to new employment opportunities" (Wilson and Wyn, 1987: 78). Nevertheless, despite the difficulties apparent in both the Kirby and the OECD reports on questions such as employment creation and the exploitative nature of the labour process itself, each exerted considerable influence on the develop-ment of government youth policy.

In August 1985, Prime Minister Hawke personally launched the Labor Government's new 'solution' to the 'youth problem'. This took the form of a policy package called 'Priority One – Young Australia'. It was the first time that an integrated and comprehen-sive policy was developed which focused specifically on young people. Recognising that "young people are the cornerstone of Australia's future and have a wide range of needs as they make the transition to adult life", Priority One "encompasses all of the Government's policies and programs which affect young people". It was to provide an "umbrella under which these can be developed and implemented in an integrated way to improve the economic and social well-being of Young Australians, and to foster growth towards their independence and sense of personal worth" (Commonwealth of Australia, 1986).

The Priority One package had a number of elements, from the introduction of 'traineeships' to campaigns against drug abuse. Initiatives were outlined in three broad areas: employment, training and education; support services; and income support. Improve-ments were to include such things as extending the options for full-time education, training and employment; developing Youth

Access Centres in Commonwealth Employment Service (CES) offices; introducing a Volunteer Community Service Scheme; increasing funding to the Supported Accommodation Assistance Programme; and eliminating the gap between unemployment benefits and education allowances. Several existing programmes were combined into integrated schemes. For example, the Jobstart Programme replaced previous wage subsidy programmes such as the SYETP, the Adult Wage Subsidy Scheme, the Special Training Programmes for the Disabled on-the-job and the Special Needs Clients Programme. Existing educational allowances covering school and tertiary education students were integrated into the Austudy scheme.

The most prominent element of Priority One at the time, however, was the massive publicity campaign launched by the Prime Minister himself. Press advertisements, leaflets, radio and television were all used to saturate the community with the message that "Young Australians should be seen, heard, educated, employed, encouraged, respected and all treated as if they're the future of this country." This type of 'feel good' propaganda campaign was characteristic of the approach to youth issues during the International Year of Youth in 1985. The fact that it was the International Year of Youth also provided the context for the Prime Minister to embark upon a campaign unprecedented in this country.

Under the banner of Priority One, Bob Hawke crisscrossed the nation in an effort to let young people 'have their say' about what concerned them most. There were toll-free telephone numbers; talkback radio shows featuring the Prime Minister; and rock concerts starring Bob Hawke and Molly Meldrum, compere of the popular ABC television music show *Countdown*, along with popular musicians. According to the Government's figures, some 26 000 young Australians used this opportunity to convey their messages directly to the Prime Minister and the Government. All up, the cost of the advertising campaign and the phone-in was about one and a half million dollars. Further to emphasise his commitment to the young people of Australia, Hawke moved the Office of Youth Affairs into the Department of the Prime Minister and Cabinet and assumed the responsibility for Youth Affairs. The newly discovered 'commitment' and 'priority' to young people was replicated at the State level in many instances. In South Australia, for example, the Bannon Labor Government created a new Cabinet position – the Minister for Youth Affairs – in 1985.

The mainspring of the ALP's Priority One package was the

expansion of 'traineeships'. Under the traineeship scheme, young people spend a one-year period in on-the-job and off-the-job 'training'. They work for three or four days per week and attend some form of off-the-job training for the remainder, either a TAFE college or private industry training programmes. All sixteen and seventeen-year-old school leavers are eligible to apply, with preference being given to those who leave school before completing Year 12. Trainees are paid only for the work component of the programme. In 1985–86, government subsidies of $1700 were given for each trainee where the training was in a TAFE college and $2000 where the training was in private industry. Higher subsidies were offered for particular disadvantaged groups. A further $1000 was paid direct to the employer for each trainee to help defray on-the-job training costs. Targeted industries included: tourism and hospitality; banking and finance; retail; motor accessories; and the public service.

In 1986 the Commonwealth Government was forced to spend $300 000 on a campaign to encourage the private-sector to participate in its youth traineeship scheme. When the scheme was introduced by the Prime Minister in August 1985, he promised 10 000 trainee places within the first year. A year later only 4858 places had been created, mostly in the public sector. Private employers had offered only 1454 places, and these were primarily in the retail sector (Legge, 1986: 5). Significantly, "In the retail industry the employers are notorious for their low wages and disregard of conditions. They have been successful in this because the workers have no experience of working in a situation where unions have been well organised and they know nothing of the benefits of unionism." (Burns, 1986: 55).

At the National PEP Conference in 1984, Bob Hawke announced that funds for government school students would increase by nearly 50 per cent by 1992. This commitment was not to be fulfilled. Instead, PEP funding was slashed in 1986 – and was further reduced in 1987. Furthermore, in the 1986–87 federal Budget, spending on labour-market programmes was actually reduced, with monies for programmes focusing on 15–24-year-olds being 24.5 per cent less in 1986–87 than in 1984–85. In addition, while spending on traineeships was up, there was a $103.6 million cutback in the Community Employment Programme (Marginson, 1986a: 4). Thus, the Government's commitment to job creation lessened, rather than increased, over time. Traineeships were offered as the panacea to the nation's youth unemployment problems – though the percentage of teenagers holding full-time waged jobs continued to fall steadily (Freeland, 1986).

In its initial stages, the traineeship scheme clearly did not 'work' for the Hawke Government, in real terms or in popular political terms. Priority One was generally seen as a failure because of the faulty implementation of the traineeship scheme. From the start there were, and continue to be, numerous problems ingrained in the whole notion of 'traineeships' as a 'solution' to unemployment. No real jobs were created as a result of the programme, nor did it guarantee jobs for trainees at the end of the one-year period. Major questions were also asked regarding the transferability of training from one area of employment to another, the monitoring of on-the-job training, the effect of contract labour (i.e., trainees) on union rights, the low pay given to trainees, and so on.

Regardless of how the traineeship programme has worked – or not worked – in practice, the scheme has played an invidious ideological role. Specifically, it has been utilised to shift the debate about unemployment away from the objective lack of paid jobs and adequate wages, to that of the 'deficiencies' in individual teenagers who are seen to need special training in order to keep up with labour-market requirements. It is but a small step from this approach to the adoption of a perspective which places the blame for unemployment directly on the young people involved. Indeed, this is precisely what has occurred over recent years in Australia.

In the first part of 1986 the federal Opposition raised the notion of 'work-for-the-dole' as part of its developing policy proposals. The Labor Government quickly criticised such a scheme on the basis that it would cost too much to implement (in the region of $700 million). Shortly afterwards, television Channel Nine's *Sixty Minutes* ran a series of stories on the 'success' of such programmes in the United States, also featuring reports on some Aboriginal communities in Queensland which were engaged in similar programmes. In the June Economic Statement of that year, Prime Minister Bob Hawke announced that he favoured a system which would provide "the opportunity, particularly for the young recipients of unemployment benefits, to undertake some community work in return for that benefit". In some circles this was seen as a response to the demise of the CEP and the failure of the traineeship scheme. As an official with the Australian Social Welfare Union (Davidson, 1986: 16) put it:

> The government has now turned to a proposal which offers only work, not award wages, a career, proper training, nor a

structured program of personal and social support. Cost cutting is only part of the reason. This also reflects a shift in the unemployment debate from 'what is the government doing about it' to 'what are the unemployed doing about it' – a blame the victim approach.

In mid-October 1986, the Australian Council of Trade Unions (ACTU) endorsed a policy based on the premise that young people between the ages of fifteen and nineteen should not receive the dole unless they were engaged in work, training or education. This 'work-for-the-dole' proposal was part of a package which the ACTU was negotiating with the Government. It was widely seen as part of a strategy involving certain trade-offs with the Government, involving questions of the abandonment of wage indexation and further cuts in real wages. The Opposition Liberal Party promptly announced that the ACTU's work-for-the-dole plan was a "stunning endorsement" of its own scheme (*Adelaide Advertiser*, 13 October 1986).

The apparent support for a 'work-for-the-dole' scheme on the part of the Labor Government, the Opposition, and the ACTU created an ideological space in which compulsory community work for the dole became a real possibility. Significantly, funding for the Youth Volunteer Programme was substantially increased in the 1986–87 Budget. And with the release of the Budget Papers, concerted media attention was given to the issue of what to do with the young unemployed.

For example, much greater emphasis was placed upon tightening up the rules of the system in an effort to weed out the cheats and those defrauding the welfare system. New rules introduced on 1 November 1986 required that unemployment benefit forms be lodged in person, instead of by mail, every two weeks. In December the Social Security Minister, Brian Howe, announced that the young unemployed would receive unemployment benefits only after a waiting period of three to six months after leaving school. Citing the need to cut welfare costs and to keep the young unemployed from joining the ranks of the long-term unemployed, Howe stated that "The idea would be to move away from unemployment benefits as the primary form of assistance and make it a matter of a last resort, or even eliminate it altogether." (Adelaide *News*, 15 December 1986). Similar to the ideas put up by the ACTU, the apparent plan would be to force young people into some kind of training or education programme if they were to receive their unemployment benefit.

The way in which 'work-for-the-dole' schemes have been presented by politicians and the mass media has redefined the nature of social-security benefits. Benefits are presented as 'privileges', rather than as 'rights'. For the 'privilege' of receiving a benefit, unemployed young people are told that they too have a responsibility to 'society' and hence they should work for their unemployment benefit. This increases the vulnerability of young people who through no fault of their own are unable to find satisfactory full-time paid work. This vulnerability is manifested in a number of ways such as increasing alienation, boredom, depression and guilt. Such public debates represent the 'dole-bludger' syndrome revisited. They create a perspective which sees the young unemployed themselves as the main 'culprits' and source of the problem.

In the end, work-for-the-dole was rejected as the Government's preferred strategy in the area of youth unemployment, although it did expand the Youth Volunteer Programme in March 1987, thereby allowing young people who carried out 'useful' work to collect their unemployment benefit while not actively looking for work. Nevertheless, the extensive discussion surrounding work-for-the-dole was remarkably successful in gaining a widespread consensus on the issue from a range of social forces, including the official union leadership. Work for the unemployment benefit is an extension of the logic behind the traineeship scheme, a logic which basically says that those less 'fortunate' in Australian society should not expect 'the rest of us' to pick up the tab for their faults, laziness, or lack of ambition and drive. The pervasiveness of such 'logic' in the debates over work-for-the-dole, in turn, served to make traineeships even more important and to justify further policy measures attacking the rights of young people to basic income support.

SKILLS FORMATION, JOB SEARCH AND ECONOMIC DEPENDENCY

The May Mini-Budget and the September Budget in 1987 consolidated the Government's concerns with training, social control and economic restraint. With the ideological groundwork laid in 1985 and 1986 for new ways of dealing with the 'youth problem', the next step was to find ways of forcing young people to comply with the Government's overall strategy.

The first inkling of what was to come was provided in the May Mini-Budget. The most dramatic element in this statement was the abolition of the unemployment benefit for those under eighteen. In its stead, a job search allowance of $25 a week was introduced, supplemented by a means-tested $25 a week for low-income families. Acknowledging the "bold new policy direction" that was being taken, Brian Howe, Minister for Social Security, said in a press statement that "The Government must encourage young people to look to the labour market, not the unemployment queue, if we are to prevent the start of the vicious circle of 'no experience – no job'." As part of this process it was further stipulated that those people receiving the job search allowance would have to attend the CES at least once every fortnight as part of their job search, and that after six months they would be required to accept the jobs or training positions offered to them by the Commonwealth Employment Service, regardless of their appropriateness.

Increases in the unemployment benefit for those aged eighteen to twenty, already lower than the rate for those people over the age of twenty, were shelved and a waiting period of thirteen weeks was introduced. These measures were seen as removing the financial incentive to leave school and as assisting in the process of increasing retention rates in schools. Several other significant measures in the May Mini-Budget included the introduction of income testing for family allowances and a change in the eligibility requirements for the sole parent benefit so that they would apply only to those below the age of sixteen.

Between the May Mini-Budget and the September Budget, national elections were held and the Labor Party was returned for another term of office. Shortly after the election, the Hawke Ministry was not only reshuffled but totally restructured as well. One outcome was the integration of education, employment and training into one 'superministry', supported by the newly created Department of Employment, Education and Training (DEET). Thus, the attention given to training, and the link between training, education and economic development, was given high administrative priority.

The manipulation of social-security benefits in the May Mini-Budget to foster more participation in training and education was complemented by a range of programme developments in the September Budget. John Dawkins, the Minister for Employment, Education and Training, announced the following measures as part of the push to get young people into some kind of full-time training, education or employment (Commonwealth of Australia, 1987; Department of Employment, Education and Training, 1987):

- a 12.3 per cent increase in funding for trade training programmes, including support for the apprenticeship system, with
some 108 000 young people expected to participate
- a substantial boost in expenditure (from $13.5 million to $43.9
million) for the Australian Traineeship Scheme, involving about
20 000 young people
- funding for an extra 3500 to 4000 intakes for school-leavers
entering universities and colleges of advanced education, with a
total of up to 5800 new places for school-leavers to be made
available by means of changes in the composition of current
student intakes (i.e., giving priority to the young over part-time
and mature-age students)
- a slight increase in the 1986 tertiary education 'administrative
fee' from $250 to $263 to keep it in line with inflation
- a new Youth Training Programme to assist some 13 000 15–20-
year-olds in vocational training courses
- increased assistance for community-based programmes, including the stablishment of seven Information Technology Centres
(in addition to the existing three centres) and expanded capacity
in the Community Volunteer Programme
- help for some 16 000 16–20-year-olds through the establishment
of a Job Search Training Programme to provide job-search skills
through 200 organisations such as community bodies, TAFE
colleges and CYSS projects
- under the same programme, the trialling of 40 Job Clubs to
provide intensive three-week training courses and practical experience in job-search skills for about 1300 16–20-year-olds
unemployed for six months or more
- the expansion of the network of Youth Access Centres to provide
young people with a central access point to comprehensive,
co-ordinated information on employment options, education,
income support and community services
- young unemployed people in continuous receipt of the job search
allowance for more than six or twelve months were also to be
given special counselling and support by the Commonwealth
Employment Service
- a real increase of 4.8 per cent in general recurrent grants to
schools, with the objective that by 1992 two-thirds of Australia's
school students will complete their secondary schooling to Year
12
- the integration of three community employment and training
programmes – Community Youth Support Scheme (CYSS),

Community Training Programme (CTP) and the Community Volunteer Programme (CVP) – into a single programme, Skill-Share.

One of the striking aspects of the September Budget was the further shift away from a positive notion of equity (based upon the ideas of equality and redistribution of wealth) to a negative notion of equity (based upon ideas of relative hardship and charity). In his Budget speech, for example, Paul Keating spoke of "only those in genuine need" being entitled to social-security payments, and of the ALP's "historical commitment to assist the most needy in our community". The Treasurer's view is succinctly captured in the following statement: "We have consistently held that people who can readily support themselves should do so, rather than putting their hand out to the taxpayer." (Keating, 1987: 6).

Equity, as defined in these terms, is based on a distinction between those who deserve assistance and those who do not. The logic of this perspective has been further extended to include a distinction not only between the poor and the not-so-poor, but also between the poor and the deserving poor. (This is evidenced by the institution of more stringent controls to ensure that unemployment-benefit claimants are in fact 'seriously' looking for work.) In effect, the historical trend, of which current policy is but an extension, has been for social policy to be constructed as providing 'charity' to the 'needy', rather than as being an instrument for the more equitable distribution of resources and the reduction of overall inequality of income in Australian society. The focus is not on how the rich can contribute more fairly, but on how to police the system against 'cheats' and 'frauds'. Ultimately this view "shifts the focus for an understanding of equity from an interest in *which* needs are unequally or unfairly met, to an overwhelming imperative to check whether a need is real or not" (Farrar, 1987a: 44).

In the specific case of young people, the 'need' has frequently been defined out of existence. For example, measures announced in the 1987 May and September economic statements relating specifically to teenagers aged between sixteen and seventeen included:

- the phasing out of the PEP and the Basic Learning in Primary Schools programme (BLIPS), both of which were designed to increase participation by 'disadvantaged' student groups
- much tighter access to Austudy grants on the basis of a family income test
- the discontinuation of CYSS Special Initiatives funding, de-

> signed to cater for the needs of particular disadvantaged groups
> - subjecting the family allowance payment for 16 and 17-year-olds
>   to a family income test
> - removing the supporting parent's benefit once the youngest
>   child reaches sixteen
> - the new family allowance supplement did not include provision
>   for young people over the age of fifteen
> - the abolition of the under-eighteen unemployment benefit
> - and the removal of the allowance for young people to undertake
>   short-term training.

Through these measures the Government was attempting to make young people less dependent on the state, and to restrict the choices open to them by channelling them into pre-defined 'career paths' centring on narrowly conceived types of education and training. Given the lack of paid work for a significant proportion of the youth population, and the dearth of job-creation schemes to accommodate those young people who do complete an educational or training programme, the question of income security becomes critical. In monetary terms, the direction of change in the Government's income transfer to young people over the age of fifteen can be surmised by noting the comparative figures in Table 1.1.

Overall the Government's policies as they affect young people, and especially those who are sixteen and seventeen years of age, have been designed to require parents to provide financial support for their children. New programmes such as the job search allowance will heighten rather than reduce this reliance on parental household resources. Indeed, it will create a number of problems, given the strict administrative procedures and rules surrounding the claiming of the allowance, as young people get fed up with the constant hassles and paperwork involved in claiming their $25 or $50 a week. Even leaving aside these considerations, it needs to be said once again that the sums listed in Table 1.1 as provided under the job search allowance, unemployment benefit, young homeless allowance and Austudy allowance are by no means generous; the poverty line is some distance away and young teenagers have adult needs when it comes to such things as food, shelter, clothing and entertainment.

In more specific terms, the changes in Government policy have had a negative effect on low-income families and young people in particular. A thirteen-week waiting period for the job search allowance, for example, will cause much hardship since it is young people from low-income families who tend to leave school and are further

Table 1.1:   Income support for young people, 1987–88

Age	Maximum rate ($/wk)	
	1987	*1988*
16–17		
In education		
secondary, at home	40	50
tertiary, at home	50	50
away from home, independent	73	76
Unemployed		
standard rate	50	25
means-tested supplement	–	25
young homeless	73	76
18–20		
In education		
secondary, at home	45	60
tertiary, at home	55	60
away from home, independent	80	91
Unemployed		
standard rate	91	91
21 and over		
Unemployed	105	112

Source: Bradbury et al., 1988: 90.

disadvantaged in the labour market. Thus, the families of such young people will be expected to meet their living costs fully for thirteen weeks, and then will be relieved only to the value of (a means-tested) $50 a week. Given that recent estimates by the Australian Institute of Family Studies show that the cost of keeping a teenager is nearly $90 per week at March 1987 prices (Maas, 1987a), the policy proposals introduced by the Government "seem destined to exacerbate rather than reduce problems such as family conflict and youth homelessness" (Maas, 1987b: 16).

For young people aged sixteen and seventeen the present must look bleak, disenfranchised as they have been from basic income supports which formerly were claimed as 'rights'. Rather than fostering the idea of independence, the Government has transformed young people who want to engage in paid work into second-class citizens subject to constant surveillance on the jobs front, and under constant pressure to join the ranks of the 'unemployed students'.

The dependency of young people does not relate solely to government benefits and allowances. It is also tied to the issue of youth wages and work conditions. Here the push from the business community has been to hold down youth wages as far as possible. Thus, an editorial in the *Australian Financial Review* (13 January 1987) argued that:

> The youth traineeship scheme has been frustrated by award inflexibilities, union opposition and the unwillingness of employers to participate. We do not need $300 000 advertising campaigns to try to cajole employers to take on more trainees. We do need much greater flexibility in awards and work conditions for young workers.

The basis for this argument is that 'greater flexibility' in these areas will open up opportunities for young people who, because of their lack of experience or training, are presently disadvantaged in the labour market.

The reality, however, is quite different. Already young people are paid lower wages than 'adults', ostensibly because the employers are helping to train the young people or because young people are less productive than others. Yet, as Boson (1986: 25) points out, "we find those who earn the lowest award rates also suffer the highest levels of unemployment. Remarkably, there is a considerable drop in unemployment rates at 18, when wages rise, and an even greater drop in unemployment rates at 21 (when all junior rates cut out)." A further reduction in youth wages, therefore, will not necessarily increase youth employment, and if it did it would do so at the expense of other workers' jobs and under conditions of above-average exploitation for young workers.

Nevertheless, the issue of cuts in youth wages is still on the contemporary political agenda. The Opposition Spokesperson on Youth Affairs, Peter Shack, for instance, argued in 1986 that employers and young people should be permitted to find mutually acceptable work agreements covering the terms and conditions of employment – in other words, 'freely negotiate' the terms of sale of their labour without union 'interference'. After all, as he put it, "I have yet to meet an unemployed person who would reject a flexible arrangement if it was the difference between getting the job ahead of a more qualified person, or staying on the dole." (*Canberra Times*, 29 December 1986). In a similar vein, shortly after the October 1987 sharemarket crash, the Confederation of Australian Industry issued a statement arguing that juniors should not receive an increase if a national wage rise was granted, because employers would be encouraged to hire more young people if the wage increase was not passed on to them.

The irony of the situation is that it is the Labor Government's policies with respect to young people and unemployment which are opening the door to even greater exploitation of young workers. The abolition of the unemployment benefit for some categories of young people, the freezing of the dole rate for others, and the requirement that young people do something in return for the payment, may lead more and more young people to look to informal arrangements with employers as a way to get money and to escape the increased government regulation of their lives. Either exploited labour, or crime; these are the options presently facing many young people.

DISCIPLINE, REGULATION AND SOCIAL CONTROL

In terms of the consolidation of a particular kind of state approach to youth policy, 1987 stands out as a benchmark year in Australia. Much of what has occurred since the 1987 September Budget and restructuring of federal government bureaucracy represents an elaboration on a theme rather than any further change in direction.

In January 1988 the Social Security Review, established by the Minister of Social Security in 1986 to examine aspects of social-security policy, released its report on income support for the unemployed (Cass, 1988). At the core of its recommendations was a concern to provide support for an 'active system' linking labour-market policy with income-support policy. For young people between the ages of sixteen and twenty, the report's recommendations dovetailed nicely with the actual direction of the Government's policy. Thus, the report stressed compulsory training and the threat of withdrawal of income support. An expanded 'activity test' was suggested as a means to monitor the efforts of young people. It did not call for an improvement in overall income support for the young unemployed, although improvements were suggested in the areas of young homeless allowance, rent assistance and training allowances. As critics of the report were to point out, there was little discussion of the nature and quality of the training to be provided; a failure to tackle the issue of lower youth payments; insufficient discussion of employment development; and more discussion needed on the potential abuses generated by the introduction of complex adminis-trative procedures (Higgins, 1988; Farrar, 1988ab).

The bringing down of the new Budget in August 1988 merely confirmed the fact that such issues and questions are indeed central to an appreciation of government policies directed at young people. While Paul Keating once again spoke of those groups "deserving" of greatest financial support receiving it, very little was said about the goal of full employment (Keating, 1988). Young people were virtually ignored in the Treasurer's speech. This time round it was two new training programmes, for the long-term adult unemployed and sole parents, which received the limelight. With respect to education, it was announced that the tertiary institution 'adminis-trative charge' was to be abolished, only to be replaced by a 'graduate tax' which requires students to pay back about one-fifth of the cost of their courses. The Budget Papers revealed that allowances such as Austudy would rise by a matter of a few dollars a week, and that the indexation of the job search allowance and the intermediate unemployment benefit (for 18–20-year-olds) would be deferred until January 1989. Measures for tighter policing of benefits were also introduced.

The dramatic changes in policy signalled in Government deci-sions during 1987 have remained at the core of the state's response to youth unemployment and poverty in a period of fiscal constraint. As a reflection of this particular approach to the issues, the Depart-ment of Employment, Education and Training has in some circles been dubbed the Department of Education, Training and Training since the 'Employment' part of the equation seems to be the one receiving the least amount of attention. Recognising the increas-ingly vocationalist direction of schooling, others have renamed it as the Department of Training, Training and Training. Such reactions are based upon grave misgivings about the direction of Government policies at the present time, misgivings which are grounded in the experience of real hardships and frustrations by a growing number of young people in Australian society.

Undoubtedly, the Hawke Labor Government has 'blamed the victims' through initiating programmes such as the Job Search Scheme. The media hype surrounding such policies has contributed to the image of young unemployed people as being lazy, bludgers, cheats and dangerous to the social body. Either they are not 'trained' the right way, or they do not have enough 'education' or 'work experience', or they are losing their sense of the 'work ethic' as they acclimatise to living on the dole. The 'solution' is to coerce or cajole them into taking up one of a series of narrowly defined 'career paths'. It does not take one long to realise that, especially in light of persistent media barrages on 'law and order', this has made it possible to extend the existing forms of social control over young people.

The 'choices' that young people are currently offered in the areas of education, training and paid employment are highly regulated through a combination of financial and outright coercive measures. These range from cutting benefits and engaging in further 'crackdowns' on suspected welfare cheats, to propagating the notion that traineeships are a viable way for young people to secure paid work in the formal labour market. In 1986, 'special investigation teams' were introduced to examine suspected cases of welfare fraud. Part of a measure aimed at tightening up the application of all existing rules, the number of teams was increased to fifteen in March 1987, and further teams were formed in 1988. Despite press reports to the contrary, comparatively few clearcut cases of fraud have been uncovered. More importantly, available evidence suggests that one of the consequences of this campaign has been to convince a substantial number of *eligible* unemployed people that benefits are simply not worth the harassment (Farrar, 1987b). Undeterred by such considerations, the Government managed to set into place further disincentives. In 1987, a Work Intention Form was introduced, to be issued selectively to clients when there were 'serious doubts about their work efforts'. In 1988, this was supplemented by a Work Effort Certificate, which requires the unemployed person to provide the signatures of employers who have been approached as part of their job-seeking efforts.

The policing of social-security benefits, coupled with a large expansion of training and job-search programmes, will lead to the creation of a permanent layer of 'transitional labour' – an underclass of unpaid and underpaid workers who will be stuck on the edge of the labour market, living in deep poverty. Most of these individuals will be working-class young people, reflecting the class-based distribution of community resources via the market and the state. Although benefits are generally paid at a fixed rate, the impact of the money received on a young person's physical survival and 'social functioning' will be dictated by the position of the young person and their family in the class structure. The latter expression refers to "the provision of, and access to, an adequate quantity and quality of material resources sufficient for the achievement of a certain minimum standard of living and a certain quality of life" (Jamrozik, 1987: 48). Both in terms of immediate survival and with regard to improving upon their present condition and life chances, young working-class people will be at a severe disadvantage under existing policies.

For those people who either opt out of the system 'voluntarily', or are forced out of it through problems on the 'job', the future also looks far from promising. To survive without a guaranteed benefit, many young people will have to look to drug dealing, petty and major property crime, and prostitution as alternative sources of income. Furthermore, what young people do in their 'spare' time reflects their depressed social and economic situation, with low self-esteem finding expression in drug use and abuse, anti-social behaviour of all kinds, and general feelings of alienation and boredom.

Allied with attempts to regulate the activities of young people in education, employment and training, the other major intention of youth policy is to control their activities and behaviour in the public sphere. Specifically, as the economic situation worsens and social tensions rise, the response of the state has been to intervene in the activities of young people on the street, in the malls, in the parks, and indeed any public space which they claim for their own. Direct surveillance in the form of police patrols, and the presence of social-welfare officials, and security guards is increasing. The extra attention paid to young people provides fuel for moral panics over the state of young people today.

At the same time, various 'hearts and minds' campaigns have been devised to not only control the 'deviant' practices of some categories of disenchanted and poverty-stricken young people (such as those who use drugs), but also to portray a positive and negative definition of the 'proper' behaviour of young people. This is manifest in the national campaign against drug abuse, the so-called Drug Offensive, which was an integral part of the Priority One youth policy package. Such campaigns, in addition to regular comments on the behaviour of young people served up in the media, provide 'justification' for the enforcement of control mechanisms, and at the same time portray the problem as *moral*, rather than economic, in character.

A vicious circle of control, response, and further control has thus been set in train. The high priority given to discipline and the social regulation of young people is evident now in all spheres of their activity from the school to the street, and in the content of programmes directed at them, whether it be a traineeship scheme or a campaign against drug abuse. The announcement in 1985 of 'Priority One – Young Australia' signalled a need by the Labor Party for a youth policy. Rather than young people themselves being the priority, however, the details and practical working out of the Government's youth policies indicate that imperatives of control are at the heart of its endeavours to deal with the 'youth problem'. As will be seen, notions of 'social justice' and 'equality' which have figured so prominently in the Government's rhetoric have in the end been bypassed in favour of approaches which are repressive in nature, and woefully inadequate in meeting the real needs of a substantial proportion of the Australian youth population. Young people may be 'priority one', but the substance of the policies directed at them suggests that this may turn out to be a cause for alarm on their part, rather than for celebration.

CHAPTER 2

Skills, youth training and a reconstructed Australia

The development of 'youth policy' by the state has been and continues to be governed by wider macro-economic considerations, and concerns which go to the core of the relationship between capital and wage labour in Australia today. Under the Hawke Labor Government a broad range of policy initiatives was introduced in attempts to generate greater levels of private investment and profit. These policies were based on ideas and proposals put forward by the 'New Right' (see Aarons, 1987; Coghill, 1987), in areas of fiscal policy (budget allocations), monetary policy (interest rates, value of the dollar), and labour-market policy (wages and work conditions). The net result of Labor's further swing to the right has been a dramatic shift in the distribution of wealth in Australian society. Recent figures show, for example, that one-tenth of the population owns 60 per cent of all wealth in Australia (Raskall, 1987); other figures show that between 1981–82 and 1985–86, the number of single people aged 15–24 with incomes below the poverty line rose by 13.8 per cent, primarily due to unemployment and the low level of unemployment benefits (Browne, 1987). The trend therefore has been for a further concentration of wealth into fewer and fewer hands, and a major increase in overall poverty at the other end of the economic spectrum.

One of the reasons why the Government's commitment to young people in the contemporary context has been restricted to education and training policies, rather than employment, is the adoption of specific policy initiatives in the area of labour-market strategy. While the Government's overall political and economic agenda has been dictated by the concerns of private capital, and has involved a complex mix of changes in economic and social policy, specific strategies affecting young people have been shaped by developments on the industrial relations front. Here, discussions between government, unions and business have led to a remarkable consensus regarding the nature of the problems of national economic performance and unemployment. In essence, these problems have been collapsed into a schematic approach which sees them as being reduced to the quality and quantity of training and education provided in Australia. The key to improved economic fortunes and greater employment growth is seen to be the improvement of the skills of the workforce, which will make production more efficient and workers more adaptable and able to adjust to rapidly changing labour processes and work settings. The success of such an approach is seen to require that the wages of workers are held in check and that relative peace is maintained in industrial relations.

The emphasis on 'skills formation' has of course long featured in the rhetoric and public pronouncements of representatives of small business and the corporate sector. Images of the ideal worker from the point of view of these sectors are commonplace in media stories, often taking the form of ad hoc 'expert' advice on how to improve Australia's national performance in relation to comparable countries. In 1987 this aspect of the economic debate took on a more formal and entrenched character through concerted systematic treatments of the issues by both the Labor Government and the Australian Council of Trade Unions. The main issues were presented in two major and highly publicised reports: *Skills for Australia*, produced as a Commonwealth Government Budget Paper (Commonwealth of Australia, 1987), and *Australia Reconstructed*, produced by ACTU representatives with the cooperation of the Trade Development Council (ACTU–TDC, 1987). The general industrial and training strategies detailed in these reports established the direction that policy development was to take. They were supported in a later government report on the state of the workforce (Dawkins, 1988a) and were influential in discussions of 'labour market flexibility' involving the Government, the ACTU and the Confederation of Australian Industry (National Labour Consultative Council, 1987).

The aim of this chapter is to show how the Government and the ACTU in particular have set a broad economic agenda to which

specific policies and proposals affecting young people must conform. Of special interest is first, to examine how the notion of skill is
presently being redefined: in essence it is being socially constructed
to match the demands of capital in a buyers' market. A second
concern is to explore how changing definitions of skill are used to
support the push for more training programmes. As will be seen, the
specific types and forms of training devised for young people cannot be separated from the underlying economic and political
assumptions of Labor politicians and union officials alike. In each
case the construction of the problem and the construction of the
solution produce a particular kind of emphasis in the sort of training
that is provided for young people.

The discussion below should not be construed as an argument
against training. To argue against the training of young people,
whether for work or for personal development, would be absurd.
But to agree with a general proposition that training is an admir-
able objective is not the same thing as to agree that the rhetoric
about training is in fact what is actually occurring. Whatever good
intentions there may be behind some training proposals, the
significance of training must be gauged by how it fits into broader
ideological debates and economic processes, and whether or not
'training' is being designed to empower, or discipline, young people.
To assert that 'training is good', and to adopt a defensive stance on
this point, is to obscure the profound social and political changes
being wrought via the introduction and extension of specific
training policies and programmes

TECHNOLOGY AND SKILL

A restructuring of the world's production and trading systems has
been under way for several decades. In large measure this profound
alteration of the international capitalist system has been the direct
result of changes in the nature and use of high technology. As well
as being the source of many of the economic problems most nations
are experiencing today, high technology is also seen as the solution.
Thus, technology is seen to have a life of its own, exerting a peculiar
push–pull effect on adjustments required for specific national
economies.

In the context of a world over-supply of both primary and
manufactured goods, technological innovation is seen as necessary
for a number of reasons (Mandel, 1975; Jones, 1982; Harman,

1984). First, new technology is seen as providing a competitive edge over other producers, because the use of it enables cheaper production of goods and thus a means to undercut the prices charged by competitors. Second, because jobs in Australian manufacturing have been declining, the development of new high technology is touted as a means to replace these jobs with others in the supply of information-based goods and services. Third, since the problem is one of over-production, the solution is to create new markets. These markets are seen in terms of developing demand for so-called 'brain-based' or 'value-added' goods. Such commodities consist of specialised products and services based upon innovative designs and applications in the area of high technology, and could include new types of computerisation, robotics, energy-saving devices, and so on.

This economic approach requires systematic development of human capital. For it to work, specific types of intellectual resources would be needed. This is because the end product – technological innovation – would require a system of flexible production, with production teams working together and being able to shift easily from one task to another (White, 1985a). This is precisely the kind of view put forward by Barry Jones (1986a) who has argued that: "We have to rethink our concept of resource. We must recognize that a nation can be richer through intellectual effort and living by its wits than through digging things up." The theme of 'living by our wits' is a constant one with Jones and with like-minded colleagues active in the government-funded Commission for the Future, a Melbourne-based thinktank that is attempting to raise public discussion about 'futures' and especially technology (see Jones, 1986bc; Commission for the Future, 1986–88).

From a parallel, but more conservative, perspective, the Economic Planning Advisory Council (EPAC) has also stressed the importance of 'human capital'. A recent EPAC paper (1986: 2) argued that "improving the quality and flexibility of labour, and through it productivity, is an imperative if Australia is to realise more fully its economic and social development potential". The paper goes on to outline how to broaden and deepen the skills of the labour force. Among other things, measures such as upgrading the quantity and quality of 'output' from the technology and business disciplines of the post-school education and training sector, and systematic regular 'standard referenced' reviews of the quality of the Australian school system, are endorsed as ways in which Australia's 'human capital' can be improved. The over-riding interest here is in "productivity growth" and improving the "quality of output from the school system" so as to ensure that "people initially entering the labour force, or those proceeding to higher education, possess broad, generally transferable competences, knowledge and skills".

During the late 1980s in Australia the arguments of people like Barry Jones and the EPAC have gradually become part of accepted economic rationality. Differences in specific goals can be discerned among those who see a 'high tech' future for Australia, but a basic unity exists in that skills development is seen as crucial. On the one hand, skill formation is seen as increasing the 'productivity' of the nation. On the other, it is seen as increasing the 'employability' and employment opportunities of greater numbers of people.

A reconstructed Australia

The Labor Government's strategy in developing a flexible workforce has been based upon the view that "Australia's economic potential has been held back by an inadequate commitment to skills formation and deficiencies in training arrangements." (Department of Employment, Education and Training, 1987). The creation of a new form of 'human capital' has forged closer links between unions, employers, government and educational officials as they have been required to accept more responsibility for skills formation.

A September 1987 Budget Paper of 102 pages titled *Skills for Australia* (Commonwealth of Australia, 1987) set out the Government's policy agenda for the years to come. It began by stating that "urgent action is needed to broaden our trading base by expanding those elements of our manufacturing and service sectors which can contribute effectively to export growth and compete efficiently with imports." (p. 3). This set the tone for the rest of the report, with the major emphasis being on "productivity improvements". Education and training were specifically seen in economic terms, as playing a "vital role in productivity performance, directly conditioning the quality, depth and flexibility of our labour force skills" (p. 4).

In laying down the foundations of a "productive culture", the report outlined objectives and priorities. These included increasing secondary-school retention rates; increasing participation in tertiary education; expanding the Australian Traineeship Scheme; assisting disadvantaged groups such as Aborigines, women, migrants from non-English-speaking backgrounds, and so on. Throughout, the report stressed flexibility and adaptability as these relate to changing labour-market demands. Thus, with respect to the traineeship scheme: "Increased emphasis on vocational competence and adaptability of skills are key objectives of these new arrangements." (p. 7). At the tertiary level, the report stated that the emphasis must be on "broad and transferable skills, and attitudes which equip the workforce to adapt to and influence change" (p. 9).

The calls for a "vocationally skilled and adaptable labour force" stem from the broad macro-economic concerns sketched above. The Government's policy has been informed by two major considerations: the need to rein in public-sector expenditure; and the economic imperative in the allocation of resources. Translated into practice, this means firstly that education and training programmes are to be critically evaluated in terms of 'productivity', with resource priority going to the most economically oriented areas; and secondly that greater attention is to be given to those programmes which establish close financial and educational links with allied industries in the private sector.

In terms of the distribution of education and training efforts, the highest priority in terms of resource allocation is to go to those areas and programmes which show a strong labour-market orientation. While the report acknowledged that educational outcomes should not be measured solely in terms of current labour-market requirements, nevertheless the Government considered that "there is scope for an approach to the use of Commonwealth funds for education and training which is more closely linked to performance, to labour market demands, and to national economic and industry development objectives." (p. 13).

These general goals are to be achieved in part by raising industry's commitment to training and education. In the context of tight budgets, a requirement that industry contribute to the training of the labour force will save a lot of money. In this regard the Government promised to take action to "achieve a more effective relationship between industry and the formal education sector in matters such as curriculum development, the sharing of training facilities and equipment, and the provision of training itself" (p. 14). In mid-September 1987, an example of this co-operation was provided when it was announced that the Business Council of Australia would be working with tertiary institutions to design speical computer-science courses for 200 students. As part of the Government's project to make education "more responsive to industry needs", in this "new approach" to tertiary courses companies would contribute staff, equipment and scholarships of $8000 a year. In what was presented as "another innovation", students would spend 30 per cent of their time in this course getting hands-on experience in industry (*Adelaide Advertiser*, 18 September 1987).

In order to ensure that labour-market objectives are being met, and that those areas and programmes which are able to obtain diverse finance occupy a privileged position in the education and training framework, the report stressed the notions of 'efficiency' and 'effectiveness'. Systematic monitoring and evaluation of each programme will be developed and the "impact of programmes will be assessed to determine their continued relevance and priority, and to ensure that desired outcomes are achieved in the most cost-effective manner" (p. 18). This reinforces the Government's plan to rationalise the education and training sector, both in financial terms and with respect to the content and orientation of existing programmes.

One of the striking things about *Skills for Australia* is that while ostensibly it is based upon concerns with skills formation, the concept of skill itself was not thoroughly examined at any stage. The general argument speaks of skills in terms of flexibility and adaptability. Where specific mention is made, the reference is usually to industry areas rather than to the content of actual individual skills. Thus, for example, potential employment growth is seen in particular areas of manufacturing, tourism and the information industries, with skill development seen as especially needed in computing, hospitality management, catering and travel consultancy. In essence, where skill is invoked as a concrete pheno-menon it tends to refer to specific industries, rather than referring to actual changes occurring within a range of existing workplace settings. Nowhere was there recognition of the notion of skill itself as socially constructed and as born out of the struggles between employer and employee over the nature of the work process.

Given current employer fixations with the idea of 'multi-skilling' as a means to break down 'restrictive work practices', and given the Government's push to get private industry more involved in education and training programmes, one might well ask how 'skill' will be defined in these programmes. A general reorganisation of the labour force is currently in train, with both public and private workplaces subject to processes of re-classification of occupational positions and the 'broadbanding' of whole layers of previously separate tasks. At the same time, the notion of upgrading one's skill level is being used as a means to convince workers of their vulnerability in the face of high unemployment. The content of training thus becomes a crucial factor not only in terms of economic development itself, but also in 'discipline' and 'control' issues in industrial relations.

Australia reconstructed

In August–September 1986 the Australian Council of Trade Unions and the Trade Development Council made a joint fact-finding mission to Western Europe, and on 27 July 1987 the report of the mission was launched in Melbourne to an audience of some 500 business and academic economists, union officials and ALP parliamentarians. The report, *Australia Reconstructed*, is a 230-page document, printed and bound by the Australian Government Publishing Service. The meeting was addressed by John Dawkins, the Minister for Employment, Education and Training, who spoke positively of the commitment of the most senior levels of the trade-union movement to maintaining Australia's international competitiveness.

The 'missionaries' who co-authored the report included union officials from a range of industries – building workers, metal workers, technical and further education teachers, storemen and packers, etc. – as well as senior ACTU officers. The report covers a wide range of issues, including "macroeconomic policies and national issues", "wages, prices and incomes", "trade and industry policy", "labour market and training policies", "industrial democracy, production consciousness, work and management organisation", and "strategic unionism". Underpinning its recommendations is the idea of developing a national economic and social objective: to achieve "full employment, low inflation and rising living standards which are equitably distributed" (p. 19). This is to be achieved through a "consensual approach" which is to be "negotiated, set and given substantial support by all major parties" such as government, unions, business and community groups.

Before considering the parts of the report dealing with skills formation and training, it is essential to highlight the general framework within which the report was written. The ideas and approach to economic and social life adopted in the report basically represent a continuation of a broad perspective embodied in the ALP–ACTU prices-and-incomes Accord agreed to in the early months of 1983. The Accord was struck just before the Labor Party came to power in the March elections. It was premised upon two central ideas: that full employment should be re-established as the principal objective of economic policy; and that achievement of economic and social objectives should be pursued through negotiation and consensus.

In the original Statement of Accord a number of specific policy measures were agreed to by the parties involved. These included policy initiatives in such areas as prices (setting up a pricing authority); wages and working conditions (return to a centralised system of wage fixation); taxation and government expenditure (increasing the social wage); non-wage incomes (restraint on capital gains); and a range of specific supportive policies in the areas of health, education, occupational health and safety, and job creation. In return for wage restraint and industrial peace, the unions were promised increased spending on the social wage and automatic cost-of-living wage increases.

In the years after the Accord was introduced a number of things happened which tested the willingness and abilities of the two sides to implement the agreement (for detailed discussion, see Stilwell, 1986). A National Economic Summit in April 1983 involving representatives from business, unions and Government established the Accord as a tripartite agreement, and saw its transformation from a statement of intention into a negotiating tool. Commitments on the social wage were undercut by the Government's adoption of the 'Trilogy' strategy in 1984, which took the form of a promise to limit taxation increases, total Government expenditure and the size of the Budget deficit as a percentage of the gross national product. Wage discounting was introduced in 1985 after a sharp devaluation of the Australian dollar. Proposed tax cuts have been consistently delayed, and promised improvements in occupational superannuation were subjected to industry-by-industry negotiations rather than being introduced across the board. In 1987 there was a change in the method of determining wage increases: the wage indexation system based on six-monthly national wage cases and (supposedly) tied to increases in the cost of living as measured by the consumer price index, was replaced by a two-tier system of wage adjustment. The first tier consisted of a wage increase negotiated on a flat rate which was discounted below the rate of inflation. The second tier permitted free bargaining in which unions could negotiate for additional wage increases. However, such increases were subject to a ceiling of 4 per cent and were to be determined by a trade-off of wages for increased productivity in the form of giving up certain working conditions (hours, allowances, staffing levels). The August 1988 National Wage Case consolidated the two-tier method of wage fixation and entrenched the notion of a 'productivity-based' wages system as the basis for future negotiations.

Since the Statement of Accord in 1983, wage levels have deteriorated considerably; unemployment has been almost static; the profit share of the non-farm gross domestic product has increased, while the wages share has declined to the levels of the early 1970s; and, especially with the 1986–87 Budget, the social wage has been subject to major cutbacks. As pointed out in *Australia Reconstructed*: "If the average wage earner's standard of living is measured as the combination of his [*sic*] actual, or private, wage and his or her social wage, then he or she is [\$240 a year] worse off than under the last year of the Conservative government and \$208 a year worse off than in the last year of the previous Labor government." (p. 53).

The consensus ideology underlying the Accord meant that the level of industrial dispute fell to a twenty-year low, even while workers' wages and living standards continued their steady decline. The Accord is premised on a notion of a basic harmony at the level of national interest, with union officials and political and business leaders working together to solve the nation's economic problems. From the point of view of the ACTU the Accord was supposed to help to achieve the objective of full employment by boosting aggregate company profits through wage restraint, and thereby increasing productive investment. In turn, this growth in productive investment would create new jobs.

This has not occurred, even though the volume of profits has grown substantially. The report points out that: "Despite high corporate profitability and historically low real unit labour cost, investment remains low in Australia." (p. 17). In responding to this situation it calls for a tripartite inquiry to examine the patterns of investment, particularly with respect to the incidence of 'speculative' versus 'productive' investment.

The report sees economic development as requiring not only more productive investment, but also greater attention to training. Thus, "Governments should not only deliver the correct macroeconomic environment, but also complement this with an aggressive and comprehensive (sectoral-specific) trade and industry development strategy, a network of 'active' labour market and training programs and a set of comprehensive supporting policies." (p. 22). It recommends the setting up of a National Development Fund, administered through the Australian Industry Development Corporation, and partly financed by the incomes of superannuation funds. This fund would be used to provide loans for investment in 'new capacity' in industry. Co-operating with this fund would be a National Employment and Training Fund to provide for skill formation and enhancement, training and general education of the workforce.

Australia Reconstructed shares with the Government a view that skills formation is central to economic development, although greater emphasis is placed on the link between skills and employment. Concern is expressed that Australia is not producing the 'right skills' as well as not producing enough skilled people. Once again the focus is on the development of new high technology as the way forward economically: "If Australian industry is to become more internationally competitive, there is a clear need for increased investment in activities which are skill and technology intensive. In order to fully realise the benefits of the new technologies, increased investment in training has to occur." (p. 123).

The ACTU–TDC report also shares with the Government a concern to forge greater links between education authorities and industry. This is particularly the case in the tertiary sector where, from an economic development point of view, to respond to changing patterns of demand "education authorities must have relevant information about changing trends in the labour market to plan their courses effectively" (p. 119). Later on, it is argued that Australian business especially needs to take a "structural and more active role in specifying the expectations of both young people and the institutions which educate and train them" (p. 124). In general, the provision of training and education is seen in terms of a tripartite framework involving business, unions and government who would work together to ensure that the education system provides adequate preparation for the world of work. In October 1987 a major step in this direction was taken by the Commonwealth Government. John Dawkins announced that the Commonwealth Schools Commission, the Commonwealth Tertiary Education Commission and the Australian Council for Employment and Training would be replaced with a National Board of Employment, Education and Training. The new board would include two representatives from the ACTU and two from the Business Council of Australia and the Confederation of Australian Industry. The ACTU alone would have the same number on the board as the representatives of all educational and training institutions and professionals.

In its discussions of the need to improve the quality and quantity of the skills of young people, the report briefly outlines the kinds of skills it sees as desirable.

> Action is needed to improve skills in communications and numeracy; to ensure Australia's young workers have a higher technological awareness and are adept in current technology; to promote more education and training in business and management skills; and to promote more cross-disciplinary study and training. [p. 124]

Except for later references to the need to develop a "production consciousness and culture" (i.e., an appreciation of the importance of wealth creation), and to expand union education (the general aims of which are "realised only by a massive, tripartite social investment"), there is little discussion of the *social* content of education and training. The education and training spoken of in the report tends to see skills in primarily *industrial* terms, and even the discussions of production consciousness and union education imply that somehow they are neutral in content, simply a matter of improving production processes and industrial relations.

By presenting skills in purely technical terms, the report is able to recommend that employers, unions and employees at the enterprise level co-operate in identifying and anticipating the future skill needs of industry. As the authors put it, "The Accord process should not stop at the national or industry level. Skills accords should be negotiated at the local and enterprise level." (p. 127). Hence, a commonality of interests is once again stressed between employers, unions and workers, and consensual negotiation is seen as the proper industrial strategy.

WORKFORCE SKILLS AND THE LABOUR MARKET

Both the Government and union leaders have perceived the problems facing Australia in the same way. Each sees future economic growth in terms of new applications of high technology and the development of new production and service areas. Each views the solution in terms of improving the overall level of skills in the Australian workforce. Each looks to a partnership of business, unions and government in reconstructing the Australian economy.

In order to assess the demand for this new kind of labour power – one which is flexible, adaptable and skilled – we need to have some idea of the kinds of skills presently needed in the workforce.

Furthermore, we need to have a basic understanding of the wider structural factors affecting unemployment, particularly as these impinge upon the Australian economy. In the context of the world economy, several interrelated trends have had a substantial impact upon economic activity in Australia. These include the extension of automation into virtually every production sphere and the impact of this on jobs (Gorz, 1982, 1985; White, 1986a; Jones, 1982); the international debt crisis and the effect of austerity measures on public-service employment and general consumption patterns; the ability of Pacific Rim nations such as Japan, Singapore, South Korea and Taiwan to take advantage of new mass-production machinery and therefore to grab a sizeable share of the world market for finished and processed commodities; the use of capital for company takeovers, playing the sharemarkets or buying commercial real estate, rather than for investment in production; and the impact of corporate borrowing on the national debt and domestic interest rates. To these trends might be added such factors as overall level of technological expertise and research, economies of scale, and distance from large markets.

Against this backdrop of international trends, calls for an upgrading of skill levels for the purpose of either economic development or employment growth must be critically evaluated. Indeed, an examination of changes occurring in the labour process and in the labour market suggests an alternative explanation for the renewed interest in skills, an explanation that focuses on specific industrial relations issues.

The Minister for Employment, Education and Training, John Dawkins, recently wrote that the task ahead in the area of training is manifold (*Australian*, 12 August 1987).

> We need to structure the transition from general education so as to ensure that all Australians gain as much benefit as they are willing and able to derive, general education being the best guarantee of a flexible and adaptable workforce.
>
> We need to ensure that training is related not to today's industrial requirements but to tomorrow's, recognising that many traditional occupational specialisations are becoming obsolete.
>
> We need to ensure that except for the largest concerns, training is industry rather than enterprise-oriented, recognising that broadly relevant and periodically refurbishable skills are those least vulnerable to obsolescence.

It should be apparent from this statement that what Dawkins has in mind is preparation of a workforce which is trained in *general* skills which would allow them the greatest flexibility and adaptability as the nature of the production process changes. What is less clear is whether this orientation towards skills in fact constitutes a general upgrading in 'average' skill levels, or whether it represents a general downgrading of skills required in the modern workforce. In order to evaluate this question it is important to analyse both the structure of the labour market and the nature of the labour process itself.

Generally speaking, the main trend in employment has been away from manufacturing and toward 'information-based' employment in service and technical occupations (Jones, 1982, 1986c; Windschuttle, 1984, 1986; Stilwell, 1986). Far from a boom at the high skill end of the labour market, the actual movement in employment status appears to be toward jobs requiring less training and less expertise (see Levin and Rumberger, 1983; Davis, 1984; Windschuttle, 1984, Sweet, 1987). Fast-food outlets, clerical work, various service industries, tourism – these are the areas in which employment opportunities are opening up. In these sectors competition between enterprises, and between prospective employees, is based less on skill (in general) than on labour costs (in general). This is reflected in the composition of the workforces in these areas.

For example, in noting that the private sector accounted for 85 per cent of the total increase in the number of employed wage and salary earners over the three years to March 1987, *Skills for Australia* also observed that:

> Among industries, the service sector has provided the greatest contribution to employment, particularly for females, with employed wage and salary earners in finance, property and business services growing by 23.5 per cent and strong growth recorded also in construction, recreation, personal and other services, wholesale and retail trade and community services. [pp. 25–6]

Significantly, the employment record over the last four years is weighted in the direction of female employment, with 60 per cent of total job growth involving women and girls. This is significant because the majority of females are concentrated in just three occupations: clerical, sales, and service. As pointed out in *Australia Reconstructed*, "Seventy-four per cent of all female employees work in community services, wholesale and retail trade, manufacturing and finance, property and business services. More than half of all female employees work in the first two of these industries." (p. 121).

The bulk of the full-time, low-paid, low-skilled workers are employed in the service sector. Not surprisingly, a substantial proportion of these workers are women, but they also include migrants (especially those from non-English-speaking backgrounds) who are likewise subject to exploitation via segregation in the labour market.

The trend in employment towards low skills and low wages is also indicated by the growth in part-time work. Overall part-time employment has grown from 10 per cent of total employment in 1970 to 20 per cent in 1987 (Lever-Tracy, 1988: 212), and over half of the new jobs created from 1973 to 1988 have been part-time (Wajcman and Rosewarne, 1986). Significantly, and especially for women, the new jobs in the service sector are mainly part-time. As Wajcman and Rosewarne (1986: 16) observe, these employees "work for low wages with few, if any, of the benefits or rights that go with full-time employment. There is no job security or promotion aspects and few of these workers belong to unions."

While the 'average' skill required in the labour market as a whole appears to reflect a downward movement, nevertheless labour shortages in particular areas have been pointed to as a means to justify the rhetoric about skills formation. *Skills for Australia*, for instance, points out that

> shortages of skilled labour have re-emerged in key areas such as the metal trades (especially in the machine tooling area), electrical trades and electronic engineering and technical support occupations. Outside of manufacturing, shortages persist in a range of important occupational groupings, including computing professionals, catering and food processing trades, business professionals, printing trades, and nurses. [p. 28]

These labour shortages cannot be explained simply in terms of lack of 'skilled' labour, since other factors such as labour mobility, labour-market discrimination and segmentation, and experience need to be taken into account in explanations of structural mismatches between job vacancies and job placements.

THE LABOUR PROCESS

Moving from labour-market analysis to an examination of the labour process, we see three types of changes in skill requirements. These are de-skilling, re-skilling, and multi-skilling.

The notion of *de-skilling* refers to those instances where, generally due to the introduction of machinery or new technology, traditional work skills lose their value. Ultimately the result is that an occupational group will not be required to have specific skills and qualifications in order to perform a particular kind of labour. For instance, a postal worker who sorts mail may formerly have needed several months' training in order to learn to recall thousands of points of distribution quickly and correctly. With mechanised plants, much sorting can be done automatically: the coders need fewer skills and less training than when they performed all of the tasks themselves. With fewer qualifications required, work which has been de-skilled is thus opened up to a larger number of potential workers. In this situation the workforce can be controlled through the mechanisms of supply and demand in the labour market. Hence, wages, working conditions and job security are less negotiable because the low skill requirement allows virtually anyone to step into a job.

At the same time as technology has led to the de-skilling of some types of work, it has necessarily created new areas of skill development. Recent areas of specialist concern, such as robotics, computer programming and bio-genetics, require personnel with new types of conceptual and technical skills. Considering that many of the areas of *re-skilling* are on the frontiers of knowledge and experimentation, the call is for trained intellectual workers. More specifically, the demand is for 'smart' labour power, that is, people who have adaptive knowledge as well as skills. Highly skilled adaptable people are desired because, in order to be competitive, enterprises need to engage in flexible-system production, so that they can shift their efforts as the industry as a whole evolves and responds to developments elsewhere.

The call for 'smart' labour power – in Barry Jones' terms, the need to work smarter, not harder – is a reflection of changing conceptions of what the 'new type of employee' should be like. However, if workers are 'smarter' in terms of the breadth, depth and flexibility of their knowledge and skills, this could in its own right cause a few problems for the employer, and in particular, for managers. As John Freebairn of the Business Council of Australia puts it:

> I think that in the long run having astute people who question what they are doing will lead to more efficient production systems, as well as happier workers, but you may get a few more ruffles in the system as management have to counter

people asking questions and sometimes being indignant. [Quoted in Kissane, 1986: 40.]

Similar concerns have been expressed by the Economic Planning Advisory Council in its discussions of the issue of "management rigidities" and the problems with "substantially outmoded approaches to management and work practices" (EPAC, 1986). Part of the solution to this dilemma is to develop workers who will be 'compliant' as well as 'smart' (Wexler et al., 1981; White, 1985a).

In order to maintain present forms of work organisation, education and training have to provide specific technical skills without a wider critical and interpretive understanding of society, or instil in the worker new kinds of work ethics and status considerations, or both. In essence, the new 'ideal' worker is prefigured in the form of the yuppie technocrat – the highly skilled, highly paid, and highly individualistic employee who finds satisfaction in personal consumption.

The concept of *multi-skilling* has recently emerged in response to the replacement of narrow job descriptions with broader classifications. In media reports it has been linked to instances where employers have attempted to rationalise existing 'work practices' in a particular factory, refinery, colliery or other 'typical' working-class workplace. The rhetoric of multi-skilling has been used to allow employers to cut down the size of their existing workforces and to increase productivity by putting pressure on workers to accept a greater range and number of tasks on the job.

The image which is presented to the public conveys a picture that workers are learning new skills and that this is 'progressive' because it will increase the marketability of each individual worker. Support for the concept has come from both businesses and unions. At its October 1987 meeting in Canberra, for example, the idea of a 'superskilled' metalworker was endorsed by the Metal Trades Industry Association and the Secretary of the ACTU, Bill Kelty. Such a worker is created by means of a rationalisation of job classifications so that workers are required to perform more than one job. Thus, the recent agreement struck between unions and employers in the metal trades will completely reconstitute all jobs in the industry through the collapsing of 348 job classifications into a dozen or less. The agreement also emphasises the "broadbanding" of skills (Australian Manufacturing Council, 1988).

Although 'sold' as re-skilling, the notion of multi-skilling is in fact best thought of as part of an immediate industrial-relations strategy, rather than part of a longer-term structural upgrading of skills. Indeed, those agencies which advocate more flexibility in occupational classifications themselves clearly recognise the negative employment outcomes of multi-skilling. It is argued that such changes in work practices will lead to "more responsibility, greater job satisfaction and security, and higher remuneration for employees" and that there will be "more efficient production techniques, improved productivity, and *reduced* manning [*sic*] levels for employers" (EPAC, 1986: 15, emphasis added). The first potential 'benefit' is highly contentious, given the inherent power imbalance between employer and worker, and the sheer number of and competition between unemployed workers, many of whom could easily become 'multi-skilled' and would be willing to be hired on the employer's terms. The second so-called benefit points to the contradictory situation where, to improve productivity, enterprises must find ways to reduce the size of the labour force, thus further swelling the pool of unemployed workers.

At a policy level, the Government has tended to equate skills formation with multi-skilling. The apprenticeship system has been criticised, for example, for not being flexible or responsive enough to the needs of industry and the advances in technology. As *Skills for Australia* sees it, "Skills training should become more broadly-based and multi-skilled in character, be moved from a time-serving to a competency basis, and become a significant component in a ladder of continuous skills development." (p. 57). The concerns of the Government in the area of youth training policy, however, are apt to conflict with the interests of the unions and their training policy. Simultaneously, the interests of unions in protecting the well-being of their members may be undercut by the Government's youth training policy.

In the first instance, the objectives of the ACTU to cater to the interests of its members already in the workforce means that on-the-job training is seen as crucial. The result will be that: "To the extent that the emerging manufacturing industry training, retraining, multi-skilling and award rationalisation packages are successful, there will be a fall-off in loss rates for tradespeople, and a concomitant reduction in apprenticeship opportunities for teenagers (male or female)." (Freeland, 1987: 8). In the second case, the increased number of workers with adaptable skills and technical training will undercut the bargaining power of previously secure skilled workers and lead to job losses in particular industry areas.

Above all the concept of multi-skilling, as currently manifest in policy statements and industrial practice, represents a political reorganisation of the workplace. If we acknowledge that skill is socially constructed, then any redefinition of skill will affect the relationship between capital and wage labour and their control over the labour process, and consequently will affect negotiations over wage rates and working conditions. An industrial definition of skill is related to factors such as: the ability of workers to gain recognition of their work as skilled; their ability to define the requirements for entry into that work; and their ability to define the requirements for entry to a particular area of training (O'Donnell, 1984). Changes in any of these areas will affect the definition of skill, and the position of workers in the labour market.

Multi-skilling effectively challenges one of the basic components of the bargaining power of workers – the holding of *specific* skills. A generalisation of the skill content of work, through the development of adaptable and flexible work practices, effectively undercuts this power of the worker. In the end, the initial upgrading of skills in terms of 'average skill' destroys previous demarcations between workers at one level, while creating the impetus for new specialisations to emerge further up the labour-market hierarchy. This process therefore represents a polarisation of skills, with the 'multi-skilled' worker eventually being seen as performing labour which is simple and routine (since it is done by non-specialists) and 'experts' being deployed for the specialised tasks.

This process of redefining skill is reinforced by the collapsing of job classifications in training as well as on the job. The broadening of the channels leading to work – by redefining what is appropriate training for specific industry areas, and by offering training for everybody – creates a labour market where workers are interchangeable. An example of this is provided by O'Donnell (1984: 20):

> Retailing, for example, is usually considered unskilled work, partly because the advent of compulsory education has taught everybody the necessary skills for the job. Only migrants with poor spoken English, or unfamiliarity with written English, are ineligible. If brick-laying was a compulsory subject at secondary school it, too, would probably be considered an unskilled trade.

Similarly, if multi-skilled work is supported by generally available and accessible training then the effectiveness of workers in pursuing industrial claims will be undermined accordingly.

So far we have examined recent developments in the labour market and the labour process. We now look at the position of young people in relation to these trends, and the specific character of training programmes in terms of their 'skill' content.

SKILLS FORMATION AND YOUTH TRAINING

Training programmes for young people have been developed, expanded and actively pushed by the Government for several related reasons. These training programmes should not be seen simply as instruments for the labour market. Their full significance emerges when we relate them to a conjunction of specific developments in three areas: employer–employee relations; government economic planning and finances; and the maintenance of public order. The factors influencing developments in these areas, especially as they pertain to young people, are those of discipline, control and economic efficiency.

The biggest problem confronting working-class young people today is that of unemployment and the problems associated with it, such as poverty, homelessness, alienation, and boredom. From the point of view of government the 'youth problem' presents itself in various ways. High youth unemployment is a drain on government resources in terms of support benefits paid out. It is dangerous ideologically because the increased public visibility of the young unemployed in the malls and on the streets reminds voters of the depth of the economic crisis and the lack of adequate political responses to the crisis. It also 'costs' the government in the area of law and order, as youth crime escalates and moral panic leads to calls for something to be done about the new street urchins and the urban homeless.

Employers' attitudes to the situation of unemployed young people reflect government concerns with the question of public order, and also their own concerns about the type of employee they would like to have. Specifically, attention has been drawn to the *skills* (or lack thereof) of young people and the *attitudes* of young people. Too much time out of the workforce, and relying on government 'handouts', is seen to erode the 'work ethic'. In addition, the expectations and behaviour of many young people entering the workforce have been criticised in terms of lack of motivation, lack of responsibility, and unrealistic expectations of the job and the employer.

The union movement sees youth unemployment as a social evil

and as an economic waste of valuable labour power. What is needed is an 'active labour market policy' which maintains full employment – one which emphasises skill formation, job placement and a reduction of labour-market segmentation, rather than a 'passive' one which relies mainly on cash payments to the unemployed. The objectives of economic development and full employment will both be met by enhancing skills and directing labour to the new growth industries.

Whichever way the problem is constructed, there has emerged a growing 'consensus' as to how it should be tackled. Namely, to ensure that all young people within specified ages are doing 'something' – employment, training or education – rather than 'nothing', i.e., living on the dole and hanging around. In order to make sure that young people will take up these more 'productive' options the Government has restructured its benefits and social welfare administration, in the process abolishing the under-eighteen unemployment benefit, establishing 'activity tests', matching Austudy allowances with unemployment allowances, and extending the waiting period for benefits. These measures have drastically reduced any choice by young people as to what they do with their time and how they respond to the situations in which they find themselves.

The changes in income supports available to young people have been accompanied by changes in the programmes on offer to them. Thus, a more rigorously policed *benefit* system has been offset by an expansion in specific training *programmes*. This has included the creation of more places in the Australian Traineeship Scheme, the introduction of a new Youth Training Programme, the establishment of a Job Search Training Programme and the provision of additional resources for the establishment of further Information Technology Centres.

These measures have primarily affected sixteen- and seventeen-year-olds and young unemployed people under the age of twenty-one. Broad support for the direction the Government is taking has been expressed by the ACTU, which goes one step further by proposing that the system be extended to the age of twenty-four. One of the recommendations in *Australia Reconstructed* (p. 125), for example, states that:

> The government should develop a specific and integrated five-year program for young people. Such a program should,

within a five-year period, guarantee that all 16 to 24-year-olds have access to full-time education specific vocational training or productive employment. At the end of the five-year program the number of persons requiring cash unemployment benefits should be at an absolute minimum.

While the emphasis here is clearly on skill formation, such a programme looks like a method of keeping a substantial proportion of young people occupied, without being employed, well into their twenties. The link to a genuine labour-market and employment strategy seems difficult to fathom if we closely consider the structural nature of youth unemployment.

Rather than posing the problem as one of 'employability', and thereby focusing on skills and abilities, a more realistic way of looking at the issue of unemployment is to consider the main factors affecting the juvenile labour market. Here the key variables are age and sex. Because of wider transitions in the labour force, away from manufacturing and toward the community services and retail industries, there has been a sharp decline in traditional male-dominated industries. As part of this transformation young people as a whole are facing direct competition for jobs from women in particular, and older workers in general. As Freeland (1987: 7) points out:

> Between 1966 and 1986 teenage males lost 80 000 full-time jobs, and 60 to 64 year old males lost 31 200 full-time jobs. For females, teenagers lost 110 000 full-time jobs and 20 to 44 year olds gained some 613 600. ... In 1966 20 to 44 year olds held 55.4 per cent of all full-time jobs and this increased to 67.6 per cent in 1986. The overall teenage share fell from 14.1 to 7.6 per cent.

In general it can be said that young people are being squeezed out of the labour market by the more experienced, the more 'mature', and the more qualified. The older a person is, usually, the more responsibilities and personal family commitments they have, and so there is greater motivation to settle into a particular job framework. Young single people, on the other hand, have traditionally constituted a more volatile and mobile workforce, tending to change jobs frequently, interspersing their paid work with periods of unemployment.

Young people have so far been able to hold their own in the job competition stakes in one area: the male-dominated trade occupations involving the apprenticeship system. This is indicated in figures which show that:

> Between 1971 and 1981 teenage male employment in the broad occupational category of 'tradesmen, labourers, etc' grew by 18.3 per cent whereas adult male employment grew by 5.4 per cent. On the other hand in the broad clerical category, teenage female employment fell by 18.0 per cent, but adult female employment grew by 59.3 per cent. [Sweet, 1987: 15.]

The overall trends, however, are for young people to be displaced by older workers in those areas of work affected by technological and structural change, and to be more vulnerable than older workers in the case of retrenchments.

That the key variable is social and economic circumstance rather than 'skill level' or 'training', is further indicated when we consider the nature of part-time paid work. While the proportion of teenagers with full-time paid employment declined by 31 per cent between 1966 and 1985, the number of part-time teenage workers increased by 355 per cent between 1966 and 1984. Significantly, and for reasons which are explored elsewhere (Sweet, 1987), employers tend to favour the hiring of *students*, as shown by the fact that "four out of every five jobs for 15–17-year-old part-time workers are held by school students rather than by young people who otherwise would be employed" (Commonwealth Schools Commission, 1987: 13).

All of this puts paid to the idea that somehow or other training, in and of itself, will provide the magic solution to the problem of unemployment for young people. This has of course been implicitly and explicitly recognised by the Government in its other labour-market strategy, education, where concerted attempts are being made to increase school retention rates as a means to keep young people off the unemployment rolls. But there is a further dimension to the training side of youth policy.

Available information indicates that while over 60 per cent of school-leavers in the full-time labour force find their first full-time job within thirteen weeks, many subsequently leave these jobs and experience periods of unemployment, particularly between eighteen and twenty years of age (Commonwealth of Australia, 1987: 43). Related to this phenomenon, in April 1987, Prime Minister Hawke 'highlighted' the problem of people on unemployment benefits turning down jobs they did not like. He conceded that he could understand why young people would be unwilling to accept jobs which were not ideal or not satisfying. He went on to say that "at least while times are tough you have got to be prepared to do those things and if you are not prepared to do those, well, then the community is not going to pay the benefits" (*Adelaide Advertiser*, 1987).

In order to 'redress' these problems, the Government now requires an 'employment separation certificate' before the unemployed can receive unemployment benefits. This is to be filled in by the employer and to show when and why the person left the job. The other response has been to insist that young unemployed people engage in a training programme of some kind. The combination of these measures provides us with further insight into the rationale behind the push for traineeships, short-term training programmes and especially the Job Search Programme (beyond that of keeping young people busy and under control). For these programmes put additional pressure on young people to take up and stay with dead-end jobs; to endure exploitation by unscrupulous employers; and to suffer the discipline of the labour process in any kind of work setting.

The social control aspects of training become more apparent when we consider who are the actual targets of the programmes. The majority of young people are not seen as a 'problem', because they are already engaged in some type of education or employment (Jamrozik, 1988). With greater financial support available from the family unit, and a greater propensity to 'succeed' in the educational sphere, the prospects of middle-class young people still remain relatively good, even if greater credentialism means that generally speaking the position of educated workers tends to worsen over time as they are forced to take up lower-level jobs (Rumberger, 1980, 1984).

The main targets for training programmes are young people from low-income families, and those population groups which have been designated 'disadvantaged'. The latter category is a broad one: it includes Aborigines, women, migrants from non-English speaking backgrounds, people with disabilities, sole parents and the long-term unemployed. In order to assess the benefits accruing to these groups from participation in training programmes, we need to have a better idea of the content, structure and outcomes of these programmes.

THE AUSTRALIAN TRAINEESHIP SCHEME

When the Australian Traineeship Scheme (ATS) was first introduced, many people in youth affairs expressed their reservations
about the programme (see, for example, *Youth Worker*, 1986). Some
of their concerns were:

- the lack of jobs at the end of a training programme
- the forcing of young people into a secondary labour force,
  thereby reducing their chances of entering the primary workforce
- the shifting of young people from one category to another
  without changing the 'real' job situation
- ensuring that accreditation for any training undertaken and that
  transfer of credit from State to State occurs
- that payments from training undercut youth and adult wages
  and lower the living standards of young people
- that very little protection for the trainee is built into such
  programmes
- that real jobs for real wages are being turned into subsidised
  traineeships
- that there is inadequate monitoring of programmes to ensure
  that the on-the-job component is in fact offered.

Many of these concerns have still not been dealt with satisfac-
torily, and indeed some of the fears raised by youth workers seem to
have had more weight than was acknowledged by government
officials at the time. In the September 1987 Budget, for example, the
Commonwealth Government announced that it would be convert-
ing the recruitment of all base-grade clerical positions for 16–18-
year-olds, without Year 12 qualifications, to traineeships in both the
Australian Public Service and in Commonwealth Statutory Authorities for those occupational categories where traineeships have been
developed.

If the British experience is anything to go by, then serious
questions about the Australian Traineeship Scheme need to be
addressed much more fully than they have been to date. In the
United Kingdom such programmes have seen young people exploited on the job and paid low wages. They have also reduced the
significance of apprenticeships; they have been characterised by sex
and race inequalities in training opportunities; and they have been
used by employers as a means of positive vetting of employees or

simply as a way to gain cheap labour by continuous use of trainees rather than creating permanent positions (Finn, 1983, 1987; Gleeson, 1986; Loney, 1986; Manwaring and Sigler, 1985; Pearson, 1985; Westhorp, 1987).

As the centrepiece of the Hawke Labor Government's youth policy, the Australian Traineeship Scheme has fallen far short of initial expectations. When first introduced it was hoped that 10 000 traineeships would be created in 1985–86, and a further 75 000 per year by 1988–89. By the end of August 1987, only some 9000 trainees had commenced the programme. As Figure 2.1 indicates, the bulk of traineeships were concentrated in the public service in

Figure 2.1: Australian Traineeship Scheme: cumulative trainee commencements, Australia, July 1986 to July 1987

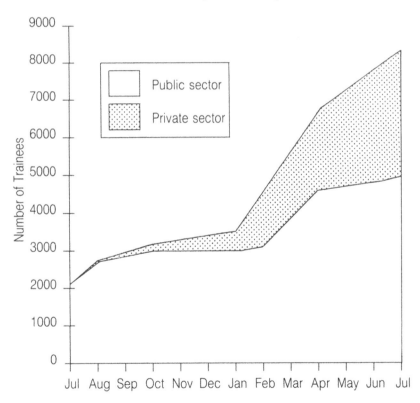

Source: Commonwealth of Australia, 1987: 49.

the early stages of the programme. Since then the Government has made highly publicised efforts to increase private sector involvement and these efforts appear to be meeting with some success. Even so, by the end of 1988 only about 20 000 young people had participated in the traineeship system since its inception.

A profile of traineeships created and commenced is provided in *Australia Reconstructed*. The figures show that, apart from high public sector involvement, the only major private sector involvement has come from the 'office and clerical' and the 'retail' sectors (see Table 2.1). The preponderance of these occupational areas in the ATS programme partly explains why young women are well represented in traineeships, accounting for some 68 per cent of commencements up to August 1987 (Commonwealth of Australia, 1987: 50). Given the high proportion of private traineeships in the 'office and clerical' area, it is instructive to examine briefly what such a traineeship course consists of.

Brochure materials provided on office traineeships in South Australia sell the programme to prospective employer participants in the following terms:

BENEFITS:
> Trained and committed staff capable of building client confidence, reducing costs and increasing productivity
> A more flexible workforce adaptable to your business needs
> Reduced staff turnover
> The chance to assess your trainee for a permanent position in your company
> Complementary off-the-job training at no additional cost
> Financial assistance to offset any additional cost incurred in training.

Some of the 'FEATURES' of the programme include: "Trainees are selected by you, with the assistance available through the CES if required"; "The wage you pay takes into account the trainee's age and time spent on the job"; "For each trainee, you will receive a $1000 training fee"; and "For each trainee, you will be exempt from payroll tax". It is also emphasised that, in addition to learning occupational skills such as use of keyboards, office records, finance and banking procedures, reception and client services, trainees will learn "broad skills in communication, and personal and work effectiveness skills".

From this outline it should be clear that the ATS has much in common with the British Manpower Services Commission pro-

Table 2.1:   Traineeships: proportion created and commenced in different employment sectors, May 1987

Employment Sector	Positions created and anticipated (%)	Trainees commenced (%)
Public (Commonwealth and State)	58.0	65.2
Office and clerical	23.7	23.1
Retail	10.1	5.5
All others	8.2	5.2

Source: ACTU–TDC, 1987: 119.

grammes alluded to above. The taking on of a trainee is presented as an opportunity to vet new staff, and as an attractive financial proposition. In the British case, it has also been pointed out that Youth Training Schemes have systematically omitted questions about the quality of work, its structure, its design and its organisation (Gleeson, 1986). In our example of office traineeships, 7 per cent of training time has been allocated for the subject of "Work Environment". This is to include both general information on business and organisational structures, occupational health and safety, industrial relations, and discrimination and equal opportunity; and industry-specific induction to the particular area of work. It is doubtful that such subjects would include critical insight into the nature of work, or do much to lead the trainee to a heightened consciousness of worker rights and union participation. This is especially so when we consider the power the employer has in determining the on-the-job training and ultimately the future prospects of the trainee.

While the cry is that unemployment is due to lack of training (the slogan of the ATS is 'Toward A Skilled Australia'), it would appear that much of the training on offer is either low quality or marginal to the needs of the employer if we view it in purely technical terms. It does not usually take a person one year, for example, to learn basic clerical, office or retail service skills. If this is the case, then what are young people involved in traineeships learning beyond initial industrial skills, and what type of labour is seen as desirable by employers? To answer this we need to return once again to considerations of the notion of 'skill'.

The demand for a skilled labour force is premised upon the notion that such a labour force would be adaptable, flexible and *disciplined*. The first two attributes imply that specific technical skills are less relevant than general transferable skills, and that therefore young people need to be trained for work-in-general within industry areas, rather than simply for specific jobs. Such general training further connotes a shift in emphasis from specifically industrial definitions of skill to psychological and behavioural concepts.

This shift in orientation means that trainees are to be evaluated on more than simply technical training grounds. In particular, skill training as translated into practice is to involve the teaching of self-control and the regulation of one's public behaviour as an essential feature of one's skill enhancement. Industrial notions of skill are thus being broadened to include other personal attributes as well. As Buswell (1986: 74) puts it: "To use a definition of skill which includes social and behaviour as well as mental attributes makes it possible to assess a person on all these dimensions, giving as much weight to features of personality, appearance and speech as to aptitude and knowledge."

The renewed emphasis on 'impression management' and 'personality' as 'skills' is, in turn, closely associated with the imposition of a new form of discipline on young workers. For if skill is redefined in general abstract terms as revolving around transferable *behavioural* characteristics, due to the fact that technical skills are subject to constant change requiring perpetual retraining, then discipline and skill become part of a unitary whole (see Cohen, 1984). The selection of young workers on the basis of personal attributes thus may mean that young people will be trained to adjust their behaviour to suit the purposes of the employer.

In part, this is already ingrained in the mode of operation of the traineeship system. As a recent advertising feature in the *Adelaide Advertiser* (30 April 1988) commented: "Employers select their own trainees and obtain motivated young people. Trainees attend formal training and use the skills learnt when they return to their employer's workplace. The employer has the opportunity to mould those skills into a very productive form." Not only do employers have a prime opportunity to "mould" their charges, to instil the idea that particular kinds of 'motivation' and 'self-discipline' are part of the skill requirement rather than aspects of management control over the labour process, but the structure of traineeships allows little room for an alternative view to be put.

These kinds of training developments are most apparent in the personal service industries, such as the retail trade and tourism, but the principle is applicable to industry training in general. This is because employers in general "cannot know what *particular* skills they require from their workers' general education and training" (Finn, 1987: 120). What they do know is that the best worker is one who is adaptable and compliant. Certainly the power of employers would be strengthened if they were provided with a workforce that was docile and obedient, thanks to a form of training which incorporated self-discipline as an essential component of skill development. In these circumstances, the rights of young people as workers are apt to be abused in the employer–employee relationship, and basic principles of unionism and notions of worker solidarity undermined.

DIFFERENT TRAINING ORIENTATIONS

The creation of a particular kind of compliance in young people is not a straightforward process; nor is it without contradictions. A brief review of government training programmes, however, indicates that the general direction of training coincides with efforts to mould a flexible but disciplined workforce. This should not be taken to imply that this is the conscious intention of all providers of training. Indeed, there is some resistance to such an orientation at the practical, as opposed to the policy formulation, level. Nevertheless, the overall framework within which training occurs bears the mark of wider concerns with social control and narrowly conceived 'human capital' formation.

Government training programmes fall into into three categories: 'vocationalist', 'social-psychological', and 'basic functional'. There may be overlap between each of these types of training, but these distinctions provide us with a means to differentiate the particular emphases in the training on offer. Table 2.2 indicates the main orientation of each type of training.

Vocationalist training focuses on so-called practical or industrial skills. The main sources of such training are the apprenticeship system and TAFE colleges. Such programmes are seen as having a specifically vocational orientation, with close links to particular industry areas. The training provided is specific to an occupation or trade.

Table 2.2:   Training programmes: characteristics

Type of programme	Characteristics
Vocationalist	
orientation	narrow vocationalist, specific application
source of training	apprenticeships, TAFE
type of training	'multi-skilling'
Social-psychological	
orientation	narrow remedial, general application
source of training	Australian Traineeship Scheme, Youth Training Programme, Job Search, etc.
type of training	'social and life skills'
Basic functional	
orientation	broad remedial, general application
source of training	English as a second language, Trade-based pre-employment courses, Aboriginal Employment Development Policy
type of training	'basic' skills, and 'equal opportunity' training

The TAFE system is seen by the Government as central to its intention to upgrade the quality of Australia's labour skills. In order to achieve this, it is expanding TAFE's total training capacity, giving priority to particular areas of existing and future skill shortage, and structuring capital grants in such a way as to reward those colleges which succeed in getting industry to make financial contributions to the purchase of TAFE equipment.

An increase in employer contributions is an aim of the Government with respect to the apprenticeship system also. Other aims include making trade training more flexible, and developing a competency-based rather than time-served approach to the acquisition and recognition of skills (Commonwealth of Australia, 1987). The intention here is to improve the productivity of the skilled labour force by tailoring the training programmes to produce tradespeople who are 'multi-skilled'. The call for 'flexibility' is thus tied to simultaneous efforts on the industrial relations front to get rid of 'inappropriate work practices and award classifications'. Uniform competency standards and arrangements for competency testing are seen as ways of responding to the needs of industry and advances in technology.

Social-psychological training focuses on broadening the experiences of the trainee, rather than on providing a lengthy core training in specific industrial skills. These programmes provide remedial training for young people who have left school early or have been unemployed for longer than six months. On the one hand there are courses which have been designed to provide the young person with work experience and training both on and off the job. On the other hand, training is to be provided in 'social and life' skills with the emphasis on helping young people to participate in the existing labour market.

The Australian Traineeship Scheme is an example of the former type of training. Another example is the newly created Youth Training Programme which is to provide a range of short-term vocational training opportunities for unemployed young people. The value of such programmes in enabling young people to find permanent work, and this is especially the case with the ATS, has been discussed previously. Just as the British Manpower Services Commission hopes that the Youth Training Scheme certificate in that country will amount to a work-based alternative to conventional qualifications (see Finn, 1987: 180–1), the Australian Government is hopeful that 'traineeships become a normal, rather than exceptional, method of entry into the workforce' (Commonwealth of Australia, 1987: 51).

The training provided is 'remedial' in character: it assumes that something is wrong with the young people in question – they do not have the right skills, proper attitudes or keen enough motivation. The implication is that such young people have no experience of the world of work, and that certain behavioural deficiencies must be overcome through a structured training programme. In commenting on the new training schemes in Britain, Willis (foreword to Finn, 1987: xviii) makes an observation which is relevant to the Australian situation. He states that:

> They are offering (institutionally) to the kids what they have (culturally) already: detailed knowledge of work; motivation to work; skills to deal with working with others – in short the

capacity to labour itself. One might say that the curse of the working class – work – has been taken from the working class, repackaged, and given back to them as a 'blessing'. It seems that it is now necessary to provide for the working class remedial learning in order for it to be properly working class!

We have already noted the type of jobs which are at the heart of the ATS, and that these mostly require low skills and pay low wages. The problem is to convince young people that these kinds of jobs are not to be resisted, and that they offer some kind of personal satisfaction. The resulting emphasis, therefore, is on socialising young people to accept particular work practices and to attempt to change their attitudes and behaviour to fit the task.

The vocationally oriented short-term training programmes are complemented by efforts to provide young people with 'skills' which will enable them to break into the labour market. The Youth Training Programme, for example, pays particular attention to the 'preparatory training needs of young people' and covers 'structured training in job search skills'. More specific programmes include Youth Access Centres which provide information on employment occupations, education, income support and community services, and the Job Search Training Programme. The latter provides intensive three-week training courses and practical experience in job-search skills (via 'Job Clubs'), and shorter-term job-search training opportunities of between seventeen and twenty hours' duration (simply titled "Job Search Training"). In addition to these, as we saw in Chapter 1, a newly integrated community, youth training and employment assistance programme (combining the Community Youth Support Scheme, the Community Training Programme, and the Community Volunteer Programme), titled SkillShare, provides young people with the opportunity to develop their work and personal skills, and to gain work experience through undertaking voluntary community work.

Some indication of the orientation of these programmes is provided in a 1988 newspaper advertisement featuring a photograph of a young woman under the banner heading of "I'm working". Part of the text ran as follows: "I went to a JOB SEARCH TRAINING COURSE where I learnt how to look for jobs, write job applications and go for interviews. I've now got a job. The course was free, and took less than a week." The content typical of these programmes is outlined in a brochure on 'The Education Bridging Course' offered by TAFE in conjunction with the Commonwealth Employment

Service (January 1986). Across the top of the brochure are the words "Hard Work", "Achievement" and "Success". The course promises to "get you up and running" by teaching skills which will help the person "be more competitive in job seeking" and "make decisions about your vocational and educational future". In response to a rhetorical question asking what the Education Bridging Course is, the answer is "revising; learning; continuing with Vocational English and Mathematics, Thinking Skills, Communication and Life Skills, Work Education, Study Skills, Learning how to Learn, and Computer Skills". In other words, how to play the job-search game by developing strategies to convince prospective employers that one is the right person for the job – with the right attitudes, work ethic, minimal skill base, and desire for continual personal upgrading of training and education. It is a training based upon particular concepts of 'employability' relating to the personal attributes of the young person, rather than to specific industrial skills.

Basic functional training refers to that training designed specifically for 'disadvantaged' groups, such as Aborigines, migrants from non-English-speaking backgrounds, women, and people with disabilities. It is broadly remedial in nature, and general in application. A newly established Aboriginal Employment Development Policy (AEDP), for example, will include a range of employment, training, education and economic resource programmes formulated to develop employment opportunities for Aboriginal people in rural and remote areas and to enhance their access to jobs within the conventional labour market. Trade-based pre-employment courses in TAFE colleges are provided to enhance the prospects of young women seeking entry into non-traditional trades; migrants can receive training in English as a second language (ESL) courses; and assistance is provided to young people with disabilities to improve their access to apprenticeships.

The emphasis in such training programmes is on providing narrowly defined vocational and socially functional skills to enable 'disadvantaged' people to compete more successfully on the labour market. Again the focus is on employability, skills and access. As in the other programmes, the concern is with individual achievement, although the necessity to redress existing structural barriers to the employment of these groups is acknowledged. The teaching of 'basics' in pre-vocational education courses is seen as essential to further the opportunities of those people most disadvantaged in the labour market, although in real terms the revamped education and training system appears to be long on rhetoric and short on dollars when it comes to the needs of groups such as women (Pocock and Windsor, 1988).

As a 'residual' category within the overall labour market population, the political importance of the 'disadvantaged' should nevertheless not be underestimated. The high profile given to 'equal opportunity' in general programme statements not only allows the Government to show its concern with equity (even if funding is not forthcoming for equity provision), but it also serves to bolster the importance of training programmes in general. For instance, the source of 'disadvantage' is seen as being deficiencies in training and education. Thus, in a discussion of disadvantaged groups we are told that "There is a strong and well-demonstrated relationship between low socio-economic status, lack of skills, and high levels of unemployment and other forms of social disadvantage." (Commonwealth of Australia, 1987: 15). By defining the problem primarily in terms of training, the logic of skills formation as the solution to the problems of unemployment and economic development is once again confirmed.

The government programmes outlined above are supplemented by traditional private sector training agencies such as secretarial schools, non-government welfare agencies such as the Salvation Army and many newly created private vocational training firms. In each case considerable emphasis is placed upon providing training in narrowly defined industrial skills, and in developing appropriate work habits.

TRAINING AND LABOUR-MARKET TRANSITIONS

The ideology of skills formation has come to prominence in a time of deepening crisis in the worldwide capitalist system. The twin evils of unemployment and weak national economic performance have been met in virtually the same manner by government, business and union – with productivity, technological development, and training and education viewed as the key to recovery and rejuvenation of the national economy.

Actual developments in production processes and the labour market, however, contradict the positive outcome which the training policies were expected to achieve. Since this is the case, the real effects of the current training push lend themselves to critical scrutiny from a different perspective than that offered by officials who publicly speak in terms of the technological future.

Specifically, it has been argued that the translation of the ideology of skills formation into practice is characterised by: a weakening of the bargaining power of workers in the labour market; a deepening of class divisions and restriction of labour-market mobility based upon differences in access to specific types of training; and the systematic use of training programmes to instil a new kind of discipline in young workers.

The content of training programmes reflects a shift in emphasis from a well-developed knowledge base for workers to a narrowly conceived skill base. Accompanying the overtly vocationalist orientation of the Government's programmes has been a move to portray social and behavioural attributes as work skills. In more general terms, such skills have tended to emphasise individual adaptation and survival, competition and personal success, rather than social skills centring on power relationships in the work setting or the collective interests and rights of unemployed young people.

A combination of labour-market policies and social-welfare policies has been used to regulate the options open to young people and to restrict their lifestyle. These measures, plus the high level of unemployment itself, constitute a means of social control over young people in the first instance. Once the young person enters a training programme, control is extended by means of the notion of self-discipline, which is often a component of the 'transferable skills' package.

A further aspect of training programmes is that they extend the age of dependency for young people. That is, they act as a holding tank for the young unemployed until they are into their early twenties. Significantly, it is when young people reach this age that economic considerations become central as marriage and personal independence begin to affect young people's behaviour in a deeper way. As Wallace (1986: 110) puts it: "It would appear that the 'stick' that finally serves to beat young people into submission to the labour process is the long-term reproduction of the domestic life cycle. This is more important at 21 than at 16." Thus, discipline arising out of the training process is due, not only to the intrinsic nature of such programmes, but also to the fact that they play an important delaying role until discipline can once again be imposed by external circumstances.

Formulating a coherent response to these trends is well beyond the scope of the present work (instead, see Finn, 1987; Sydney Independent Study Group, 1985). Nevertheless, it can be said that a progressive training policy would need to consist of a wider curriculum which deals with the politics of work, unemployment and leisure; it would need to reflect the interests and needs of trainees and the unemployed, rather than business; it would need to be based on democratic and accountable structures which put the interests of workers ahead of those of employers; and it would need to be integrated into a full employment strategy from the outset, rather than being constructed in terms of employability for places in an economy which, sometime in the unspecified future, will be operating at a capacity which provides all those who want to work with the opportunity to do so.

There are problems associated with the link between training programmes and labour-market realities, but it is essential to place questions relating to the form and content of training at the centre of the political agenda. Until this is done, training will continue to reflect the interests of the powerful, and young working-class people will continue to suffer the burden of the economic crisis.

CHAPTER 3

Back to school and minimalist education

Young people today are being forced into education and training programmes. They are being told that such programmes are the only way to get a job. There may be shortages of skilled workers in some areas, but this should not obscure the fact that there is an overall lack of demand for significant numbers of skilled workers in the Australian workforce, much less other kinds of paid work. Education is therefore primarily and actively being sold as job preparation in circumstances which are inappropriate to such a strategy.

This chapter takes as its theme the decline of 'education' in the broad sense of the word. It is also about the steady 'de-schooling' of Australian society. The issues discussed revolve around two concerns. The first is the demise of broad, liberal education while greater emphasis is given to more narrow, technical types of 'education' and 'training'. The second is the future prospects of an ever-growing proportion of young people in Australia. It is argued that the goals of institutionalised 'education' are being oriented more toward employment or labour-market ends which ostensibly reflect a concern with technological development and expertise. This is the case even though the objective opportunities for finding full-time paid work in general are declining. The results are a sharpening of the educational contest for better credentials and qualifications; and the development of even greater disparities between young people from different class backgrounds.

The consequences of these two trends are first, that young people in Australia today are being denied an adequate education; one which is not only desirable in terms of their roles as residents and participants in Australian social life, but also one which is in fact needed in broad economic terms as well. Secondly, the types of 'education' and 'training' which are being promoted as the solution to problems such as unemployment will not and cannot resolve such problems at all. Indeed, the basis of the current economic crisis, and in particular the phenomenon of unemployment, is such that an *educational* response will necessarily fail unless it is accompanied by fundamental changes in economic and social structures.

If present policy and bureaucratic initiatives within the educational sphere continue to hold sway – toward 'technical' approaches to subject matter and methodology in most areas of teaching and research – then 'education' as we currently understand it will disappear. Education in this broader sense is characterised by such features as breadth of information, informed criticism, lively conceptualisation, analytical rigour, philosophical depth, and ethical debate.

Nor is it simply a question of education not having a future. For the immediate and long-term losers in today's educational system are young people, and especially young working-class individuals, be they young men, young women, young Aborigines or young migrants. Not only are many of these people unlikely to 'succeed' in the world outside schooling, they are also being robbed of the intellectual resources essential to a full understanding of the reasons for their exploited, alienated or oppressed condition. The reasons for their probable 'failure' in the labour market relate to the nature of changes occurring in work-in-general, rather than to problems with schooling. The reasons for their possible lack of adequate 'education' relate to the school itself, insofar as the educational system is being forced to take on narrowly conceived labour-market problems as its own problems, while being subject to considerable constraints on finance and resources.

SCHOOLING AND THE ROLES OF EDUCATION

As an institution, the school exhibits a number of characteristics which reflect the wider social, economic and political context within which it is located. In other words, what happens in the school is shaped by the broader system of power relations which govern the general nature of a particular society. In any society, power and the exercise of authority tend to reflect the interests and concerns of the dominant groups and classes. In the case of Australia, power and wealth is concentrated in the hands of a relatively small group of white males, who own and control most of the productive resources of the nation.

The maintenance and perpetuation of structures of inequality, and the social divisions arising out of the unequal relations between the powerful and less powerful groups in society, is a complex process involving a number of social institutions. One of the most important of these is the school. At an abstract level the school, while appearing to be a 'neutral' institution providing everyone with the same 'good thing' (i.e., education), performs three important roles in sustaining a particular kind of social order. The school contributes to the maintenance of the economic and political status quo through its influence in the areas of labour power; ideology; and intergenerational reproduction.

First, the school provides employers with an educated labour force 'free of charge'. This is a labour reserve which as far as possible is technically and socially prepared for capitalist forms of commodity production and work practices. Secondly, at the same time, the education system is geared to legitimating the existing social order. This is done through the teaching of selectively chosen and narrowly defined 'fundamental' and 'essential' values ('parliamentary democracy', 'individual achievement', 'the national interest') to the exclusion or marginalisation of others ('class interest', 'women's liberation', 'socialist democracy'). The chosen ideas and values serve in the end to 'naturalise' the status quo by presenting it as the only possible social alternative and by mystifying the nature of exploitation and inequality in society. The third major role of the school is to ensure that working-class kids get working-class jobs, that girls end up doing 'women's work', and that ambitious members of the middle-class wind up as the captains and lieutenants of industry and commerce. In other words, it ensures that each specific group of young people will almost inevitably follow in the footsteps of the previous generation, either by directly engaging in the same types of paid or unpaid work as their parents, or by doing something which in the end does not represent a closing of the gap between the less powerful as a whole and the more dominant groups and classes.

These general processes are not uniform, nor are they without their own internal contradictions. That is, the emphasis on, and performance of, these social roles by the school will vary considerably, depending upon specific historical circumstances. Nevertheless, as a broad generalisation, there is convincing evidence that the development of free, compulsory and secular schooling in Australia was intimately tied to the wider project of fostering conformity and obedience in the interests of a status quo divided along class, gender and ethnic lines (Ely, 1978; Angus, 1986; Miller, 1986). The ability of the school to undertake such a project can be explained in terms of the *content* of the educational curriculum and the *selection* process whereby certain individuals are deemed to have 'passed' or 'failed'.

The issues of educational content and selection processes are inextricably linked when it comes to consideration of school outcomes (see Bourdieu, 1976ab, 1977; Apple, 1979, 1982). On the one hand, the school provides individuals with certain types of knowledge and skills, what becomes 'commonsense' knowledge in terms of general perceptions of the world. On the other hand, the school selects students on the basis of how well they deal with the knowledge that the school has to offer. In cultural terms, the school incorporates a range of specific skills and information into a 'hegemonic' curriculum – that is, one which provides a selective view of the world that is predicated upon maintaining wider unequal social structures. Students whose backgrounds and social status do not match the dominant culture of the school are at a disadvantage, insofar as the school evaluates them on how well they can relate to what the school has to offer. With the onus being placed upon individual achievement based on 'objective' criteria (because education has ostensibly been opened to all), 'disadvantaged' students often do not look to the social structure and the educational system as reasons for their failure, but to 'deficiencies' within themselves. Furthermore, the limited social mobility of some 'disadvantaged' students, especially in light of the continual rhetoric about 'equality of opportunity', is seen to legitimate traditional school practices as both neutral and fair, and hence also serves to legitimate the existing social order.

Themes such as 'equality', 'social mobility', and 'national efficiency' have long characterised debates and discussions over education in Australia. The school's labour-market orientation, its ideological functions and its preservation of social status divisions have produced potential contradictions between the economic role of the school and its presumed egalitarian role. The historical compromise between these demands is to be found in a three-tiered educational system – fee-paying schools catering for a socio-economic and political elite, Catholic and State high schools designed for upward mobility and workforce preparation, and a technical system for the provision of a vocationally trained workforce. Inequalities in education, then, exist not only in terms of systematic discriminations within a particular school which affect individuals from different social backgrounds, but also with respect to different sectors of the overall educational sphere and the placement of particular schools within the institutional hierarchy.

Historically, the transitions and expansion of schooling to the present system of mass, compulsory education cannot be characterised in simplistic terms as being a smooth process of development. That is, educational change has always involved numerous conflicts and confrontations, including overt resistance by particular sectional interest groups. However, the long-term consequences of educational change and 'reform' have done little to alter or challenge the economic and political status quo in any fundamental or permanent way. This is reflected in the nature of educational debates and changes in policy over the last two and a half decades.

In the 1960s and early 1970s Australia was still enjoying the fruits of a long boom of economic development. The concern in educational circles was with questions of 'inequality' between individuals, and the 'quality of life'. 'Progressive' education became the popular approach to pedagogy as many teachers devised new ways to respond to the individual needs of pupils and to take greater responsibility in the development of curriculum materials. The emphasis on child-centred education was reinforced by the publication of the Karmel Report in 1973, with 'devolution of responsibility' (but not power), 'equality' (but within the meritocratic framework), and 'diversity' (but accompanied by a centralised bureaucracy) as the catchphrases of the day. Problems with the 'system' were identified, but reform was seen and acted upon in terms of piecemeal changes in education, rather than in terms of challenges to the basic economic and political foundations of the system.

By the late 1970s the economic context had changed dramatically. Australia was in the midst of a major economic downturn and unemployment was on the increase. The ideals put forward in the preceding ten years were quickly cast aside. Schools were blamed for the nation's economic ills, and progressive education heavily criticised for not providing the right kind of schooling, including training in the 'basics'. The supposed mismatch between education and the demands of the labour market was used to justify education cuts and the movement within education away from concerns such as equality and the value of a liberal arts education to a form of training which was more or less 'productive' for the national economy (Williams et al., 1979; Freeland and Sharp, 1981; Johnston, 1983).

The recession of 1981–82 reinforced the view that education was much to blame for the nation's ills. Public debates centred on the need to make education more 'relevant' to the needs of the labour market and to prepare young people for the world of work. At the same time greater government concern with increasing budget deficits meant that education was to become a target for financial austerity measures. While money for private schooling was increased by the Fraser Government, and later by the Hawke Government, the government school system was to suffer a period of chronically inadequate funding.

Since the early 1980s the main concerns in education have had to do with 'rationalisation' of the system, making it more 'efficient' and 'cost-effective'. Whereas previous educational ideals focused on questions such as educating the 'whole child' and 'progressive' pedagogical techniques, the more recent concern has been with the 'quality' of schooling within a tight budget, and with provision of the minimal skills needed in an era of high technology. Today, the school still performs basic economic and ideological roles for the maintenance of a particular kind of social order in Australian society. However, the character of these roles is changing. Many of the changes in education are the result of a particular conception of the issue of 'technology', as it relates to the educational enterprise.

TECHNOLOGY, SKILLS AND SCHOOLING

It is significant that political, educational and business leaders have become vocal about the need to develop Australia's technological expertise and to use education as a crucial mechanism in the training of highly skilled workers for the newer high-technology industries. A succession of reports on education and training have raised the issue of the labour-force orientation of schooling, often stressing the qualitatively different type of society that will be brought about by the impact of technology (Williams et al., 1979; Australian Education Council Task Force, 1985; Keeves et al.,

1982; Kirby et al., 1985; South Australian Education and Technology Task Force, 1986; Economic Planning Advisory Council, 1986).

Prominent among those calling for Australians to transform the 'lucky country' into an 'intelligent country' has been the federal Minister for Science, Barry Jones (*Adelaide Advertiser*, 21 January 1986; see also Jones, 1982, 1986abc). Susan Ryan (1986: 21), former Labor federal Minister for Education, has also presented ideas very similar to those of Jones. During the period when she held the education porfolio, for example, she commented that:

> We need to increase our levels of education participation so that the skill base on which Australian industry can build will be broadened. If, as a nation, we upgrade our levels of general skills then, in turn, we have a better base on which to develop specific vocational skills. The restructuring of industry and the impact of rapid technological change mean that adaptable skills are the most valuable and re-training assumes more importance.

Such pronouncements are typical of the way in which the Government has intervened in the education debate over recent years. They have often been backed up by extensive research and policy development work, a notable recent contribution being a report prepared by the (now defunct) Commonwealth Schools Commission in 1987 titled *In The National Interest: Secondary Education and Youth Policy in Australia.*

As the title suggests, this report assumed a unity of interests in Australian society. Its basic theme was that, in the midst of competing demands made on secondary education as a whole, there is a need to shore up the relationship between schooling and the economy. Thus, "the main contribution of the education system to the economy is to facilitate and shape economic change by providing a higher order of knowledge and skills amongst all entrants to the workforce and to create cultural preconditions favourable to economic and technological development" (Commonwealth Schools Commission, 1987: 41). The familiar issue of skills formation was once again canvassed, as were the issues of "equality of opportunity", "equality of outcome", and "democracy".

The major rationale behind the report, however, is found in its concerns with increasing the retention rates for secondary-school students. Discussions of the content of schooling and the need for adaptable pedogogical methods and the like were to a large extent premised upon the ideas of both improving the economy and keeping young people in school for a longer period of time. This should be seen in the context of a situation where, as Sweet (1987: 11) points out, by the mid-1980s almost all fifteen-year-olds, and most sixteen-year-olds were involved in one form or another of education, and nearly two-thirds of seventeen-year-olds were involved in one form of education by 1984, as were over 40 per cent of all eighteen- and nineteen-year-olds. More young people in the 1980s are already participating in education, whether in schools, TAFE colleges or higher education courses, than in the 1970s.

The importance of retention rates from a social control perspective becomes apparent when we consider who in fact is leaving school early and who is staying on. In this regard there are clear class differences in school participation rates. As the Schools Commission report indicates (1987: 60), retention rates differ considerably for different types of schools. In 1986, for example, apparent retention to Year 12 was 42.3 per cent for government schools, 57.4 per cent for Catholic schools and 89.2 per cent for other non-government schools. The 'problem', therefore, is how to get students from working-class backgrounds (i.e., those who attend government schools in particular) to come back to school in even greater numbers than at present. The 'solution' is found in: making changes to the incentives and disincentives for school attendance (like the levels and types of financial benefits available); tinkering with the curriculum so that 'appropriate' education is provided which is compatible with the perceived interests of the student; and stressing the greater importance of educational credentials and skills training in getting paid work.

The technology debate is significant for the form and content of education, and the limitations of proposed courses of action both in theory and in practice. To understand this, it is essential to examine closely some of the assumptions guiding current discussions. The role of the school in meeting skill requirements in the workforce is usually presented in terms of the teaching of new skills. These skills are required for new forms of production; but different levels of skill are recognised. The specific role of the school is to create a new type of 'smart', but 'compliant', labour: that is, workers who will be innovative and flexible in their work practices, but who will nevertheless conform to the requirements of managers and employers. With an emphasis on practical, technical skills, school selection is ideally to be based upon different levels of appropriation of these skills. In other words, there is a hierarchy of skill levels, and those students with the 'right' cultural capital will, as usually is the case, be the ones to succeed in the school and subsequently in the workplace.

The high levels of unemployment, coupled with the decreasing demand for skilled labour relative to the workforce as a whole, has been translated in the schools into what can be described as *minimalism*. This refers to the attitude and policy of evaluating students on the basis of minimal pass requirements, rather than demanding greater levels of work and creativity. While minimalism is the broad orientation of the school today, there is still strong support for the 'gifted child' and those students who are likely to succeed in the new specialist areas. Thus, 'minimalism' and 'achievement' stand side by side in the school as means to quite different ends. Although seemingly contradictory, they in fact constitute two parts of the same whole.

Minimalism is a result of the emphasis on the labour-market function of the school: to provide the basic skills necessary in today's labour market. With the ideology of the day regarding schooling as an instrument (rather than viewing schooling as 'good for its own sake'), the curriculum is subject to rationalisation and standardisation. In part this stems from State attempts to cut costs in education. In a period of economic 'restraint' the bureaucrats' concern for financial efficiency fits well with notions which see the school first and foremost as providing a 'practical' education.

The labour-market demand for workers with narrowly defined technical skills, and the transition within schooling toward cost-effective education of a minimalist type, raises the question of whether the school does in fact have a role to play in economic development. If most new jobs are created in low-wage, low-skill areas, it is possible that most of the direct training for these jobs can be done equally well or even better outside the secondary school. The Higher School Certificate, for example, may eventually lose its value if job opportunity proves to be more strongly linked with traineeship-type schemes.

Education in Australia today is in flux, with a vast array of teaching methods, course curriculums, and educational ideologies being promoted, each reflecting the different interests of student organisations, union bodies, professional groups, business people and so on (see Hunt, 1986; Marginson, 1986bc). Generally speaking, and based upon the trends outlined above, three broad changes are taking place in education at the moment. These are: the polarisation of education between achievement and minimalism; new attempts to create compliance in the school; and the movement away from 'education' and towards 'training'.

POLARISATION IN EDUCATION

High youth unemployment, a general downturn in global economic performance, and greater competition for all types of jobs have led to the emergence of very sharp divisions in the educational system. The role of the school as an agent of social selection has been heightened as individuals scramble to find a place in a tight labour market. The school is called upon to guarantee paid work, mainly by teaching subjects which will be immediately 'useful' in the workforce.

The lack of adequate financial and human resources in the government school system has coincided with greater allocations of government money to the private schools sector. This has occurred at a time when governments are trying to reduce or offset State expenditures in education and hence to rationalise spending in this area. The emphasis on economic restraint has been accompanied by renewed emphasis on 'vocationalism' in the school. For instance, so called 'practical' subjects, such as computer training, can be 'taught' through the use of a standardised format, including the use of computers themselves to perform a tutor-like role. By such means, two of the immediate goals of government in the area of schooling can be achieved in an integrated way; namely, the transfer of practical skills, and a relative saving of costs (White, 1985ab).

For traditionalist educators the renewed interest in standardisation, competition, examination and so on has resurrected and given much status to the notion of 'measurable individual differences' between students. Concepts such as 'educability' or 'equal outcomes' are shunned. From this perspective the key words are 'quality', 'standards' and 'efficiency' and these translate into the wholesale pre-packaging of courses; uniform testing of material; pseudo-scientific justifications of educational success and failure; and the resurgence of psychology as the 'science' most suited to finding ways to determine differences between individual students. Any notion of *social* difference between groups of students is carefully avoided or regarded as a question of secondary importance.

Conversely, in other educational circles there is still a strong professed concern with entrenched inequalities in educational and social outcomes, and in equipping young people to meet the challenges of social and economic change. This perspective is evident in initiatives carried out by the Victorian Ministry of Education in the mid to late 1980s. In addition to an emphasis on 'collaborative decision-making', which includes the devolution of responsibility for curriculum and administrative decisions to local School Councils, the Victorian Government has stressed the concepts of 'access' and 'success'. Thus, the stated goal is to provide real access for all students to genuine educational experiences.

The means of achieving this goal nevertheless reflect an overriding concern with 'skilling' students rather than making them knowledgeable. Education is seen in terms of the individualisation of learning and the gradual growth of qualities that are seen as innate in each individual. This pedagogical approach tends to not make reference to the hierarchy in knowledge, or of the necessity of moving beyond learning details and specific skills to synthesising what is learned into a general unified whole (see D. White, 1988). In its own way, this model of education, like that of the more traditional, equates society with the market. In the marketplace, "the object is to enhance the power of negotiators" (D. White, 1988: 79). The role of education within this framework, therefore, is to facilitate the process whereby students gain individually owned skills which they can then negotiate with potential employers. While students in this education system are not subject to the same kinds of testing as that favoured by traditionalists, the concern with accountability, evaluation of performance and outcomes means that even school-based assessment of pupil-centred learning is subject to pressures to document 'measurable individual differences'.

In real terms, however, the playing down of group differences and the renewed interest in individual differences among school pupils have widened the gap between particular categories of students. In this situation one's 'achievement' is generally based upon the cultural capital that one brings into the school setting, and the school has moved away from recognising the social nature of differences in cultural capital. Clearly, in this setting, class, gender, and ethnic differences will become stronger over time.

A key factor in determining school outcomes today is money. Thus, in addition to the streaming which may occur within particular schools under the rubric of 'measurable individual differences', there are also major divisions based upon different categories of schools. Private fee-paying schools are, through government policy and financial assistance, booming in Australia. Public or government schools are faced with tremendous problems, due to a concerted failure on the part of decision-makers to maintain, let alone improve, their overall position and to stop siphoning off funds to private schools. In its baldest terms, the growth of the private-school sector represents the ability of the middle classes to protect their own by investing in something which will presumably ensure that their sons and daughters will wind up with paid work.

There is indeed an increasing polarisation of schooling in Australia. The main dividing line is that between private and public. The basis of this is the distinction between 'education for all' and 'user pays', the outcome being that those who can afford to pay more will have a better guarantee that their children will inherit the privileges of their parents. Ideologically, the new orthodoxy in the economics of education is based upon a 'free market' approach that assumes the desirability of competition and which stresses the 'value' of education primarily in terms of the benefits accruing to the individual rather than social benefits. The state-school system itself is not immune to the influences of this perspective. In concrete terms, for example, it has been manifested at secondary-school level by the selling of places to fee-paying overseas students in a Western Australian State school in 1987, with close to thirty other Australian tertiary institutions and schools accredited to sell student places in 1988.

The free-market approach to education has its roots in 'human capital theory', which sees education as an individual investment in future earning power: it disregards all but the economic aspects of education. This approach incorporates a range of ideas and values which directly challenge the notion that free, accessible and quality education should be provided for everyone in Australian society (see Marginson, 1986bc). Conservative forces therefore emphasise vocationalism while neglecting political, social, cultural, and other aspects of education. As Hunt (1986: 11) points out, "Such a more limited preoccupation can also reduce the magnitude of the educational efforts and, correspondingly, the burden of public expenditure on taxpayers. At the same time, the concept of privatisation complements those strategies by denoting that education beyond some minimal program is a private responsibility."

The idea that education is a social right and a social benefit has steadily lost ground as, in practice, the process of privatisation has continued unabated at the schools level. Furthermore, the division between those who can pay, and those who cannot, has been exacerbated by developments at the tertiary level. Here we can point to the Hawke Labor Government's introduction of the $250 'administrative' fee in 1987, the announcement of a 'graduate tax' in the August 1988 Budget, and the recent opening up of private fee-charging 'universities' such as the Bond University in Queensland, as developments which will harden the divisions between the classes. 'Equality of opportunity', in this context, is rapidly being relegated to the goals of the past; the hardline politics of greed are steadily supplanting a social vision based upon collective rights and the humane society.

The heavy reliance on credentials – whether these concern specific subject matter, or attendance at the 'right' school – is publicly justified in terms of an elitist meritocratic educational philosophy. For the sake of 'standards', and of holding the standard on high, the private fee-paying schools push their students to excel. The ideology of 'achievement' is embedded in the students, as is their 'rightful' place in society as future graduates of the school in question. The main thing here is to teach people what 'success' really means, for each of them individually and as members of a class. (In specific terms it should also be noted that elite State schools – well-resourced middle-class institutions such as Melbourne High School and Adelaide's Norwood High – share many of the objectives and attributes of their private competitors.)

This approach can be contrasted with the defensiveness apparent in the government-school system. Here the concern is with holding the line – with minimalism. Students who 'succeed' are applauded, as all exceptions are. For the rest, however, the idea is to provide them with a few minimal skills which they might be able to use in the world outside. Everyone 'knows' that many of these pupils will not be able to find work, that many will become 'burdens' on the system in some way or another. 'Achievement' in this context is measured by how well the school can help to prevent students from breaking the law, or destroying themselves through despair or wanton act. The key, therefore, is control.

A minimalist education assumes that vocationalism is the main task of schooling. That is, schools exist to prepare students for the world of work. The stress on vocationalism manifests itself in the allocation of resources to science subjects in preference to the humanities, in the use of technological devices in the school and as part of a study programme, and in greater attention to 'hands-on' types of courses in so-called practical subjects. The concept of 'minimum competency' sees the school's role as to provide students with the bare essentials they need to pursue a particular occupational or life path. Put differently, the concept of minimalism concerns itself with requirements of 'minimal acceptability' in contrast to the notion of 'maximal quality'.

The origins of minimalism do not lie solely in the financial costs of education. According to political leaders, some form of economic cutback is needed, but this does not necessarily imply the particular shift in educational philosophy currently under way (although in practice it does masquarade under the present rhetoric of pedagogical reform). Minimalism is also a result of the fact that, in an economic climate distinguished by structural transformations in the nature of work, there simply are not enough jobs for every school-leaver to have one, regardless of the level of their skills and knowledge.

In order to legitimate its role in society, and to counter criticisms that blame it for the economic misfortune, the school has had to present itself as sensitive to changes in the labour market. Thus, the 'new vocationalism' is as much as anything an ideological response to a crisis of institutional legitimacy, rather than a practical solution to the crisis of the economic system in general. Although ideological in nature, and unable to address the structural issues surrounding employment in Australian society, the strategy adopted by educational planners and policy-makers does have real and significant effects on what occurs within the school.

As mentioned above, one of the effects has been a reorientation of the curriculum toward more technical and practical subjects rather than the conceptual and liberal arts. Another significant development in the last five or six years has been the considerable emphasis being placed upon standardisation and central bureaucratic control of curriculum development (B. Ryan, 1982, 1986; Marginson, 1985; White, 1985b, 1986b). Standardisation takes place through a number of means, including central administrative control over curriculum guidelines, accreditation systems, promotion, and reviews (which impinge upon 'school-based' decision-making structures as well as traditional educational structures); manipulation of funding and resource allocation at both Commonwealth and State levels to ensure conformity; a concentration on accountability and thus placing emphasis on demonstrating 'quality' and 'standards' by reference to an 'objective' system of measurement; and fostering the idea that there is and should be an ideological consensus on the purposes and form of schooling – that the new order in education be taken-for-granted and that there be uncritical acceptance of the broad educational agenda. Although perhaps originating in a desire to cut administrative and staffing costs, the thrust of bureaucratic moves has been to stifle creativity for the sake of managerial expediency. The centralisation of decision-making power and the integration of formerly disparate policy areas has taken its most substantive form to date in the creation of the National Board of Employment, Education and Training by the Commonwealth Government in 1988, an example of administrative and ideological rationalisation which has not been lost on State Governments around the country.

Accompanying these trends has been a greater emphasis upon the testing and measurement of individual 'progress' through comparisons of standardised examinations or equivalent systems of evaluation. Competition is constructed in terms of the 'individual'. Differences between social categories tend therefore to be obscured, because 'intelligence' as 'scientifically' measured 'proves' that some individuals are 'brighter' than others (McCallum, 1986; B. Ryan, 1986). Significantly, a report released by John Dawkins in May 1988, *Strengthening Australia's Schools*, hinted at the possibility of the introduction of national testing, and pressure has been building up in a number of quarters at both the national and State level for more extensive use of 'quantitative performance indicators' in order to assess the success of students, teachers, schools and systems and as part of a push for better 'corporate management' of the system (Preston, 1988).

These broad changes in schooling are the result of interrelated factors which affect the operation of the education system today. Perhaps what is most striking, however, is the utter failure of these changes actually to address the problem which they highlight; that is, the school has failed to guarantee jobs for students. This has a whole range of implications and has led the school to take on other tasks in order to remedy possible conflict.

Schooling is being portrayed as a necessary prerequisite for paid work. Retention rates have risen in the secondary-school systems, and the number of individuals trying to gain places in tertiary education is well beyond the number of places on offer. On the other hand, and somewhat ironically, 'education' as a commodity is steadily losing its 'value' on the labour market. Since most new jobs, as we have seen, are at the low end of the skill and wage spectrum, employment does not depend upon high educational credentials and academic prowess. The high-skilled, high-wage jobs are small in number and cannot accommodate the sheer quantity of graduates leaving the system each year.

Schooling is still seen by many young people as important,

however, if only as a means to hedge their bets when it comes to employment opportunities. More precisely, the school *credential* is seen as important. And this is what could attract many early school-leavers back into the system after a spell of unsuccessfully trying to find secure, paid work. If you are between the ages of fifteen and nineteen, where else do you go if you do not have a job? That increased school participation rates are more closely tied to 'credentials', rather than 'skills', is illustrated by recent work done by Sweet (1987: 18). Large numbers of teenagers decide to stay at school for only one or two extra years beyond compulsory school-leaving age, yet still leave before completing Year 12. The reason is that:

> They were staying at school to enter essentially the same sorts of jobs that they would have obtained had they left one or two years earlier: office jobs, trades, sales work or similar jobs. Their extra investment in education was undertaken with no prospect of an additional return in the form of social mobility or increased life earnings streams.

However, increased retention rates cannot be explained only in terms of credentialism. Changes in state benefits and administrative procedures have also had an impact. It would appear that the introduction of the job search allowance, with an activity test and parental income test, plus greater policing of the system of alloca-tion and the introduction of 'Employer Report' certificates, has proved to be a disincentive for many young people eligible to claim this benefit. At the same time, as Bradbury et al. (1988: 92) point out, recent changes in Government policy mean that "for low-income families with older secondary student children, the in-creased level of assistance may save many from poverty". Thus, going to school may be seen by some young people primarily as a source of income, rather than in strictly educational or labour-market terms. This is borne out in part by the findings of the South Australian Youth Incomes Task Force (1988: 117) which produced information that showed that some 60 per cent fewer young people in metropolitan Adelaide were in receipt of the job search allowance in February 1988 than were receiving the junior unemployment benefit at the same time in 1987. Concomitant to this, the Task Force found that post-compulsory school retention rates appeared to be improving, and that there was a 28.8 per cent increase in the number of actual applications for the Austudy secondary allowance over the figure for the previous year (1988: 59–60).

In addition to a general push toward vocationalism in educational provision, the needs of schools themselves as institutions provide much of the impetus towards minimalism. In the context of falling enrolments in relation to number of schools and financial cutbacks, there is also pressure on schools to ensure that teenagers complete their formal education. To attract senior students back into the system, and to retain those already in the system, schools must be able either to prove their 'worth' in terms of labour-market credentials, or to vary their courses enough to make them 'interesting' for the young person. Not only is this strategy essential in order to bolster the numbers needed by the school for further funding, but it also assists in the process of maintaining discipline and control in the classroom. By widening the extent of course offerings, and even perhaps giving the students more say in the courses in some cases, the pupils may behave in a manner which does not threaten the order of the school.

The apparent 'democratisation' of some aspects of schooling does not in any way offset the other tendency occurring in education: the shift to standardisation and more authoritarian forms of direct control over teachers, curriculum and students. For where rules and regulations have been loosened up, or innovative courses developed and offered, this tends to be in the nebulous area of 'life skills' training or in 'alternative' types of schools. (In addition to high schools, such courses are also provided by TAFEs, CYSS projects and community agencies such as the Salvation Army.)

Interestingly enough, a Victorian review of post-compulsory schooling (Blackburn et al., 1984) found that attempts to broaden the focus of upper secondary schooling by extending the number of alternative subjects was not successful in increasing choice, because of the dominance of the academic curriculum. It would appear that for many students, choosing a narrow academic path may be a way of keeping their employment options open, something which 'life skills' or pre-vocational courses may not offer.

Nevertheless, recent developments in educational debate and policy indicate that moves are under way to standardise school credentialling, which would institutionalise "minimum competency for the disadvantaged and excellence for the elite" (Marginson, 1985). The recent and very influential report of the Quality of Education Review Committee (Karmel et al., 1985) implicitly argued that schooling should be organised around two major occupational streams, requiring 'higher order' mental skills and 'lower order' mental skills respectively. This would be done in the context of standardising the school curriculum by means of a substantial expansion in the number of compulsory common-core subjects, each of which however would be designed to cater to several different levels of 'ability' and 'competence'.

Those students who are deemed not to have much hope in the 'traditional' school practices are usually the ones for whom alternative methods and objectives have been devised. Thus, divisions in the school are increasingly apparent between those at the upper end of the school hierarchy who are pursuing the mainstream 'academic' curriculum, and those at the bottom of the school hierarchy who are doing pre-vocational generalist courses.

While the system as a whole is orienting around notions of 'achievement', skill training, competition and so on, in the lower echelons of the government school system 'minimalism' has been promoted to such an extent that often even the barest pretence of 'vocational' or 'academic' education is difficult to find. Instead, the concern in many 'life skills' courses is the production of 'correct attitudes' rather than skills – by teaching young people how to dress the right way, to speak the right way, to act the right way, if they are to succeed in gaining an 'adult's' job (see Cohen, 1984). In their own way, 'life skills' courses represent yet another form of standardisation. Here, however, what is being moulded into uniformity is not one's technical aptitude or academic skill, but one's basic character. To succeed is to conform; life skills teach one how to conform.

Juxtaposed with 'life skills' courses are low-level 'vocational' courses designed to be of interest to those young people who are likely to end up in menial work or unemployment. In general, these tend to be 'Mickey Mouse' busy-work. Course proposals coming before the New South Wales 'Participation and Equity Programme' Committee in 1984–85 provide an illustration of the types of courses on offer (Sydney Independent Study Group, 1985: 24–5):

One Sydney suburban high school proposed (under the rubric of 'socio-economic'!) the following:
1. Typing
2. Cake Making
3. Macrame
4. Word Processing
5. Film Study and Photography
6. Driver Education and Car Maintenance
7. Child Development
8. Garment Construction

The list is not atypical. One country school proposed a unit on free-range chicken farming for young Aborigines. A school in another country town offers Urban Landscaping. A country technical college runs a course on 'Hospitality' for the 'Geographically Isolated'. In Sydney's West another Tech proudly boasts in a press release, that 'PEP Takes to the Racetrack'. Yes, the young unemployed of the western suburbs are to find jobs as jockeys!

The content of the courses leaves much to be desired in terms of vocational opportunities; serious questions must also be asked about the form and process of such education.

MINIMALISM AND THE CREATION OF COMPLIANCE

One of the declared aims of the minimalist approaches is to prepare students to be self-reliant and to enable them to take on responsibilities. However, in real terms minimalist approaches cannot be squared with liberal-progressive points of view, despite official and unofficial claims to the contrary. For it is nearly impossible to prepare students to be self-reliant in the context of a contracting public-school system. This is highlighted by the comments of a senior official at a high school in the South Australian city of Whyalla (White, 1988):

> It's absolutely ludicrous to be asking schools to do more things like develop more applied type courses, practical type courses which require smaller numbers, like provide for individual differences, and help remediate problems, which require smaller numbers – it's ridiculous to expect schools to do that and then to reduce the resources which they've got, that is, the personnel resources.

Without adequate resources, there are only very limited options possible with respect to things such as subject 'choice' and class 'participation', and there are major limitations on providing much more than superficial attention to the development of critical thinking, action, and the intellectual and political content of ideas. Under these circumstances, educational practices may in fact stifle the individual, encouraging conservatism, and thereby prevent the opening up of new avenues for creative thought and collective action.

Minimalism is necessarily designed to cater in the main to the 'underachievers' and the 'non-academic' stream of students. The curriculum at this end of the educational spectrum is in essence vocationally useless; it is only this fact which allows space for experimentation with liberal ideas such as group participation in decision-making and so on. Yet, ironically, it is precisely the concentration on such attributes and characteristics of human interaction which may render some of these pupils more 'saleable' in the labour market.

A recent study of the educational needs of teenagers in Whyalla (Salagaras, 1985: 70–1) examined the kinds of skills and qualities that employers felt to be the most important in employees. The overwhelming characteristic cited by the employers at the interview stage was personal appearance. Beyond this stage of the hiring process, employers were looking for the following:

> Attitude; Being able to communicate well with both staff and clients; Keenness; Polite and friendly disposition; Neatness; Willingness to learn and take direction; Maturity; Qualifications in subjects required for position; Initiative; Good attitude to safety procedures and policies; Honesty; Ability to listen carefully and react quickly; Responsibility; Good presentation of self physically and verbally; Manners; Mathematical/bookkeeping skills; Ambition; Desire to obtain particular job; Good Health; Common Sense; Attention to detail.

Most of these qualities are based upon appearance and attitude. As such, they are perhaps best catered for by programmes which stress 'life skills' and an individual's ability to interact with other people.

On the surface, a minimalist approach would appear to be 'useful' in this regard. A vocational orientation that is neither skills-based in any traditional sense nor part of a broader liberal education can, paradoxically, prepare many students even better for the demands of the labour market. Catering to different needs, abilities, interests and cultures may produce a form of relationship between people which is desirable in general social and cultural terms. But it is precisely this *form* – without its critical content – which is being demanded by employers. Given that the growth in job creation in Australia is in low-wage, low-skill labour, is minimalism then simply a better way to produce the 'ideal' worker of the 1990s?

Minimalist education, therefore, may actually assist young people in getting paid work, although it is seen as a school stream which is pastoral in orientation. Nevertheless, this stream is still regarded as inferior to the academic curriculum, both in terms of content and in terms of the student population groups that tend to be in it. Because of a lack of adequate time, energy and resources, the sort of education which is provided is often piecemeal and lacks any external perspective on paid work or social change. Without a specific focus, it sustains the myth that what is identified as 'liberal' education is 'soft' and has little direct relevance to a pupil's future prospects. This reinforces other forms of 'education' which are clearly and self-consciously vocational, incorporating traditional teaching methods and 'objective' testing and curriculum content.

In the end, liberal education in general has been devalued by the focus on a narrow version which has a restricted application to the 'less successful' streams in the school hierarchy. The general concept has also been weakened by the reduction of any rigour and conceptual content in these streams in efforts to dissociate what is being done at this level from the high-status academic curriculum. The specific character of the type of education on offer has been shaped as well by the limits imposed by the systematic withdrawal of government resources for public schooling.

TRAINING AS AN ALTERNATIVE TO SCHOOL

If 'education' is reoriented toward instrumental vocational goals, and if 'education' is to consist of technical and practical types of courses, then it is but a small step to remove 'education' from the school.

In fact, in some ways training which takes place outside the school may appear to be more desirable than that offered within it. There are several interrelated reasons for this. Inside the educational system the student is often treated like a child (or a prisoner), with few rights and many obligations. This has long been a source of resentment and resistance among certain categories of students (see Corrigan, 1979; Willis, 1977; Hawkins, 1982; Thomas, 1980). There has also been a general devaluation of education as a means. of enhancing a young person's chances for getting paid work. Some students might wonder whether the whole exercise is worthwhile. Compounding this is the fact that if a 'vocational' education is what is called for, then it is best achieved either on the job, or at a college of Technical and Further Education.

A further factor is the effectiveness of school streaming. If students are slotted into a particular category of school, fitted into a specific course, officially labelled as this or that kind of pupil, then this could affect how they view staying on in the school system. If one is not in the top categories of the educational hierarchy, then there may be little incentive to stay in school. After all, as the media and many politicians keep telling young people, Australia needs highly educated workers and that is where the jobs lie. In these circumstances, it would seem to make much more sense to leave school early, and attend a TAFE college or a training course of some kind.

A survey of young people undertaking training in the visual and performance arts in Whyalla (White, 1989) highlights some of the concerns raised above. One of the outstanding features of the survey was the experience of schooling by the participants. Virtually all of the respondents were very negative about their school experience, citing course relevance, teacher attitudes and the institutional framework of discipline and regulation as the main problems.

The survey findings included the following observations as to why the young people did not like school:

> No freedom of speech, generally a prison.
>
> irrelevant stuff
>
> constantly competing against a system of teachers, students, friends, parents, exams and many more
>
> the segregation of students and all the contradictions of the hierarchy
>
> They didn't teach me about life which is more important than Maths, English, etc.

With respect to the teachers they did not get along with, the young people replied along the following lines:

> Teachers who use authority as a weapon and not a teaching aid. Teachers who were incompetent and couldn't control a classroom full of kids.
>
> All the teachers who believed in their own safe world of unreality. The verbatim regurgitation teachers. Assembly line education
>
> authoritative teachers – teaching machines
>
> Teachers who get upset at anybody regularly. Also teachers who stick to the book of rules 100%.

patronising teachers

bossy, rude teachers

In contrast to these comments, most of the respondents also pointed to "good" teachers who "treated them as human beings", and "good" subjects which sparked their creative interests, as being positive aspects of their formal schooling. Indeed, there appeared to be a strong link between the teaching methods used in school, and the students' interest in particular subjects. For instance, the movement of many of the respondents into the arts area was due in no small measure to the attitudes and practices of their art and drama teachers. Comments such as "I got along with teachers who were down to earth and treated me like a human instead of an uneducated animal" and "teachers who spoke to you on the same level, because I realised they were human and not teaching machines", described the kind of teacher the survey participants liked.

What is significant for present purposes is the fact that the interest in art, drama and music generated at school was carried over into the participants' post-school plans. Whereas in school such subjects were primarily taken for interest or as alternatives to boring subjects and repressive teachers, they were now seen in terms of training for future employment. Importantly, the choice of performance or visual art was linked to a desire for greater autonomy in the sphere of paid work (fostered by individualistic notions of creativity and skill development), and as a response to the 'dead-end' nature of work in the local area and the dearth of paid employment in general.

This training and employment orientation, in turn, created tensions between the teachers and the students. For the goals of the teachers included handing over control of the programme to the students themselves. This was seen as both part of a general 'empowerment' strategy, and as helping to establish an ongoing community arts movement in Whyalla. For their part, the students were primarily concerned with the training side of things, the process of which was seen as temporary in nature and as personally rather than collectively benefiting them. The participants overwhelmingly preferred the training programme to school: because they were "treated as adults"; because it was seen as immediately vocational in orientation; and because it was seen as assisting them in finding paid work in the area they wanted to work in. The survey findings seemed to confirm that a major shift is occurring in young people's, as well as teachers', views of 'education'.

The reasons for this are not hard to find. The buzz word today in discussions about unemployment is 'training'. Even in debates over the position and role of the school, the main focus is on the 'training function' of the educational institution. Training is seen as the panacea for the nation's economic ills, and of course as the solution to the problem of youth unemployment. It is important to recognise that the ideological climate which has been created, based upon the notion of skill formation, determines the way in which 'education' is viewed. In immediate terms, it means that young people may eventually view undertaking a training programme, such as those provided under the Australian Traineeship Scheme, as the best way to get a solid credential for work purposes. If school is oppressive, boring, irrelevant, and unchallenging, then traineeships seem pretty attractive. The student is a 'schoolchild'. The trainee is not just a 'trainee' but is also often a 'worker'. Differences in status, pay, duration of programme and curriculum are wide enough to gener-ate doubts as to the usefulness of schooling.

At the same time, the expansion of traineeship schemes puts even more pressure on schools, especially those threatened with closure due to falling enrolments, to compete for student places by offering a more diverse range of vocational and pre-vocational courses. Work-experience programmes are being devised and further links made with local enterprises and industries in an attempt to be seen as providing job-oriented 'education'. Thus, in addition to Govern-ment policies which favour a vocationalist orientation, a spiral effect is developing as training outside the school fosters the development of further training programmes inside the school.

The question of where one does one's 'training' is largely ir-relevant – except for one thing. The training provided must enable the young person to end up with a credential of some kind, something they can use on the labour market in order to compete for the limited work available. As we saw in Chapter 2 (p. 65), the *content* of the training or 'education' is increasingly being relegated to secondary importance. While the cry is that unemployment is due to a lack of training, the fact is that much of the training on offer is either of low quality or marginal to the needs of the employer.

This applies both to school-based programmes and to traineeship schemes. In the school, for example, work-experience programmes are often far too short, unplanned and poorly administered to be of great value. Just as importantly, the prominence given to such programmes ignores the fact that a large proportion of school students are already working part-time (see Commonwealth Schools Commission, 1987; Sweet, 1987). To take just one example, a survey of school students in Whyalla found that 51.3 per cent have at some stage had a part-time job (Salagaras, 1985: 274). In other words, a sizeable proportion of students already have 'work-experience' of one kind or another. Whether working as shop assistants or in fast-food outlets will help them to get permanent paid work is another matter, as is the job potential generated by staying in school long enough to receive their school certificate.

As in the case of the school, much of the training which occurs outside the educational system aims to create a particular kind of compliance in the young person. This can be achieved in several ways, although it is never totally successful. The young person is made to feel guilty and at fault for their immediate or future unemployment by the constant attention given to 'training' as the source of the problem. Traineeships offer short-term relief, at low wages and often without union rights and protection. The emphasis is on keeping one's nose clean in order to impress upon prospective bosses that one is an 'ideal' type of worker. Skills are kept to a minimum; partly through expediency on the part of the agencies involved which do not have time to devote to training exercises, but also because low-level skills are more and more all that is required for many enterprises. Without special skills or expertise, the trainee does not necessarily gain anything on the rest of the people in the unemployed labour pool (see Sweet, 1987; Finn, 1983; Pearson, 1985).

The crux of the matter is that, regardless of whether 'training' occurs in the school or outside it, there are not enough jobs to go around. The present economic system is simply not structured in a way which permits greater participation in productive paid work. The trends outlined above – ranging from increasing polarisation both within the school and in the educational system as a whole, through to the growth in non-school training as an alternative to what is offered in the educational system – will not alleviate this situation. On the contrary, the direction of change outlined above will exacerbate the divisions in Australian society, and will lead to real hardship and turmoil for the less powerful groups and, indeed, the majority of residents of this country.

THE FAILURE OF THE TECHNOLOGICAL DREAM

One of the central factors in the relationship between education and work is the way in which the 'problem' has been constructed. The issue has been portrayed in such a way that the only socio-economic choice offered is between full-time work, or full-time unemployment. There is irony in this.

Technology has long been conceived as a *liberating* force in society. New technological developments and innovations were supposed to free people from the tyranny of work and the drudgery of the daily grind. In practice, technology has created a whole new economic and social climate, one which is characterised by fear, insecurity and loss of control. It has directly affected the number and types of jobs in society and has now advanced to the stage where a qualitative leap in human history is occurring. Never again will there be full employment or anything approximating it as we understand the term today. A new era is beginning. The direction of this new era is one of the most profound questions of our age.

Because of such things as the concentration of power and decision-making into the hands of a few, and the pressures on businesses to cut costs by lowering wages and introducing new tech   logy, the problem of unemployment will not be dealt with in a substantive fashion. The existence of a large reserve army of unemployed people allows employers to pick and choose their workers, to dictate the specific ways in which their labour power will be used, and to reduce expenditures on the 'labour unit' component of business. The lack of a credible or concerted attempt to tackle the employment problem, therefore, has had and will continue to have repercussions throughout the rest of the economic and social system.

Certainly the neglect of the employment issue has had a major influence on State budgetary decisions and government policy in the education sphere. Education has been more closely tied to economic strategy, the idea being that as the economy grows and changes so more jobs will be created. The failure to come to grips with the structural nature of changes in work, and the stolid refusal to acknowledge that economic success often means less jobs rather than more, has resulted in a form of schooling which is totally inappropriate for present needs.

The rationalisation of government spending, plus the emergence of conservative ideologies and practices in education, reflect the interests of the powerful and wealthy in Australian society. As the economic crisis worsens, these interests will be more nakedly revealed; already the process has been set in train. When we examine recent developments in education we need to be aware of the political and ideological dimensions of change, in addition to the economic. The relationship between these is complex and at times contradictory.

In its economic dimension, educational change has been characterised by a new emphasis on vocationalism and training. Education in this framework is seen in terms of efficiency, technical skills and the provision of rudimentary knowledge. Ideologically, education is being constructed in terms of 'measurable individual differences' and meritocracy, whereby those with the most 'ability' will rise to the top academically and in the labour marketplace. Politically, control is being exercised via a number of mechanisms. Some of these are: standardisation of classroom materials and practices; greater emphasis on enforcing discipline in the school; promoting the ideology of competitive achievement; and teaching life skills which match employers' demands for obedience and presentation of self.

If we survey a few of the developments over the last decade or so, the picture is a disturbing one indeed. They include: a reduction in needed spending on education; moves to centralise the curriculum; further privatisation of education at all levels; the emergence of 'training' schemes in direct competition with educational institutions; and a shift to minimalism in educational provision. It is also important to recognise how liberal notions of education – based upon the notion that everyone is educable – have been applied in practice. This general pedagogical perspective has tended in the late 1980s to be associated with a narrow preoccupation with exceptional cases and experimental programmes. But the 'success' of the latter does not guarantee a wider application *across* student groups. It merely highlights how the 'special needs' of the 'less able' can most 'constructively' and 'effectively' be met. The net result of the above trends thus has been to negate progressive pedagogical approaches and to undermine the development of a broad liberal education. A large proportion of young people are still not getting jobs, and no amount of generalised training will remedy this situation. But not only are these young people facing a future of no work and much poverty, they are facing it without the tools with which to understand and change their world.

A well-informed population which has been provided with an education based upon democratic practices and critical thinking would be in a much better position to resist authoritarian and elitist measures which omit the bulk of the people from consideration or involvement. Indeed, the need for liberal education has never been greater. For as the economic crisis worsens, and society polarises into distinct social, economic and political groupings – the powerful and advantaged, the less powerful and the disadvantaged – justice will come into conflict with greed. The disenfranchisement of young people from education in the broad sense of the word highlights the particular role that schools are being forced to play in perpetuating social division and structures of inequality in Australian society. If liberal education is under threat, then crucial questions need to be asked as to whose interests and needs are being served by this development.

PART TWO

YOUTH CRIME, MORAL PANICS AND PUBLIC ORDER

Media images, the 'youth problem' and social regulation

Historically, attempts by the state to control the behaviour and activities of young people have consisted of two major strands: extending the scope of complusory education or training programmes; and tightening the net of the criminal justice system in regards to law enforcement, surveillance and punishments directed at young people. While education, training and social security are generally seen as the key components of 'youth policy', developments relating to 'law and order' and 'youth crime' are significant elements of the state's response to the 'youth problem'. Significantly, many of the procedures and sanctions usually associated with the operation of the criminal justice system are now also being integrated into education and training in various ways. In addition, when we analyse what the role of youth workers who are involved in short-term training courses for the young unemployed means in broad social control terms, it becomes apparent that social regulation outside schooling is not a matter left solely to the police.

In recent years in Australia, public concern over questions of 'law and order' has gained momentum. Virtually every State election in the last few years has featured considerable debate over what to do about rising crime and the operation of the criminal justice system. Very often the term 'crime' is in fact used as a shorthand expression for 'youth crime'. Usually presenting the issues in sensational fashion, devoid of detailed statistical or theoretical analysis, the mass media has helped to exacerbate public fears about crime in general, and young offenders in particular. The moral panics generated over youth crime have an impact far beyond the issue of crime per se. In today's world, according to the mass media, merely to be 'young' can be enough to betoken an incipient 'criminality' and 'deviancy'.

Media images of young people are by no means static in nature, nor is the information that is conveyed uniform in content. Nevertheless, it can be said that as wider social, economic and political circumstances change, and as young people are affected by these changes, so media reportage will shift accordingly. In the 1980s, the particular ways in which young people are rendered visible, due to high levels of unemployment and homelessness, coupled with increasing fears about the safety of one's property and person in the context of a depressed economic state, have fuelled media stories which are very selective in their highlighting of youth activities.

The thrust of contemporary media reports has been to present young people in a negative light. Consistent media coverage of this type prompted Justice Michael Kirby, head of the Australian Law Reform Commission, to comment in 1987 that: "The media ... have become the modern-day replacement of the medieval monks giving us a daily homily on young people ... as bad-news brats. They've manufactured a stereotype of young people as misfits, moppets, druggies, dole bludgers ... and lumped them in with the strikers, criminals and radicals." (*Adelaide Advertiser*, 19 September 1987). To understand why this is the case, it is essential to consider first, why and how the media selects certain images and stories over others, and secondly, which categories of young people are in fact being presented in the terms outlined by Justice Kirby.

The concentration of print and electronic media in Australia in the hands of five or six businesspeople provides the context of media reporting. To acknowledge media as big business should sensitise us to the particular social interests which the media ultimately serve. They do so, practically, by complex processes of selection and presentation. The net result of these processes is a particular view of the world and a particular interpretation of the events selected as being significant. Fundamentally, what is constructed via the media is a consensual viewpoint that assumes that we all have the same interests in society and that we all have roughly an equal share of power in society (see Hall et al., 1978).

The construction of a commonsense consensual view of society is 'achieved' through continual processes of typification. Through these processes, what is 'normal' and what is 'deviant' become naturalised as everyday perceptions of the nature of social reality. By highlighting what is 'abnormal' or 'deviant', the media both passes judgement on what is seen as 'bad' behaviour and implicitly reaffirms the presumed status quo. To put it slightly differently, the media "selects events which are *atypical,* presents them in a *stereo-typical* fashion, and contrasts them against a backcloth of normality which is *over-typical*" (Lea and Young, 1984: 64). Much the same can be said about the stereotypical images of young people currently in vogue with the media and the specific social content of these stereotypes.

Contemporary media stereotypes of young people can be put into four broad categories: the 'ideal' young person; young people as a 'threat'; young people as 'victims'; and young people as 'parasites'. The *ideal* young person is the one most associated with commercial advertising. This 'typical' young person is presented as one who has a range of 'positive' attributes such as a slim or muscular body and a perfect toothy smile, radiating good health and a fresh and wholesome appearance. The 'all-Australian' young person is bronzed by the sun, definitely heterosexual, white, and of European descent. Women and men are attractive in conventional terms, with men being presented as active and women as smiling and pretty. The overriding message is that to be young is to experience freedom, mobility and affluence.

The ideal young person is also the 'exceptional' young person, as indicated in stories about young people who are brilliant musicians, artists, award-winning students, or people showing some kind of initiative in paid work or leisure activities. The media image here is one which concentrates on the achievements of specific individuals, achievements gained through exceptional talent or by serious hard work.

Young people as a *threat* form a more common theme in news items about the behaviour and activities of the young. In this case much attention is directed to the lack of respect for authority on the part of young people and the breakdown of moral standards of behaviour. The way young people dress, the use of drugs and alcohol, overt sexual behaviour, different kinds of music, all of these and more constitute reasons for worry on the part of the news makers. Anything which is seen to challenge 'conventional' ways of doing things is presented as a threat to the moral fabric of the nation and as something which must be responded to with specific measures.

More directly threatening are images of young people as juvenile delinquents and budding criminals. This category of young people includes school cheats through to those who engage in vandalism and physical aggression. The proliferation of graffiti is frowned upon as a wanton destruction of private property, and 'hoons' and 'larrikins' are constantly referred to as creators of disorder and fear among 'ordinary law-abiding citizens'.

The treatment of young people as *victims* is an increasingly popular aspect of media stories. Issues such as the high incidence of youth suicide and increasing youth homelessness go hand in hand with reports on alienated youth and the problems of youth unemployment. In this instance, the problems of young people are personalised in the form of 'case studies' of this or that unfortunate or disadvantaged young person, and sensationalised in the form of particular 'horror' stories of the difficulties faced by some young people. As Frith (1984: 63) indicates, the change in objective circumstances affecting young people has created a new awareness of youth problems. Thus, "From being an object of adult envy, youth have become, it seems, an object of adult pity." But this 'pity' is usually expressed in voyeuristic terms, or as a simple comparison between how lucky are those who 'have', and unlucky those who 'have not'.

The fourth media stereotype is that centring on young people as *parasites*. They are presented as 'dole bludgers', as ripping off the welfare system, as lacking incentive and wasting their time. Living off the fruits of the labour of 'the rest of us who have to pay taxes', young people are presented as lazy, lacking initiative and as simply hanging around the shops and malls. With no real pressure to do something with their lives, they 'do nothing' but leech off the economic order, taking drugs and upsetting their elders by showing no respect for those who have to work hard for their living.

While the first media image idealises the consumption of leisure by young people, or sets up role models to follow in establishing good work habits and standards, the latter three typifications are negative in character. They are also often intertwined. The 'victims' may be sympathised with, given their sorry state of affairs, but at the same time criticised as being 'parasites' because they are not doing anything about it, and condemned as a 'threat' for resorting to illegal or irrational behaviour when they do act.

The construction of young people in the media therefore consists of a range of separate and interrelated images and concepts. The typifications provided do not in substance refer to all young people, but each set of typifications tends to correspond with different categories of young people. For example, the 'ideal' young person bears the mark of middle-class white Australian attitudes and values, the presence of other cultural and class groups carefully filtered out or only fleetingly acknowledged. The portrayals of males and females similarly tend to conform to traditional stereotypes of masculinity and femininity, the implication being that this is the way things are and should be.

The negative stereotypes tend to focus on working-class males in the first instance, with particular 'problem' young people such as Aborigines singled out for special attention. While the 'ideal' image conveys a sense of 'normality' and 'proper' behaviour, the latter images make reference to the 'abnormal' and the 'deviant'. The actions and attitudes of working-class young people in particular are those that are made problematic in the media. Specific events are abstracted from their social context, and evocative labels are attached to people, places and practices linking them with notions of danger, irrationality and immorality. In this way specific categories of young people are stereotyped as being 'good' or 'bad', as warranting our praise or condemnation. Young people's apparent rejection of middle-class values and aspirations, their challenges to 'legitimate' authority, and their adverse responses to the helping hand of welfare professionals are cited as reasons why young people, like those portrayed in the media, should be treated as a source of concern one way or the other.

The moral panic that is created and sustained by the media does of course have some basis in the real situation confronting many young people. A general deterioration in the lifestyle and life chances of working-class young people has created the conditions for greater social unrest and, at a personal level, identity crisis. The working through of contradictions generated by economic and social forces at the personal level is bound to produce a variety of responses in young people. The wide-ranging quest for answers to questions of survival, autonomy and dependency in turn fuels particular media images of the 'lost generation'. Young people are seen at the crest of a new crime wave. They are seen as at the centre of moral degeneration. They are seen as the main culprits in the welfare cheating scandals. They are seen as irresponsible pawns in the bad parenting game.

The 'solutions' offered in and by the media are as varied as the ways in which the 'problem' is defined. One solution is to blame the victim, to call for enforced conscription of young people into some kind of work, education, training or national service. Another is to target parents and to exhort them to do a better job in controlling their offspring. Yet another is to demand better policing and increased legal measures to regulate the behaviour of young people. Appeals to greater charity provision for the unfortunate are another type of response.

Negative media images of young people feed into a circle of concern involving the public at large, politicians, police officers, judges, youth workers, teachers and parents. As concern grows, and as the material circumstances facing many young people worsen, the state is called upon to play an ever expanding role in restoring order and placating a nervous public. Often this is done without reference to the reasons for the plight of many young people, and with little sensitivity to the specific conditions giving rise to the actions of particular categories of young people. In the end, legal and welfare-oriented solutions to a problem constructed as one of 'law and order' and 'social regulation' beg the question of the underlying foundations of youth activity, constitute unwarranted intrusions on the social and legal rights of young people, and will do little to alleviate the overall situation of young people in Australia today.

CHAPTER 4

Car theft and the crime of no space

If young unemployed people do not enter into a training programme or stay in school for the longest possible period, and if they
are denied adequate social-security benefits, one of the few options
remaining to them may be to engage in crime. This is due to a range
of negative and positive pressures: firstly, reduced income sources
and choice of activities; and secondly, general cultural processes
and particular local economic factors.

This chapter assumes that the social construction of crime and
the engagement in criminal activity by young people is determined
by the position of specific categories of young people in the social
structure. It is argued that, in order to understand why certain
categories of young people commit and are charged with offences,
we must look at the question of 'space' – both 'social space' and
'physical space'. In the context of the increased visibility of young
people due to high youth unemployment, and the subsequent
attempts of the state to regulate the public sphere more closely, the
search by young people for a space of their own has taken on even
greater significance. The tensions arising from the economic and
social situation of some categories of young people, and the restricted nature of their access to 'adult' status and lifestyle based
upon waged work, manifest themselves in a number of ways,
including crime. The nature of the crimes committed reflects basic
social divisions and inequalities in Australian society.

The specific issue of car theft will be used to illustrate these general observations. It will be shown how car theft is intimately linked to, and best explained in terms of, specific ideological, political and economic processes which taken together constitute a particular social milieu which engenders this kind of activity. More concretely, the chapter provides a profile of car theft offences in Adelaide – according to the age, sex and economic status of the offender – and examines some of the interrelated factors such as accessibility of mass transport and leisure facilities which help to explain why certain young people are charged with car theft.

CAR THEFT AND CRIMINOLOGICAL ANALYSIS

> Seven minutes to become statistic No 38 176 ... That's how long I was in physical possession of my new car on Friday night, which is one minute less than the average time between stolen cars in [New South Wales]. ... It was finding out the hard way about Australia's car-theft epidemic which is expanding faster than the national debt. [Alan Farrelly, editor of the *Australian*, 17 August 1987.]

The issue of car theft is important from the point of view of criminological analysis itself, as well as being integral to a 'youth studies' approach to young people. According to recent figures, car theft seems to have reached 'epidemic' proportions in this country. Between 1965 and 1986, the number of motor vehicles stolen increased by approximately 400 per cent, and the ratio of cars stolen to number of vehicles on the road went from 6.3 cars stolen per 1000 cars registered in 1965 to 13.4 per 1000 in 1985–86 (Mukherjee in Australian Institute of Criminology, 1987). As car theft has become more common, so too has concern regarding the fact that, on the basis of arrest statistics, it is young people who are disproportionately identified as being car thieves.

The 'official' responses to car theft have tended to centre on ways to prevent the crime, by both technical means (mechanical and electronic devices) and social control measures (publicity campaigns and schemes like Neighbourhood Watch). The key concern has been to protect private property. The approach to prevention is generally based on analysis of the crime itself, rather than its significance in the wider scheme of things in the lives of young people. Thus, for example, insurance companies examine car theft from the point of view of the orientations of car thieves (recreational, transport, money-making) and by developing typologies of the 'key players' (professional, petty, fraudulent, and joyriding thieves), in order that campaigns such as "Make Life Hell For Car Thieves" in New South Wales can be better organised and car thefts thereby reduced (Lamble, 1987; Challinger in Australian Institute of Criminology, 1987).

Just as the official measures taken to combat car theft cannot be isolated from other social control measures directed at crimes such as prostitution, vandalism, drug use and shoplifting, so too car theft shares much common ground with other 'youth crimes'. Indeed, a major aim of this chapter is to develop a conceptual framework which will allow us to appreciate and acknowledge the complexities of what on the surface may appear to be 'simple' events. This raises several methodological issues which we will look at briefly.

First, the analysis provided below assumes that the social context within which young people are situated is more important at the level of explanation than the event itself. If we think of this in terms of the personal choices 'offered' to young people in their daily lives, then the argument is simply that individual decisions are mediated and shaped by wider social limits and pressures. In terms of method of analysis, this means that primacy will be given to the structural conditions (economic and ideological) which 'allow' or foster particular types of crime and which influence the meaning(s) attached to these kinds of activities.

Secondly, the approach adopted here acknowledges the 'silences' in traditional criminological investigation and attempts to address them. In recent years much has been written in youth studies and criminology about the lack of attention paid to young people who do not fit the category of white, working-class male. This has especially been the case with regard to studies of youth subcultures and criminal activity. Criticism has been particularly directed at the failure of social scientists to focus on young women as the *subject* of their analysis. While acknowledging that this does indeed constitute an instance of (male-dominated) academic myopia, the problem is not restricted only to the topic or subject of analysis. It is also found in the very *method of analysis* itself. The 'silences', then, pertain not only to gaps and emphases in social scientific research, but also to a consistent failure to grapple with the relational character of social practices.

To clarify the issue, and to indicate how a relational approach might be undertaken, the chapter focuses on three types of relations which are of considerable importance in trying to explain car theft.

The first is that of spatial relations. Given the wider context of unemployment and dependency on the parental home, it is shown how the spatial location of young people in the city determines the work and leisure options available to them.

The second concern is that of gender relations. It is argued that discussion of 'masculinity' only gains credence in terms of its linkages with the ideological and material manifestations of 'femininity'. In other words, a specific focus on young working-class males is not the issue here. The methodological point is that gender bias resides at the level of explanation; it is at this level, as well as at the substantive empirical level, that steps must be taken to see 'masculinity' as part of a relation between the sexes. One cannot adequately deal with one side of this relation without acknowledging the dialectical interplay between the two.

The third relation which is discussed has to do with economic situations. In many analyses the relationship of young people to the waged economy is given much attention. However, this emphasis may sometimes obscure or underestimate the position and activities of young people in the 'informal' or 'irregular' economy. An examination of the relationship between the 'informal' and the formal economy can provide valuable insights into the behaviour and choices of young people and the meanings they attach to their actions.

The main concern of this chapter therefore will be to develop a general analytical framework with which to examine young people and crime. As such, the chapter attempts to explore a range of theoretical issues via examination of car theft, rather than to simply provide an in-depth empirical investigation of its incidence.

CAR THEFT AND THE LOCAL DISTRICT

The absence of waged work for growing numbers of young people has effectively and some might say permanently changed the traditional pattern of transition from youth to adulthood. No longer can young men and women expect to move from the parental home, through school, to the paid workforce, to marriage and their own home. This has created tensions in the personal lives of young people, which have been exacerbated by recent developments in government policy where the push for greater education and training is simultaneously being undermined by a lack of concern with job creation and major cuts in programme spending.

Wider developments in the spheres of employment, education, training, benefits, and housing – supported by the general ideological prominence given to 'the family' as a supposed emotional haven and source of material support – have created a new dependency on the parental home for young adults. At the same time these developments have confirmed the diminished lifestyle options and alternatives available to many young people.

The specific response of young people to these broader political-economic trends will be mediated by their experiences in the local neighbourhood. More precisely, the impact of wider structural processes will not affect all categories of young people the same way. The fact that one is male or female, black or white, migrant or established Australian, working-class or middle-class, will obviously affect one's lifestyle and life chances. But the *spatial location* of young people in the urban environment is also a significant factor in terms of the activities they engage in and where and how they spend their time.

The statistical relationship between place of residence and offences committed shows that specific local factors affect regional crime levels. In South Australia, the Central Northern Region is a district defined by the Department for Community Welfare as including Elizabeth, Salisbury, Ingle Farm, Tea Tree Gully, Enfield, Windsor Gardens, Nuriootpa, Gawler and Clare. Of the six such defined districts, the Central Northern Region has the highest proportion of appearances before the Children's Aid Panel and Children's Court per 1000 persons in the juvenile age group. The latter half of 1985, for example, saw 30.0 persons out of every 1000 in this group make an appearance before an Aid Panel or Court, as against the State average of 25.5 persons. Within the Central Northern Region itself, 49.2 persons per 1000 from Elizabeth made appearances, and 32.7 persons per 1000 from Salisbury (Office of Crime Statistics, 1986: 84).

The regional and local variations in figures pertaining to juvenile offenders could be explained in terms of such factors as the ethnic background and social class of the offenders charged. For present purposes, however, our concern is to examine features relating to the local context within which the offences occur, rather than the specific characteristics of the offenders. As a case study, we shall be looking at the Northern Adelaide Development Area, an area which starts at the southern boundary of Salisbury Council and extends to include Elizabeth, Munno Para and Gawler Council areas.

This area contains more than 170 000 people, with about 80 per cent of households owning their own home. Nearly 30 per cent of the area's workforce is involved in the manufacturing sector. The area's largest employer is General Motors-Holden (GMH) which employs more than 4000 people, and many others are employed in the supporting industries. Proportionally, there are fewer people engaged in professional occupations in this area than in the metropolitan area as a whole, and levels of educational achievement are proportionally lower. While labour-force participation rates are declining for men and increasing for women, the area's male participation rate remains consistently higher and the female participation rate consistently lower, than the metropolitan average (Northern Adelaide Development Board, 1987ab).

In terms of age distribution, more than one-third of the population in the Northern Adelaide Development Area is under fourteen years of age, compared with the metropolitan figure of 23 per cent. Unemployment rates for both men and women are higher in this area than in the metropolitan area as a whole, and significantly, the area contains one-quarter of the metropolitan total of unemployed aged between fifteen and nineteen and has one of Australia's highest rates of unemployment amongst its young people (Northern Adelaide Development Board, 1987ab).

Adelaide has the highest per capita level of car ownership in Australia, in part due to the impact of industrialisation from the late 1930s onwards (Sandercock, 1977), and partly because reliance on the motor car was actually built into the layout of urban centres such as Elizabeth (Oakley, 1973). Generally unsatisfactory public transport, in terms of routes and times, also in effect encourages automobile ownership.

Owning a car, in lieu of adequate public transportation, is now more than ever a crucial factor in employment prospects for people in the Northern Adelaide Development Region. In 1981, for example, "there were only 62 local jobs per 100 employed local residents, implying that over one-third of the region's workers travelled to workplaces outside the region." (Northern Adelaide Development Board, 1987a: 1). Given the restructuring of manufacturing industry, and especially the motor-vehicle industry, the problem of attracting enough business to support the area's population has taken on even greater significance.

As it stands, locales such as Elizabeth have been particularly hard hit by the economic crisis, with a high percentage of welfare-dependent households (because of the preponderance of Housing Trust homes in the area) and poor access to jobs and services.

Recent figures compiled by the Department of Social Security, for example, showed that Elizabeth and Salisbury receive the highest amount of social-security payments in the State, with unemployment benefits, pensions and family income supplements constituting a major proportion of the payments (Willcox, 1987: 1). The need for cheap accommodation through government assistance means that low-income persons are being forced into areas which are characterised by their distance from possible job sites and better services. Furthermore, studies have shown that those who are disadvantaged in access to private transport also tend to be disadvantaged by inadequate public transport (Adrian, 1984).

For young people in the Northern Adelaide Development Area, the physical and social constraints on their activities are acute. Youth unemployment ranges up to 50 per cent in some areas (Presdee, 1985), probably reflecting the impact of parental 'disadvantage' which has been shown to be associated with high unemployment probabilities among teenagers (Bradbury et al., 1986). Not surprisingly, the question of what to do in one's 'spare time' and where to do it is subject to constant debate and friction. Measures announced in the May 1987 Mini-Budget and the September 1987 Budget, such as the abolition of the under-eighteen unemployment benefit (see Chapter 1), certainly did not make things any easier.

Lacking sufficient monetary resources, young people are effectively cut off from using commercial outlets to pass their time. The general demise, in demographic terms, of the teenage consumer as an economic force in the area, coupled with a substantive reduction in spending power due to unemployment and low wages in the paid workforce, has further lessened the 'welcome' they might receive when wandering the shops and malls. The lack of community-based recreation and leisure facilities has, ironically, fostered the use of 'public spaces' such as shopping centres not as places for consumption, but as gathering places for young people to spend their time socially. The increasing use of these centres as places for social activities has in turn led to the installation of further security arrangements to monitor and regulate their behaviour (Presdee, 1985).

For many young people their enforced 'leisure' has made them extremely vulnerable to negative experiences associated with 'being on the dole'. Since they have little social space of their own, the street is one of the few territories to which they can lay a claim. Yet here they are subject to constant surveillance and harassment from businesspeople, welfare officials and the police. If we consider the specific case of Elizabeth, the evidence suggests a serious deterioration in general in the relationship between the police and the young unemployed. Presdee's recent study (1987) of the pattern of policing in this area refers to the charge book for one week at the Elizabeth Police Station. Of the people listed who were aged between fifteen and twenty-five, nearly 70 per cent were unemployed. On the basis of his research and observations Presdee concluded that 'the essence of any patrol is to visit spaces it is thought young people might occupy' and that there is a major push to keep them off the streets and under tight control.

To 'escape' this kind of close neighbourhood surveillance is not the only reason young people in the northern region migrate away from their local residences in search of alternative social spaces. One of the biggest complaints by young people in the area is "There's nothing to do!". In a video produced in 1986 by young people of the northern region this came through as a theme. The video, 'A Rough Cut', was part of a CITY (Community Improvement Through Youth) effort to let young people say for themselves what living in the north was like, as well as to enable the participants to learn new technical and social skills. The young people interviewed in the video consistently returned to the problem of having "nowhere to go" and "being bored". Police harassment was seen as causing problems, as was the feeling that no-one really seemed to care about their problems from their perspective.

The lack of 'leisure' opportunities in the northern area and a flat and uninteresting urban environment makes Adelaide city centre seem all that more attractive. The attraction of the city is reinforced by a desire to leave the immediate vicinity of one's parental home, the links to which have been strengthened not necessarily by choice but by economic circumstance and government policies. Besides, the bright lights of Hindley Street and the crowded congregations of all manner of 'weird and wonderful' individuals who flock to Rundle Mall on a Friday evening are tempting to those who need some excitement to break the tedium of everyday life without money.

The lack of physical and social space to 'do their own thing' means that transport becomes a big issue for many young people in the northern area. As we have previously noted, public transport is inadequate in the northern area, and has the further disadvantage that it shuts down early. For young people wanting to travel to the city centre and back this can create problems, especially considering the distance they may have to travel from their place of amusement to the appropriate train or bus stop. For example, the last bus available from the city centre departs from King William Street at 11:48 for Elizabeth and 10.45 for Salisbury (there is no bus for Gawler). The last train for Elizabeth, Salisbury and Gawler leaves the platform at 11.35. As well, it needs to be remembered that much of the layout of the northern area is designed for the private motor car, which means that if a car is not available via one's friends and family then moving from one place to another about the neighbourhood can be very difficult.

The accompanying tables show the incidence of car theft in South Australia in 1985–86. Table 4.1 shows that car theft is overwhelmingly a young person's offence (i.e., from the point of view of apprehension and arrest), with well over half of offenders being under the age of eighteen. The more specific age breakdown in Table 4.2 is significant in that it allows us to observe that the largest proportion of car theft offenders are aged between fourteen and seventeen.

While more detailed study is needed, elements of an explanation for the relationship between age and car theft can nevertheless be offered. One of the conclusions to be inferred from the data is that there is a correlation between the legal school-leaving age (fifteen) and the incidence of car theft. The age at which offences start to

Table 4.1: Offenders involved in motor-vehicle larceny, by age and sex, South Australia, 1985–86

Age	Male	Female	Total
Under 18	898	100	998
18–24	492	51	543
25–34	127	13	140
35–44	23	2	25
45–59	7	–	7
Over 60	1	–	1
Total	1548	166	1714

Source: South Australian Police, Annual Report 1985–86, *1987: 129.*

Note: Statistics based on details of offenders recorded by the Police Department.

Table 4.2:   Alleged offenders involved in motor-vehicle larceny, by age and sex, South Australia, July–December 1985

Age	Male	Female	Total
Under 14	54	7	61
14–17	418	43	461
18–19	123	21	144
20–24	120	13	133
25–34	55	8	63
35–44	11	–	11
45–59	3	–	3
60+	2	–	2
Total	786	92	878

Source: Office of Crime Statistics, Crime and Justice in South Australia, *1986: 24.*

Note: The term 'alleged offender' describes persons allegedly involved in offences cleared and apprehended by the police during the relevant period. Not all of these people would subsequently have been found guilty of an offence in court.

occur in larger numbers could also be related to the fact that at sixteen young people are eligible to gain a motor-vehicle licence in South Australia and thus the car becomes more significant in their personal plans and ambitions. In either of these instances the issue of economic resources becomes important to consider.

Young people from middle-class backgrounds not only tend to stay at school longer than young people from low-income households but they are more likely to be able to draw upon parental resources for transport. That is, they are more likely to have access to a motor vehicle: a car may be given to them as a gift, or a 'family' car may be 'lent' to them when outings warrant it. Furthermore, as students they are more likely than non-students to be in part-time work. Staying at school thus appears not only to enhance future employment opportunities but also one's immediate access to paid work, the monetary income from which could be channelled into the buying or use of cars.

Many young people in the northern area, however, live in poverty or near-poverty. Unemployment and reliance on state benefits affects not only them, but their parents as well. The low-income character of the northern region also means that paid employment is no guarantee of sufficient consumer power to maintain a two-car household. There are other factors to consider: both parents (if there are two) may have to work, and their employment may entail irregular working hours or shift work. Furthermore, even if a car was accessible there is still the question of finding money for petrol and other expenses.

The dearth of employment opportunities in traditional paid work means that many young people are denied the chance to purchase their own vehicle. Since many of these young people leave school at an earlier age than middle-class youth, given the different conceptions of 'work', 'school' and 'finding a job' among working-class young people (see Corrigan, 1979; Willis, 1977; Thomas, 1980), the lack of money and abundance of 'spare time' produce frustration, alienation and general feelings of boredom.

Some indication of the effects of leaving school in a period when the transition from adolescence to 'adult' status in economic terms has been severely disrupted is found when comparisons are made of employment status and appearances before the Children's Court or Children's Aid Panels. The nature of the offence and the response of social control agencies to the offender appear to vary considerably depending upon employment status. For example, from 1 July to 31 December 1985, unemployed young people made up almost half of the juvenile population appearing before the Children's Court (out of the figures pertaining to the known status of the offender), while they constituted a significant minority of young people appearing before Children's Aid Panels (Office of Crime Statistics, 1986).

The economic status of the offender is a key variable in explaining the incidence of car theft. However, questions still remain as to the meaning of the offence to the young people themselves. The next two sections consider in greater depth the 'cultural' and the 'economic' significance of car theft as this relates to young working-class men and women.

WORKING-CLASS CULTURE, GENDER RELATIONS AND CAR THEFT

One of the more striking features of Tables 4.1 and 4.2 is the marked difference in rates of offences between young men and young women. The intention of this section is to explore the reasons for this difference. Specifically, the objective is to provide an explanation, not only of why young men steal cars, but of why young women by and large do not (for a case study of a car theft group involving both young men and young women, see Wrennall, 1986). As will be seen, in each case the explanation offered revolves around the different position of young men and young women in the social structure.

A further concern of this section is to suggest that car theft (as with other similar offences) may constitute, for young men, one possible avenue to reaffirm their gender identity in a period when the disappearance of waged work is undermining many of its traditional foundations. For young women, the situation is quite different: the options open to them reflect their 'traditional' place in the domestic sphere and the general constraints placed upon many of their activities in both the private and the public spheres. The altered social state within which many young people find them-selves lends itself to various kinds of response, many of which are shaped by the general status quo of class and gender. As Roberts (1983: 56–7) puts it: "Family backgrounds, educational attain-ments and job opportunities set young people apart, on masculine and feminine, then separate social class trajectories, and youth cultures do not overwhelm but respect these boundaries, and assist in transporting young people to conventional adulthoods."

We have already noted that the largest employer in the Northern Adelaide Development Area is GMH. This is significant, since it provides a material base for the particular cultural milieu of the area. The motor car is a key part of the economic and social life of the northern region. Indeed, since the late 1940s the car has become "a central feature of working-class life and culture, a basis of the economics of everyday life" (Connell and Irving, 1980: 295). The motor car is integral to a range of production and consumption relations and activities for working people in the northern area. An examination of the ways in which these relations and activities are structured can provide us with some insight into the nature and meaning of car theft.

The patterns of ownership and use of motor cars have been historically shaped by a range of cultural and material forces in Australian society. The relationship between gender identity and motor vehicles is socially constructed, and in it males are at the centre and females at the periphery. The close association of 'masculinity' with car ownership and use is intertwined with the processes of production and consumption. Explication of the complex web of relationships surrounding 'a man and his car' is a difficult task. Nevertheless, several observations can be provided which indicate the nature of these relationships.

Initially it can be said that, for men in particular, a car is (and is seen as) a necessity for paid employment. For working-class men in the Northern Adelaide Development Area this is especially true. The 'necessity' is twofold. First, the making of motor vehicles and the provision of associated parts and services is a major source of livelihood in the region. The car therefore represents not only a means of transport, but is the very lifeblood of economic existence. To own a car is, at this level, in itself a form of recognised 'productive' (rather than simply 'consumption') activity, being tied into the reproduction of the conditions of one's labour. Secondly, given that there is insufficient industry in the area to maintain the resident population, the car also represents for many workers a necessary means of travel to work sites distant from their homes.

These 'necessities' are not of themselves *necessarily* gender specific; for example, female workers have an equal need for transport. They become gender specific because of the primacy attached to the male as breadwinner in our society, and the low status ascribed to women in wage labour and domestic work. The fact that males in the region have a higher rate of labour-force participation than females seems to suggest that the workforce is highly segregated, as well as indicating the strength of patriarchal ideologies in relation to the allocation of paid work generally. Another contributing factor could be the status of many women in the region as sole parents, which may discourage them from entering paid work.

The strong identification of working-class men with paid work, and a particular kind of relationship to this work, reaffirms their notions of sexual identity while confirming the 'domestic' and 'feminine' status of women (Donaldson, 1987; Connell, 1983; Dwyer et al., 1984). As Willis (1979: 197) comments: "The male wage packet is held to be central, not simply because of its size, but because it is won in a masculine mode in confrontation with the 'real' world which is too tough for the woman." Where there is widescale industrial production broadly perceived as being 'masculine' in nature, as in the case of the northern region, there are characteristically a number of measures (discrimination in hiring and on the job, sexual harassment) which can be used to exclude women. In a period of high unemployment, female 'intrusions' into traditional male domains are more difficult than ever.

The conjunction of elements of manual labour power with certain kinds of masculine gender definitions is not only an essential feature of the shop floor, and access to work on the shop floor, but it carries over into consumption as well. For example, the emphasis on practical ability and 'lived knowledge' is an important characteristic of working-class culture (Dwyer et al., 1984). Young men are brought up in a cultural setting which places great importance on 'practical things' and 'aggressive physicality', attributes that fit the pattern of work practices they may in the future engage in.

Aggressive physicality is expressed in a number of ways, many of which centre on motor cars. This is rendered visible culturally and materially in several ways: through the exhibition of prowess in mechanical skills, and through the connotations associated with control over the machine. In a discussion of the relation of masculinity to machinery, for instance, Connell (1983: 23) comments that: "The 'maleness' of such work is maintained by a network of social practices, in which teenage boys' involvement with motorbikes and cars is an important transitional form." The emphasis on mechanical skills and basic principles of operation (knowledge of mechanical and electronic equipment) is fostered by popular images in the media relating to the motor car. Connell and Irving (1980: 298) make the observation that "The rising popularity of motor sport, massively publicised by the motor and oil industry from the Redex reliability trials of the early 1950s to Jack Brabham's international racing triumphs of the 1960s, spread the gospel of technique among working-class youth." In the 1980s, much the same can be said about the impact of the yearly Grand Prix motor car race in this city.

For many men, the Grand Prix means licence to assert their masculinity publicly through drinking, through driving, and through collectively proclaiming their virility to female passers-by. The danger, the speed, the noise, the thrill of it all is very much physical, and 'sexual', in character. The streets throb with the power of machines that only 'real men' can control, the vehicles whizzing past admirers jampacked into stands set close to the narrow centre stage. The traditional champagne shower and kiss from a local 'beauty' caps off a performance which tells the world that success with motor cars equals power, sex and excitement. As Cunneen (1985: 85) puts it: "The male relationship to the car or motorbike is one of power. Power over objects, power over the 'world', power over women." Thus, for men, to 'consume' the Grand Prix is to consume the knowledge that 'potency' lies between one's hands. For many, the car becomes indelibly stamped into their consciousness as a key symbol of masculinity. Cars are toys for the boys.

Getting a driving licence, much less easy access to a car, is of course a different experience for young women. Virtually excluded from popular 'lifestyle' constructions of 'the car' (except perhaps as sex-object 'accessories'), young women are likely to see it in functional terms. If the motor car is viewed symbolically, it is in terms of 'freedom', rather than 'potency' or 'power'.

However it is viewed, young women encounter greater obstacles than young men in the use of and familiarity with the motor car. For a start, priority in the use of cars (including tinkering with their mechanical operation) tends to go to young men who, with their 'mates', 'need' the car as a 'natural' part of establishing themselves in the public sphere. Young women, on the other hand, tend to 'need' greater parental protection and guidance as buffers from the evils that may beset them in the 'outside' world. Besides, for many young women it is still the case that their 'value' lies in the domestic sphere, their 'contribution' measured in dishes washed, clothes ironed, meals cooked and children cared for.

The sexual division of labour in the 'public' and 'private' spheres, and the different cultural space occupied by young women and men (McRobbie and Nava, 1984; Game and Pringle, 1979; Wallace, 1986), have affected how the 'broken transitions' to adulthood are experienced in each case. These divergent experiences are important to bear in mind when we consider the nature and meaning of car theft.

In terms of life experiences many working-class young women grow up with a very specific idea of women's role in society. In areas such as northern Adelaide, for example, many share their mother's isolation from the outside world. They are aware of the limited options open to them for paid employment. They see that they will likewise suffer from the lack of adequate child care and family support services, the lack of transport and the consequent additional time spent on doing household tasks such as shopping.

Leisure and recreation facilities designed for their specific needs or at least accommodating their interests are at a premium as well. And, as sociological research has shown, the limited 'leisure' pursuits available to young women tend to be organised in ways that reinforce traditional gender stereotypes, involving non-group non-participatory activities (Poole, 1986). As McKay (1986: 357) summarises it: "Boys' games provide them with opportunities to rehearse competitive, individualistic and organisational skills that are akin to the demands of work and the public sphere. Girls' games feature mainly co-operative, intimate and socio-emotional traits that are more suited to the private sphere and maternal roles." It is the boys, then, who are active and orienting toward adult-type activities in the public sphere; the girls are more passive and generally locked into the privacy of home and bedroom.

An analysis of socialisation patterns can indicate some of the influences on the behaviour of young men and women in our society, and why young men are more likely to be actively engaged in 'public' events than young women. But we also have to recognise the additional impact of unemployment and poverty on the 'options' open to young women. For example, housing is in the midst of a crisis in South Australia as it is elsewhere. In 1986, 39 600 individuals were on the South Australian Housing Trust waiting list, an increase of 13.1 per cent from the previous year. Information prepared by the South Australian Council of Social Service (1987: 10) further indicates that young people who are not in paid employment (or who are on low incomes) may find it impossible to get suitable accommodation. Even taking into account Department of Social Security payments including rent assistance, SACOSS figures indicate that *no* private rental stock is affordable for unemployed single persons.

The low wages of young women who find paid work, and the low unemployment benefits for young people, are forcing many young women to stay in the parental home or return to it after a spell on their own. One consequence of this is the 'infantilisation' of many of these young people: treated like children, they are subject to numerous constraints on their behaviour and coerced into performing an excessive number of domestic duties in order to 'pay their keep' (Presdee, 1984; Brake, 1985). Placed in a position of virtually total dependency, a dependency complicated in this case by age differences and particular authority relations between members of a household, young women constitute a readily available and exploitable resource in the private sphere. Significantly, the time spent on domestic labour appears to have increased rather than decreased, even though the introduction of a range of new household technologies (dishwashers, microwave ovens) have changed the specific features of this work (*New Internationalist*, 1988; Game and Pringle, 1983). Washing, ironing, cleaning and cooking, as well as tasks such as childcare and shopping, can be used as a measure of a young unemployed woman's contribution to the household. However, if her 'worth' is to be measured in terms of a trade-off between parental support and domestic labour, then great pressures will be put on her to continually 'prove' her 'value' to the household. The problem here is that there is no set working day or specific times allocated for domestic labour and, as Game and Pringle (1983: 125) observe, "since the value of household work is not clear, non-employed women feel pressure to spend long hours at it to ensure that an equal contribution is being made". Hence it is not only the activity itself that may constrict the activity of young unemployed women: the difficulties in measuring domestic labour, and its perceived lack of real value, will also add to the pressures already experienced by them. The net result of such processes is a situation which reinforces the isolation of young women from friends and peers and which erodes their confidence and ability to get along in the world outside.

The movement back to the parental home is due to a combination of economic circumstance and public policy which places greater 'responsibility', including financial responsibility, on the family unit to care for its own. In depressed areas in particular, this process is often accompanied by greater incidences of family tension and violence in the home. Young women's expression of the frustrations they feel in this situation is not the same as young men's. For young women the response to stress of this nature is linked to an ideological definition of 'female problems' that see them as internal to the individual woman. Thus, as Alder (1986: 221) points out, "as a consequence, the response of women to situations of stress often takes the form of privatized and self-destructive behaviour such as alcohol and drug abuse".

For young men in a similar situation – that is, unemployed and living at home – the avenues for action are quite different. Without the same pressures to perform domestic labour and subject to different types of parental sanctions regarding their public behaviour, young men have a lot more freedom of movement and thereby action. On the street they will find ready peer support, support which is expressed according to the various conceptions of working-class masculinity.

Theft of a car reflects this concern with establishing a masculine identity in several ways. The sense of 'being a man' is tied up with being able to do physical work, and being paid to do so. The 'sacrifice' of work, and the expected role played by males as the breadwinners, have been undercut by unemployment. This constitutes a major crisis in the development of a male working-class identity. And, as Willis (1984b: 13) suggests, "One way for young men to resolve their 'gender crisis' may be an aggressive assertion of masculinity and masculine style for its own sake." This assertion of masculinity will logically have as its focus objects which are an integral part of constructions of the masculine ideal – in this instance, the motor car.

The theft of motor cars holds an appeal for young working-class men because of life experiences which stem from their position in the class structure. The offence is 'made necessary' by factors such as lack of transport, or even lack of shelter for those who may be homeless. It is also rich in excitement, a dramatic break from the tedium and boredom of being wageless in a consumer society. The 'joy ride' is aptly named, for it brings with it exhilaration far beyond the normal routine. It is also grounded in the cultural attributes of working-class life: to steal a car requires certain practical knowledge and skills: which cars to choose, how to gain entry, and how to start the engine without the correct key.

As young men, those who steal cars have a basic familiarity with the object of their actions. The impersonal nature of the offence lends the act further 'legitimacy'. Motor-vehicle insurance and the knowledge that no one will be physically hurt by their actions gives credence to the offenders' belief that the crime is not a serious one. Since they are without economic resources of their own, an occasional 'borrowing' from those who are well-off is not seen as particularly bad. At the same time, the fact that the act is illegal is an important element both in the immediate excitement and in the assertion of male bravado. In the act of stealing a car is the self-confirmation that one is indeed 'a man'.

But 'being a man' in hard times can also have an economic dimension. The next section explores the significance of car theft from the point of view of activity that takes place outside of the realm of the 'formal' economy.

ECONOMIC ACTIVITY AND THE INFORMAL ECONOMY

The contraction of the formal economy is having an impact on all facets of the lives of young working-class men and women. The formal or market sector of the economy is, generally speaking, characterised by the following features: (a) it is centred on a 'workplace'; (b) it involves the production of goods and services for exchange, rather than for personal consumption; (c) it is regulated by legal and administrative agencies of the state; (d) it consists of work organised into regular or fairly continuous blocks of time; (e) it involves particular power relations between employer and employee (control over the labour process, distribution of income from the sale of commodities); and (f) it involves a flow of labour power from individuals into the formal production system in exchange for money wages, which in turn are used to buy goods and services from this system.

In a capitalist economy the wage received from work in the formal sector is seen as having paramount importance in the lives of young people. The wage represents a means to an end – for young women, to escape the parental home and establish a sphere of relative independence and autonomy; for young men, to enable them to buy consumer items and to 'buy' space for themselves in commercial outlets such as discos, pubs and sporting venues. While the long-term aspirations of both sexes may include thoughts of establishing a separate personal household (see Willis, 1984a), the immediate goals of young working-class people seem to reflect the division suggested above.

Recent studies undertaken in Britain (Griffin, 1985ab), the United States (Weis, 1987) and Australia (Presdee, 1984; Alder, 1986) provide strong evidence that young women do not regard waged labour as marginal. On the contrary, most young women want to obtain waged work and indeed many view such a goal as being more important than marriage and a family. This view of waged work is linked to two factors: men cannot be counted on to 'support' women, for a variety of reasons including unemployment; and young women feel oppressed when they are stuck in the parental home due to wider economic and political circumstances.

Being dependent upon the parental home means something quite different to young working-class men. This difference relates to the nature of 'work' in the home, a topic which we will take up shortly. While waged work for young women opens the door to freedom from the parental home, for young men freedom and independence are often defined in different terms. A useful illustration is provided by Robins and Cohen (1978: 9) who make the observation that:

> The assertion of youthful independence conforms to the fundamental class divide. On one side, those who embrace student-hood, accept continued wageless dependence, on their families or State grants, and whose struggle is for *a place of their own to be who they like in.* On the other, those who take for

granted the fact of continued domestic dependence, because their target is *a wage of their own to do what they like with*. If dependence and autonomy are conditional on one another, so is the tension between the two.

As these authors further indicate, working-class young men use their wages to buy substitutes for the things they lack, in this case space of their own *outside the parental home*.

The lack of waged jobs available to young people, and the low wages and part-time nature of the jobs that do exist, severely restrict the ability of young women to take control over their residential requirements, and of young men to utilise fully the spaces open to them outside the parental home. Lack of an adequate income, whether from waged work or unemployment benefits, gives impetus to other kinds of economic activity. Increasingly, then, the 'informal' economy is playing a larger role in the livelihoods of both households and individuals.

It is important at this stage to distinguish 'waged work' from other kinds of work in society. A labour-market focus on waged work and market relations outside the home obscures the significance not only of 'irregular' work outside the home, but also of the labour that takes place within the household. For most women the home is a workplace, regardless of their employment outside the 'private' sphere. The centrality of domestic work in the lives of young women is crucial to the isolation women feel and the impetus behind their desire to leave the parental home. Finding time for any 'leisure' outside paid work which is performed in conjunction with unpaid domestic work thus becomes "difficult, if not impossible to achieve" (Griffin, 1985b). Just as domestic labour constitutes a major part of young women's unpaid work, so too it accounts for much of the paid work they perform in the 'informal' economy (and, we should add, domestic commitments also affect the employment opportunities available to women in the formal economy).

The 'informal' economy involves a diverse range of activities, some of which resemble activities undertaken in the formal economy. The features of the informal sector are that economic transactions are unregulated, they are untaxed, and they are not officially measured (Mattera, 1985). The informal economy involves activity outside the formal network of market relations and accounting frameworks. Unpaid domestic labour is one example of the informal economy at work. The present concern, however, is with those activities which involve money payments – the so-called 'cash' economy.

The 'cash' economy means different things to different groups of people. Its essential characteristic is that it is illegal, involving the avoidance of tax and the transgression of various state regulations. Gershuny (1983) outlines three types of 'underground' economic activity which provide background for discussion of the place of car theft in the informal economy. First, there are activities which are closely associated with formal employment and production. These include such things as occupational theft; from the relatively trivial (a waiter lifting food from a restaurant) to major actions (tax evasion and tax avoidance). Secondly, Gershuny talks about production processes which feed into the normal production system but are not part of it. The example here is outworkers in the clothing industry whose employment may not be recorded in the books of conventional firms. The third category of underground employment is that of providing services and goods directly for consumers. This is most visible in the form of 'self-employed' persons doing house repairs, cutting lawns, ironing, house cleaning, doing renovations and so on.

It has been suggested that, especially in a period of high unemployment and with the advent of new technology which allows more productive activity to occur in the household, the informal economy is becoming independent of the formal economy (Dorn and South, 1983; Gershuny, 1983). That is, goods and services are increasingly being provided informally at the local level in systems of household/ community production which are not tied into the formal market economy. This has specific implications with regard to the types of activities engaged in by young men and young women.

We have already noted that young women bear extra burdens of domestic labour. In the 'cash' economy, the sexual division of labour is reproduced. In this case, paid work for women usually consists of home-based activities. If tied into the normal production system and commercial enterprises, it could include, for example, doing piece-work for a clothing manufacturer or hospital laundry service. Childcare is another type of paid work, and the conditions and payment often parallel those in the formal sector (as indicated by the 'dollar-an-hour' per child which some caregivers receive while working under the federal government's Family Day Care scheme – see Powell, 1987).

In the local neighbourhood, the classic example of 'young women's work' is babysitting. As Dorn and South (1983: 32) point out, this is "a significant source of funds for some girls, and which gives them access to other household's facilities (magazines, television, audio, sometimes food and drink, escape from the pressures of home, and space for the entertainment of friends)'". People living in areas such as the northern Adelaide region, which is characterised by a high proportion of low-income households in Housing Trust estates, are doubly disadvantaged: by the lack of adequate public services and by their inability to afford any services that might be on offer. In these circumstances one could expect that greater reliance would be placed upon finding assistance through the informal networks and readily available 'workers' in the community.

These examples of participation by young women in the informal economy show that it is based on gender stereotypes, and it takes place in the household. The location of women in the household sphere precludes them from taking part in many other kinds of activities, including illegal ones, in the 'public' sphere. For example, criminal offences committed by young women tend to centre on objects and activities related to their place and roles in society, as with shoplifting which is connected with their role as the 'shoppers' and their dependence on income from sources outside themselves (see Smart, 1976; Alder, 1986).

For young men the experience of activity in the informal economy is 'public' in nature. In addition to 'handyman' work, the popular British television programme *Minder* reminds us that much of this activity is of a shady character. To relate this to the topic under discussion, if we are to understand the possible economic and cultural attractions of car theft for young men, then we need to locate it within the context of the operation and specific nature of the informal economy.

While more study of these questions is needed, it can be suggested that wider transitions taking place in the labour market – the growth of part-time work, the rise in sub-contracting, and legislative efforts to deregulate relations between employers and employees – will affect the opportunities of young people in both the formal and informal economies. It could be argued, for example, that young people will be squeezed out of some sections of the informal waged economy due to the availability, vulnerability and work experience of other categories of workers, most notably older women and non-English-speaking migrants, who are in a position to displace young people from many of the arrangements that have characterised the cash economy. Under these circumstances, it is likely that young people will be forced to be active in the criminal economy, obtaining or supplementing their income through irregular criminal activity.

The position of car theft in the framework of activity of the informal economy is not the same as those practices which, although themselves illegal, are more closely related to the formal production sector. Car theft is unambiguously illegal and 'illegitimate', especially when compared with the 'softer' categories of small business 'enterprises' in the informal sector. In opposition to 'victimless' crime, the act of motor-vehicle theft immediately calls attention to itself – it invariably demands a response of some sort on the part of the state, if only in that the offence is reported to the police.

It is partly this aspect of 'danger' which is so attractive to young people who steal cars. A further reason why young people steal cars is to give themselves a measure of control over their environment. In a study of a group of car thieves in Sydney, Wrennall (1986: 5) makes the observation that:

> Poverty is associated with feelings of powerlessness, vulnerability and impotence. The stealing of cars is a result of kids' attempts to overcome economic exclusion. They break into a world which becomes theirs. Inside the car, their own social relations prevail. It's their world, for once, and it is populated by friends.

Another attraction is the 'irregular' nature of the activity. Involvement in these kinds of illegal activity is marked by a 'bunching together' of intensive work, interspersed with a "continuous activity of searching for further opportunities and of surveillance for potential dangers" (Auld et al., 1984). As 'work', car theft certainly offers much more excitement than the drudgery of normal paid work or the boredom of life on the dole. These dimensions of car theft – danger and excitement – explain why young men who *do* have paid employment (but low wages and little job satisfaction) might also look to the criminal economy to supplement their income and gain a few 'kicks' at the same time.

Young people who steal cars for economic reasons need to know what to do after the 'merchandise' has been picked up. This applies to the sale of the car itself (or parts thereof, including stereo players and cassette decks) or to the items garnered by some other form of 'irregular' activity which may involve a stolen car for transportation purposes. The main target of car thieves is motor vehicles ten to fifteen years old. New vehicles tend to be targeted for the stripping of accessories, while with older ones the objective is to strip them for parts (Lamble, 1987). The social networks required for transactions involving the sale of accessories and parts tend to be male-dominated. This is so for several reasons.

The most obvious explanation lies in the different spaces accorded to young men and young women in society: the former encouraged to move out into the public sphere at an early age, the latter generally restricted to the private home. The claiming of public space as their own also brings young men into contact with other young men. Hence peer groups and subcultures develop in a manner unlike the more isolated experiences of young women. This entrance into the world of 'grown-ups' is reflected in the greater preference by young men than young women to engage in adult-oriented leisure activities such as drinking and going to clubs (Poole, 1986).

The mobility experienced by young men, coupled with peer support and expectations regarding 'manly' behaviour, afford young men the opportunity and cultural resources to connect with the appropriate people in the informal economy. However, the impediments facing young women cannot be explained in purely cultural terms relating to stereotyping. Nor can they be explained simply in terms of cultural and physical space. There is an economic factor here as well. Put simply, men tend to monopolise the opportunities existing in the criminal economy for themselves. Women are systematically excluded, except with regard to the sale of their most intimate 'commodity' – their bodies (Auld et al., 1986). The masculine nature of the criminal economy is based upon male concerns to protect their economic territory from possible competition from their female counterparts.

Whether the stealing of cars in the context of the informal economy is primarily for economic survival, or so that the persons involved can be provided with resources with which they can participate and enjoy leisure pursuits (see Muncie, 1984), is subject to debate. How one interprets the *meaning* of car theft, however, ultimately depends upon how the nature of 'the problem' is perceived and the viewpoint from which it is investigated.

SPACE OF THEIR OWN

The arguments presented in this chapter have revolved around the interrelated concepts of 'space', 'gender' and 'economy' and the efforts of young people to create their own identities in relation to these constructs.

Stealing a car represents an assertion of control over the machine and a short-lived but important sense of independence in terms of physical space. Living in an urban environment hostile to their needs and desires will only kindle the flame of resistance and the search for 'more to offer' on the part of many young people.

For young men specifically, car theft also provides an outlet to express aggressive masculinity which, in the face of restricted opportunities in other realms of their experience, appears to offer some solace for their decline in social status. The low proportion of reported cases involving young women should certainly not be seen as something to be celebrated. For disclosure of the reasons for the 'silences' in the statistics brings home once again the oppressive conditions young women are subject to in the 'normal' course of events.

The theft of an automobile can also be seen in terms of defiance and economic independence. The act itself marks a sharp break with authority, but when linked with activities in the informal sectors of the economy it carries other connotations. The checking by Department of Social Security personnel of young unemployed people receiving benefits, the rules and regulations surrounding the job search allowance, the pressures on young people to consume although they are without the resources to do so, the patronising tones used by those who encourage young people to engage in voluntary community work – all of these pale into insignificance when juxtaposed with the excitement and no-strings-attached financial return of the informal economy.

The view advanced in this chapter has been that if an 'answer' is to be found to the problem of car theft, then we have to look beyond the offence itself. The problem lies not in the act, but in the oppressive economic and ideological structures within which young people are situated. In the end, issues such as youth crime emerge from and, in many ways, reproduce the basic inequalities and oppressions of Australian society.

An escalation of youth crime, of which car theft is a part, will provide ammunition for those calling for campaigns for 'law and order', and lead to even greater intervention by the state in the lives of young people. Such intervention characteristically uses regulations and coercion as a means of containing social problems. As the previous discussions have indicated, however, a 'big stick' approach to social control will not address the underlying problems confronting young people. Nevertheless, it is this kind of approach which has characterised contemporary state measures designed to deal with the 'youth problem'.

CHAPTER 5

Young people, law and the street

The topic of 'young people and the law' is often framed in terms of young people in 'trouble' with the law. In part this is due to the strong historical links between youth studies, which have focused on the nature and 'style' of youth subcultures, and the tradition of research into delinquency. It is also related to recurring public statements of concern about the 'problems with young people'. As Pearson (1983) vividly demonstrates in his study of 'hooliganism', there is a long history of public outcry and 'moral panic' over the issue of 'youth' crime, which shows that the 'law-and-order' campaigns of the last century have much in common with those of the present.

The high profile given to the academic study of youth crime, coupled with periodic outbursts by the media, politicians and police over the unruliness and disorder of the younger generation, has been responsible for a peculiarly narrow view of the relationship between young people and the law. The phrase 'young people and the law' as normally used can be read as meaning 'young people in *confrontation* with the law'.

This view of the relationship between young people and the law is unsatisfactory for a number of reasons. Firstly it tends to examine the link between young people and the law only in 'exceptional' circumstances – that is, the analysis is an examination of specific intervention by law enforcement officials in situations involving the criminal justice system, or by state welfare officials where the welfare system is involved. As a result the study is limited, in terms of who is studied (i.e., a select category of young people), and what is examined (i.e., a particular set of circumscribed situations). One might assume from such an approach that the *only* point of contact between young people and the law lay in immediate and observable instances, such as when a young person is arrested by the police for a criminal offence.

Secondly, this approach directs our attention to the issues of crime and delinquency, and thus to questions of law and order, with the conditions of life for young people being relegated to secondary importance in the analysis. The circumstances are examined only in terms of their impact on wrongdoing, not as crucial questions in their own right. If we shift our attention to these 'conditions of life', however, we find that whereas crime and delinquency are often on the periphery of young people's experiences, the law is absolutely central.

The law is central in all aspects of the social life of young people. The 'law', in its many forms (legislative, administrative, criminal, civil), institutionalises the relations between young people and society. All young people are, in some way, affected by the law all the time, but the specific manner in which the law actually intervenes in their lives depends on their social background. This chapter shows how the position of young people in the legal system puts particular categories of young people 'at risk' of direct intervention by the law in the form of police or welfare personnel.

The chapter begins with a discussion of the legal status of young people. This is followed by an examination of the interrelationship between generation-based contradictions and situation-based contradictions. This interrelationship is illustrated by reference to how young people use the 'street', and in particular how female 'street kids' and young Aboriginal people use this space. It will be shown how the contradictions arising from the position of young people in regard to the law generate further contradictions and further interventions by the law in their lives. The latter part of the chapter explores the nature of some of these recent interventions by examining the functions and consequences of state campaigns such as the so-called Drug Offensive. Significantly, while such campaigns are ostensibly aimed at curbing and modifying the behaviour and attitudes of *some* young people, nevertheless the whole youth population is the target. Because of this, they have serious and profound implications with respect to the particular kinds of controls and regulations being placed upon *all* young people in Australian society.

YOUNG PEOPLE AND THE LAW

If a reader is to pay any attention to the media's opinion of teenagers, the reader would find that teenagers are constantly drunk and are addicted to drugs. The reader would also find that teenagers even when appropriately licensed, are incapable of driving safely at night.

The reader would also discover that while teenagers are not drunk or on drugs, we fill our time in other ways. For example, we are all supposedly cheating our way through high school or we are happily unemployed. [Fonovic, 1987.]

These words were written by a young person who is concerned about the "negative image of teenagers expressed by politicians through the mass media". In recent years residents of Australia have been subjected to media barrages detailing the 'youth problems' afflicting their particular town, city or State. These have ranged from cheating in the high schools to underage drinking, from poor driving records to the problem of 'dole cheats'. The current moral panic over the affairs of young people has been accompanied by calls for even tougher laws to govern their behaviour – to the extent that proposals for a youth curfew have been seriously considered by local authorities and State governments, and in some cases actually implemented on an informal basis. Little of the public debate has involved young people themselves. As Aldo Fonovic adds in his letter to an Adelaide newspaper, "I think I speak for the majority of teenagers when I demand to be given a fair go and at least some say in the legislation and restrictions that are placed upon us."

The negative public image of young people – and the moralising tone used in judgements about their attitudes and behaviour – are important parts of a concerted movement to regulate young people more closely. This push for greater social control is bound up with the failure of governments to deliver the goods in the areas of youth employment, income security, housing and so on. The economic tensions felt by young people today have brought them out into the open, with the struggle over space, and its regulation and use, increasingly critical in their lives (Presdee and White, 1987). It is a struggle *for* a space of their own, and it is a struggle *against* measures designed to restrict this space, to keep them off the streets, to make invisible the many and varied social problems they are experiencing as a result of the considerable change and crisis in the Australian economy.

What young people do with their time and where they do it is subject to a wide range of legal and extra-legal constraints. We will consider how some of these constraints operate in distinct, though interrelated, spheres of activity (for further discussion, see Children's Interest Bureau, 1985; Boer and Gleeson, 1982; Youth Affairs Council of Australia, 1988). There are significant variations between the States in laws affecting young people, and each State has adopted its own particular approach, age categorisation, and legal provisions and services for young people. In each case, however, there are laws relating to the custody, care and control of children by a parent or guardian; laws compelling young people to go to school and regulations governing their actions within the school context; laws delimiting the age at which they can start paid work, and the wages deemed appropriate for young workers; and laws pertaining to the ability to make legal agreements or contracts, gaining a driver's licence, consumption of alcohol and cigarettes, sexual intercourse and marriage.

But there are many other laws and regulations which affect the position of young people in Australian society. Other notable areas of concern include provisions relating to Children's Court, political party membership, voting rights, and medical services. These laws pertain to the status and rights only of young people: in addition, young people are subject to the provisions of the criminal and civil law which bear upon every resident and citizen of Australia.

This brief description indicates the highly regulated nature of the young person's world. It is interesting to contrast this picture of 'growing up' in contemporary Australia with that of Llewellyn Fowler, born on 25 March 1893. As Davey (1986: 375) recounts Fowler's story:

> His passage into the adult world was almost entirely unregulated. It was achieved with little or no guidance or restriction, either familial or institutional. Even at school he had one foot in the classroom and one in the workplace. The final step would have passed unremarked. He never really had an adolescence as we understand it.

The development of a highly regulated passage from adolescence to adulthood, and the array of laws pertaining specifically to young people, has been characterised by the virtual absence of young people themselves from the decision-making concerning the limits and scope of their rights.

The complexity and unevenness of the law, and the fact that it is something which is imposed upon young people, creates problems for young people who have no say in shaping the laws that affect them. The operation of the law in practice also gives rise to difficulties. For instance, recent studies have highlighted the fact that the legal knowledge of young people is poor, and that their rights are frequently overlooked in their interactions with the police (Staden, 1987; Gray, 1987). Other research has pointed to the inadequacy of much of the legal information currently provided for young people, and the fact that the legal needs of young people are largely unmet in areas pertaining to the family, schooling, income support, accommodation, employment and the consumer market (O'Connor and Tilbury, 1987; White, 1987).

At a theoretical level, each young person has the same 'rights' and 'obligations' before the law. According to the 'rule of law' each person is to be treated alike, equally and impartially, in society. Thus, for rich or poor, male or female, white or black, the law is supposed to act in equal fashion (see White, 1986a; O'Malley, 1983). The very existence of the rules and regulations outlined above also serves to indicate at an abstract level the common ground shared by diverse groups of young people.

In practice, however, the law does treat different categories of people differently depending upon their social background (White, 1986a; Smart, 1976; Fine et al., 1979). The present concern is not to document these differences; rather it is to indicate how the *general* positioning of young people in the wider legal matrix shapes the *specific* social realities which they experience. To illustrate the nature of this process the next section will examine how the 'street' is used by different categories of young people, and how public responses are constructed in relation to this usage.

THE SOCIAL NATURE OF THE STREET

Age and circumstance combine in a complex fashion to produce a wide array of street activity and behaviour among young people. The legal and social position of young people in society, which is determined on the basis of age, gives rise to what can be called 'generation-based' contradictions in attitudes towards them. For particular individuals these contradictions mean different things, depending upon class background, sex and ethnicity.

The character of generation-based contradictions is such that young people are provided with a range of formal and informal rights which co-exist in uneasy fashion alongside each other. For example, young people may in one moment be treated as 'adult' consumers with certain 'rights' based upon money, or chided by parents and teachers that they must 'grow up' and act like 'an adult', while in the next moment they may be told that they cannot do something because they are 'too young' or because the school or parent makes the 'rules'. Similarly, at an ideological level young people are constantly reminded that 'adolescence' is the time to be 'different', and that they are indeed 'different' from other generation groups. For the most part, however, they are rarely provided with enough resources actually to express this difference.

The different and at times confusing ways in which young people are treated in society creates tension at a practical level. Much of the activity of young people in general is directed to escaping the authority figures of school, home and work. In order to do this, there are several options available to them. These include frequenting cinemas and games arcades, and participating in organised spare-time activities such as Boy Scouts or Girl Guides. The 'problem' with these options for many young people is that money is a prerequisite for commercial-based activities, whereas activities organised by adults often involve measures designed to dictate their behaviour in one way or another.

The 'street', therefore, is one of the few havens for young people who want to please themselves about what they do, when, and with whom (although even here they are subject to numerous restrictions). In other words, the street is "free in both commercial terms and in terms of close control" (Corrigan, 1979: 123). As a place to 'hang out', the 'street' in fact refers to specific well-defined locations, locations where young people have a degree of room to move, as well as an opportunity to meet (or simply 'watch') other young people. Familiar sites where young people congregate in the Adelaide area, for instance, include places such as Hindley Street and Rundle Mall in the city centre, and various shopping centres such as the Elizabeth Town Centre. The reasons why young people migrate to these areas at various times of the day and week appear to be directly linked to the availability of specifically youth-oriented facilities in the area (see Department for Community Welfare, 1985; Hindley Street Youth Project, 1986, 1987; Presdee, 1985; Wakim, 1986). Similar sites are found in other Australian cities; for example, Kings Cross in Sydney, or Fitzroy Street, St Kilda, and the Bourke Street Mall in Melbourne.

The street is significant in the lives of most young people, regardless of their social background. This is due to their position in society and the inadequate provision of overall resources available to them (since young people as a category lack any significant social power in their own right to 'win' these resources). The manner in which young people 'relate' to the street, however, varies considerably depending upon situational factors. Indeed, there is a continual contest among young people as to who will 'own' which section of the street. Hence, the street can be seen in terms of specific 'territories', spaces which can be mapped according to the specific activities carried out by specific groups of young people. Hindley Street, for instance, is known as being 'rough' as well as the major entertainment 'strip' in Adelaide; Rundle Mall on the other hand tends to be actively used by a much wider variety of young people, probably due to the emphasis in this location on shopping, and is seen as relatively 'safe' by the users.

Different groups of young people are on the street for very different reasons. Their lack of power in other spheres, and the lack of other available 'space', explain why the street is so attractive to them. On this larger canvas there are many variations. For example, it can be said that the street is the place which young people "can take over as their own by the forceful presence of their numbers, their looks, their music, their spray-can graffiti and, sometimes, their petty crime and violence" (Winship, 1985: 28). In the very process of 'owning' their patch of the street, young people are also forging specific identities – as students at a particular school, as punks, as skinheads, as Koories or Nungas, and so on. But the construction of these identities themselves is dependent upon the material circumstances surrounding each group of young people.

For instance, a series of reports published during September–October 1986 in the Adelaide press discussed the deep divisions between young people known as 'the trendies' and the 'street kids'. These labels are by no means unambiguous. The term 'trendy' has been applied to two groups: private-school young people who at one stage were making use of the Second Storey facility in Rundle Mall as an after-school drop-in centre; and to a particular group of 'fashionably'-dressed young people who frequent some of the night spots on Hindley Street.

The first group of 'trendies' used Second Storey as a secure meeting place where they could indulge in behaviour that might be frowned upon at home or school (smoking cigarettes, speaking freely about a range of topics, expressing an interest in sexual matters). Ostensibly an agency providing health services, the Second

Storey Youth Health Centre caters to a range of youth needs, including the need for 'space' of their own. At the time when public attention was focused on the centre, the former director commented that "There is no doubt that a mixture of young people aged between 12 and 25 do use the centre – we don't discriminate." (*Adelaide Advertiser*, 16 September). This provides some indication of how the 'target population' was constructed at that time. That is, it was primarily constructed on the basis of age, with class, gender, and ethnic background as secondary considerations. It is these latter differences among young people, especially that of class, which partly explain the antagonisms that developed between the 'trendies' and other users of the centre. The second group of 'trendies' – those who parade up and down Hindley Street – are there to be seen and to consume what the commercial outlets have to offer. There was and is a vast social distance between either of these groups and the 'street kids'.

The term 'street kid' is also somewhat ambiguous. In one sense, 'street kids' can be defined in cultural terms. Thus, Brake (1985: 190) describes street culture in the following terms: "It is desperate, anti-authority, raw and violent, involved in the defence of symbolic territory. It occurs outside the home, in the urban street, itself a tough environment. It is neither safe nor nice, and hence very attractive." This portrayal of street culture assumes several things about the material circumstances of young people who might be described as 'street kids'. For present purposes it is sufficient to point out that 'street kids' do not have the consumer options that other young people might have, nor do they view the street as one of a range of alternatives when it comes to how and where they will spend their time. In many cases the street is the only option – whether because of lack of money or because other venues are not appropriate or open to them.

A distinction amongst 'street kids' can be made on the basis of temporary and long-term use of the street. For some young people the street is a temporary site, used for recreation or adventure-seeking, but not as the sole or permanent living space. For others, the street is an escape from authority and abuses of the parental home or welfare institutions, an escape which may eventually separate them from support networks and the usual social institutions. As 'outsiders', these street kids are generally regarded as 'social junk' (Wilson and Arnold, 1986).

To indicate the lack of choice available to this latter category of young people, it is useful briefly to consider the issues of accommodation and the violence of street life. With respect to accommodation, a number of 'street kids' do not wish to use existing accommodation services and refuges because they object to the rules and regulations they feel are imposed upon them. Where this is the case, it tends to imply that decisions are made and transmitted in a 'top-down' approach that excludes the young people using the service. As a result some young people may see such services as simply an extension of the paternalistic, authoritarian attitudes they encounter in most other spheres of their lives. They may be in need of shelter, but they object to the regimentation and discipline which accompanies the social responses to their need.

Reluctance to use provided accommodation is due to such things as management committees which are insensitive to the 'power' needs of young people, through to government regulations which specify that accommodation is for short-term use only, thus fostering the continual movement of young people in and out of refuges. Without a stable environment, and subject to rules laid down by staff who are trying their best to preserve some kind of order and care for a transient population, young people can feel trapped and uncertain about where they stand. This can be compounded by the fact that different refuges have different rules and regulations, and staff often hold markedly different views on how to work with young people.

The street is often romanticised in fiction as being a place of adventure, where 'streetsmarts' are at a premium, and where a positive experience of 'real' life takes place. The reality, of course, is far removed from the idealised portrayals of street life in books, magazines, movies and television programmes. As a youth worker (Wakim, 1986: 3) with the Service to Youth Council in Adelaide has commented: "It is surprising how still so many people deny that child prostitution, paedophiliacs, hard drugs exchanged for sexual favours, child pornography, organised car thefts, violent territoriality and other exploitative industries are still alive and well, albeit more insidiously, in inner city Adelaide." The key issue here, then, is the extent and the variety of ways in which young people are actively exploited by others on the street.

In this context, being 'streetwise' does not mean having control over one's circumstances; but rather finding ways to cope with the violence and exploitation characteristic of the darker side of street life. The entrapment process and sense of despair and isolation which are part of this process are captured in the accompanying poem, written by a "street kid whos trying to get his shit together" (see Wakim, 1987).

what is a thirteen year-old kid meant to do on the streets no
parents no money nothing. he is expected to live free and easy
bullshit. some kids watch movies and see big tough guys and
think f—— how street life must be fun because of a f——
movie, then theres others who dont get on too well with their
oldies so they leave home. then theres the runaway sees tom
sayer and thinks it must be so easy to live out there. but they
soon realise how wrong they were . . . then theres the kid who
gets kicked out of home, stone broke, hungry alone feels
deserted begins to hate and hate with a vengeance. he feels hes
got nothing to lose and most of kids dont he gets his tattoos to
be one of the boys, learns how to fight, learns how to drink gets
into drugs just to stay mates with the boys, eventually every
street kid gets into trouble with the cops; I always said no not
me never but I've had my fair share of trouble most have
families to go back to. but then theres some like me who dont
have no family alone in a strange environment that has no love
no one to run to nobody to love you. alone having to fend for
yourself. no big strong dad to protect you no mum to hold and
love you. JUST YOU ALONE. you have to fight your own battles
kill or be killed. hunt or be hunted. the streets aint no good
times as the movies make it out to be. the streets consist of
savagery, hate, violence, blood this may all sound great fun
but its not that much fun when its YOUR blood dripping into
the gutter from an iron bar across the head, or some f——
stick is tryin to screw you up the ass. you have to fight tooth
and nail to survive these are the things the movies dont show.
no street life is good times. for one good time theres one
hundred bad times. some eventually wise up and start getting
their shit together before its too late. but the stupid f——wits
who dont wake up end up dead from a bullet, needle, iron bar,
knife. these are the real streets not hollywoods streets.

jnr, SPIDER

The street, then, is not the romantic site portrayed in television
drama and adventure stories. It is not a way of life young people
want to engage in. It becomes a preferred 'choice' for 'street kids' as
a result of external factors (like abusive home situations), and due
to the fact that strong peer networks can develop among people in
similar situations. Thus, the hardships of the street may to a certain
extent be counter-balanced by the excitement and emotional
support provided by friends, and by the fact that intense bonds can
develop among young people on the street.

While 'street kids' do not form a homogenous group – being distinguished from each other in terms of use of the street and length of time spent on the street – their economic position is generally similar. In terms of social response, however, the specific form of police intervention in the activities of 'street kids' often reflects the particular social characteristics of the group or individual in question. In the Adelaide suburb of Newton a reported case of police harassment indicates how ethnicity, for example, can influence attitudes and behaviour. One of the young people involved was to comment that: "They follow us around all night from park to park. They call us garlic-breath, Italian stallions, and tell us to go home and have a shower." (*Eastern Times*, 1986). As will be seen, attributes such as gender and ethnicity affect the relations of different groups of 'street kids' to one another, as well as to state officials such as the police. The differences between 'street kids' also mean that there are differences in what they need to know in order to look after themselves on the street: the definition of 'streetwise' is different for different groups.

The following sections briefly examine two particular 'types' of 'street kid' – young women, and young Aborigines. In the first case, the main emphasis is on examining the situation of 'homeless' young women who live on the street as a way of life; in the second instance, the concern is with a social group which uses the street as a venue for spare-time activities.

FEMALE STREET KIDS

The female street kid is understandable only in terms of the position of women in a male-dominated class-divided society. There are two reasons why young women may be forced to scrounge a living on the streets: abuse and violence in the home; and the economic realities facing young women today.

The need to escape from the family home is often due to domestic violence and sexual assault, or to rebellion against restrictive gender-role expectations. In the case of sexual assault, the trauma of the actual violence perpetrated on a young woman can be compounded by the wall of silence and disbelief she encounters when she raises the issue. The psychological reaction to lack of response and support is acute and profound, as this poem (see Wakim, 1987) indicates.

She needs someone to love her
but there's no-one there to love
No-one will believe her
They think she's lying
But she's not – it really happened
They believed him cos he's a friend
But she's their daughter
They should believe her
They do but they don't want to
They don't want to think it could happen
Not to their daughter
Why didn't they see it happen
Why couldn't they stop it.

Becky, 15

At this point two options present themselves to a young woman in need. One option is to move out: to live with other relatives, or to establish her economic independence. As we shall see in a moment, the question of economic security is particularly problematic for working-class young women at the present time.

The second option available to parents and daughters is to become involved with the state welfare system. For a young woman trying to improve her welfare by this means, the problems are enormous: they range from unsatisfactory and arbitrary interpretations of situations on the part of state officials through to inadequate financial, emotional and accommodation support (see Neave, 1986). In the case of legislation and procedures affecting young people, Hancock and Chesney-Lind (1985: 249) are particularly critical. They argue that:

> Present policies and practices intended to 'protect' young females actually expose specific categories (most often the socially and economically disadvantaged) to negative social experiences, dependency and social rejection. Official intervention may place them further at risk to drug abuse, prostitution and premature motherhood.

Another difficulty facing young women, especially those who have reached school-leaving age, is that of unemployment. Young working-class women are particularly vulnerable to the narrowing of job opportunities, and to the consequences of being unemployed.

The way in which unemployment benefits are structured – with a means-tested job search allowance, and with the under-twenty 'youth dole' pegged at much lower rates than the adult rate – is the result of, and reinforces, the legal and social view that parents are responsible for the care and maintenance of their children. Furthermore, as Fopp (1982: 306) remarks, "different families have differing abilities to meet this ascribed responsibility and as such the burden is not distributed evenly and fairly among those families affected". The implications which arise from this observation are forcefully brought home in a study by Presdee (1985: 7–8) of young people in Elizabeth. Of the people surveyed, 36 per cent of the unemployed had unemployed fathers compared to 22 per cent of those in paid work; 53 per cent of all mothers were not in waged labour.

On top of the pressures on young unemployed women to find financial support in environments where such support is not possible, or at best woefully inadequate, there is also the issue of a young unemployed woman's role within the home. As we have seen in Chapter 4, her situation is often oppressed; it has been described as follows: "for unemployed young women there is not only a forced and unwelcome retreat into housework, but a retreat into the unpaid chores of the child, in many cases 'board' being paid and collected on top of the value of work in the home" (Presdee, 1982: 13). The tensions that emerge in such an atmosphere of stress and dependency see parents telling their daughters to leave home, or else the young women are subject to attitudes and practices which give them little option but to leave.

Young women tend to be more closely controlled by their parents than young men; they have to spend more time doing domestic tasks in the home; and they are expected to spend more time on their 'appearance' before leaving the home for leisure activities. These are features of how space is constructed in relation to young women in general in society (Thomas, 1980; Brake, 1985; Griffin, 1985a). Any attempt by young women to break out of this constricted structural and cultural space is met with concerted resistance. Here the position of young women in relation to the law is of vital significance. For example, parents' exercise of their authority over their children is often directed at females in ways which focus on developing specifically 'feminine' behaviour (lack of assertiveness, emotionalism, an overriding concern with appearance). Generally barred from the public domain, young women are thereby also restricted in learning how to handle themselves in the 'wider world', much less protect themselves.

These kinds of attitudes are confirmed in the ways in which state agencies intervene in the lives of young women, whether it be in the form of sex discrimination and lack of concern with women's issues in the school, or in discriminatory marriage laws. Then there is the case of the use of status offences with respect to young women. When young women are apprehended by justice officials their 'offences' are 'sexualised': young women are predominantly charged with 'status offences', that is, such things as 'ungovernability', 'being in need of care and protection', or 'running away'. The evidence consistently shows that the laws governing such offences are "used categorically to regulate the morality of females" (Hancock and Chesney-Lind, 1985; see also Alder, 1985; Naffin, 1986; Stratman, 1983). The 'morality of females' does not refer only to sexual activity, but more fundamentally to situations where young women have rebelled against authority. Moreover, many young women who are placed in the care of the state are in this situation as the direct result of parental complaints, indicating a parental bias in assessing the seriousness of male and female misconduct (Hancock and Chesney-Lind, 1985).

For female street kids, 'other options' to the parental home or state welfare agencies are difficult in their own right; and once again, they are often structured in such a way as to emphasise their sexuality above all else. The first problem for a female street kid is to find accommodation, an extremely difficult task given the large gap between the level of need and the spaces available in refuges and institutions. Since many such kids leave home in the first place to escape authority, the rules and regulations of youth refuges often do not seem to be much of an improvement. As we have seen, even kids who need shelter may object to the regimented accommodation provided for them.

Within the shelters and refuges, there are other pressures that can negatively affect young women: the sexual expectations imposed upon them by young men. For instance, McDivett (1986: 37) points out that: "Because male youth culture predominates inside as well as outside the shelters, young women often offer their bodies as a means of acceptance into the group. This makes the enjoyment and development of themselves as young women difficult." As Nava (1984) also points out, the vulnerability of young women, coupled with the lack of adequate support networks, can thus lead them to be 'policed' by young men on issues relating to 'femininity' and sexuality.

Even if a young woman was interested in joining the 'refuge hop', there may be problems depending upon her age. Because of the special offences which in some States and Territories pertain to girls under sixteen years of age, and the misconceptions relating to penalties for assisting a girl who has left home without her parents' consent, some refuges may be reluctant to offer shelter. As O'Connor (1985: 63) comments:

> The result – many girls find it difficult to find anywhere safe to live. Many refuges readily accept young boys, but when a young women arrives contact is immediately made with police, welfare, or parents. Consequently, many young women are forced to remain at home, or return home, or are forced to avoid places like refuges, which are presumably operating for their benefit.

To survive on the street, young women are likewise subjected to pressures arising from their sexuality. They must deal with sexual violence and harassment from men; but often to survive economically they have to prostitute themselves in some form or another, either by finding a man to live with who will provide them with food and shelter, or by finding work in the 'male entertainment' industry. Homeless young women are prime targets for pimps, who find them "hard workers and easy to control", and because they can be forced into prostitution through desperation, physical force or addictive drugs (Harvey, 1983). Drugs and sex in turn put female street kids at risk of disease and even death: a problem which has been exacerbated by the advent of the AIDS virus.

The combination of family relations, social welfare policy and practice, and criminal law forges a specific life option for female street kids. In every area they are confronted with varying forms of sexist practice and gender oppression. For these women, 'femininity' as constructed out of their own experiences, runs counter to middle-class notions of 'femininity'. With an emphasis on toughness, streetsmarts and anti-authoritarianism, it further complicates an already complicated situation when state law or welfare officials attempt to intervene 'for the sake of the young woman'.

YOUNG ABORIGINES

While young women who can be characterised as being 'street kids' tend not to be visible in a collective sense, because they do not generally hang around in large groups, the same cannot be said for young Aboriginal people. Here we can examine the situation in

Adelaide as a focus for discussion. Every weekend night and often during the week as well, stretches of Hindley Street constitute the gathering place for these 'street kids'. For these young people Hindley Street is a main source of attraction as a meeting place and as somewhere where 'things happen'. Many of them have histories of truancy, family breakdowns, homelessness and substance-abuse.

The use of the street by Aboriginal young people is once again partly because young people have no space of their own. It is notable that during 1983–84 there were a number of facilities open to young Aboriginal people, and consequently fewer frequented Hindley Street. However, towards the end of 1984, "things began to change again as the Otherway Centre suspended its youth pro-gramme, the Youth Worker attached to the Community Centre focused his work more in the suburbs and most significantly, the Woodville Blue Light Disco, the most popular and accessible, was closed down" (Hindley Street Youth Project, 1986: 11). Since that time every Friday and Saturday night has seen one hundred or more young Aborigines venture out to Hindley Street.

Aboriginal young people's use of the street differs significantly from that of other young people in the inner city. The reason for this can be traced to the position of young *black* people in Australian society. From the first days of the British white invasion Aboriginal people have suffered greatly at the hands of non-Aboriginal society. Without going into the details of the oppression of Aborigines, it is apparent that the depressed social and political conditions of Aboriginal people have been sustained by a racist ideology which affects all aspects of their existence. It is not surprising then that the specific character of Aboriginal youth subcultures is premised upon a fundamentally distinct cultural heritage and identity.

The cohesiveness of young Aborigines on Hindley Street has been fostered by a number of factors. For one thing, their physical appearance, and economic situations, immediately mark them off as a separate group of young people. Victimisation and racist treatment by the general public, Hindley Street businesspeople, and the police have consolidated a shared sense of identity, forged in the need for mutual protection from outside threats. Furthermore, the fact that Hindley Street has, through circumstances relating to the unavailability of other venues, become the key location for 'leisure' activities has served to unify diverse elements within the Aboriginal community. Hence, "They are a very cohesive group, no longer small groups based on place of origin but nowadays 'the Nunga mob' conscious of their cultural identity and the strength of numbers." (Hindley Street Youth Project, 1986: 11). 'Aboriginality' is further consolidated by shared experiences of non-Aboriginal authority, similar backgrounds and familiarity with Aboriginal family structures and culture, and the development and use of a 'lingo' which is specific to the Aboriginal community.

Having 'nothing to do' because of the lack of other facilities and resources, the young Aborigines could well appear to be 'doing nothing' to the observer on Hindley Street. In fact, as Corrigan (1979) discusses fully elsewhere, 'doing nothing' represents a chance for young people to get together and talk things over on their own. But it is also much more than this. Hindley Street is the place for a whole range of activities – from simply talking with other young people to providing a stage for a variety of collective and individual activities, including drinking alcohol and taking other drugs.

The public nature of Hindley Street, however, carries with it certain features that influence the young people's behaviour and actions. For example, the sheer number of Aboriginal young people at any one time shapes the character of their interaction with people outside of their immediate group. On a Friday or Saturday night, for instance, the large number of young Aborigines can mean that sections of the footpath are virtually closed off to passers-by. For those people who wish to cross the path of the Aborigines, the response may vary from no reaction at all, to requests for spare change, through to threatened or actual violence.

With respect to this latter point, it should be pointed out that a random lashing out at non-Aborigines is the result of a complex set of factors relating to the socio-economic position of Aboriginal people. Rarely does this kind of activity express much more than despair and alienation. The only sign of political consciousness on Hindley Street is to be found in cultural symbols, such as the wearing of a land rights T-shirt, rather than in purposeful political action. We might also add that if a confrontation occurs between the Aborigines and another identifiable group on the street (such as the 'trendies', some of whom are linked to an Italian-Australian group that frequents Hindley Street), the result may be a highly charged atmosphere in which any passer-by could become a target for verbal or physical abuse. At this time, although not only at this time, the police often intervene.

There is little goodwill between Aboriginal young people and the police. From the Aboriginal point of view the police have partici-pated in many abuses of their people. For instance, Aborigines are the most imprisoned indigenous people in the 'free world', with rates far exceeding that of the non-Aboriginal population in Australia. In South Australia, Aborigines are twenty-eight times more likely to be sent to gaol than non-Aborigines. Although they make up only 1 per cent of the population of the State, they make up 15 per cent of prisoners in the gaols (*Adelaide Advertiser*, 21 November 1987).

Not only are Aboriginal people as a whole over-represented in the prison system but, as a national tour of the Committee to Defend Black Rights highlighted, they are subject to dramatically different treatment by 'justice' authorities (Spring, 1986). This committee toured the country to publicise the deaths of five young Aboriginal men who had died in police or prison custody. The people who died were from different parts of Australia, and each had died in suspicious circumstances. In each case their relatives indicated that they felt that investigations into the killings were highly unsatisfactory and bore the mark of a cover-up by the authorities. The actions of the committee led to the establishment of a Royal Commission on Aboriginal Deaths in Custody in 1987, while the extensive publicity surrounding the issue led to revelations that as many as ninety, and perhaps many more, Aborigines died in custody between 1980 and 1987 (Wilson and Scandia, 1987).

On top of the negative feelings engendered by these kinds of charges, and the actions of individual police officers which appear to be supported by the 'system', the official police organisations themselves often add fuel to the rage of Aboriginal people. At its October 1986 meeting in Adelaide, for example, the Police Federation of Australia publicly called for Aboriginal legal services to be scrapped, ostensibly because they are 'discriminatory against non-Aborigines'. In response, the acting director of the Aboriginal Legal Rights Movement remarked that: "The fact that the police are so worried about the service proves it is effective." (*Adelaide Advertiser*, 7 October 1986). The black deaths in custody, coupled with a generally aggressive stance taken by police unions toward Aboriginal people, provides the context of a broader struggle in which young Aboriginal people are an important part.

On the street, the wider issues facing Aboriginal people manifest themselves in the form of a deep hatred of the police. The 'rightness' of this hatred is confirmed through experience, and more generally by the problems experienced by other 'street kids' in their contact with the police. Contact between police and youth can include: police intervening unnecessarily; police responding to provocation

in a punitive fashion that is often extreme; police failing to discriminate between minor and major offences; police hassling young
people who are 'known' to them; and police assaulting young people
during on-street questioning (Ashley, 1983: 7). The general and
growing antipathy between police and young people in a variety of
situations is shown in Table 5.1. This information was gathered as
part of a survey undertaken for *Streetwize Comics*, a series of publications that provide practical information about health and legal
matters to young people in crisis with the health, legal and welfare
system (see Mohr, 1986ab). The table shows the issues that young
readers of the comic in different settings regarded as relevant or
important.

In the particular case of young Aborigines, workers with the
Aboriginal Legal Rights Movement in Adelaide point to a range of
factors which specifically affect relations between police and Abo-

Table 5.1:   Issues seen as important by young people in various
situations

| | *Situation* | |
Youth centres	*Supported accommodation*	*Schools*
Police violence	Police violence	Police violence
Anti-racism	Anti-racism	Anti-racism
Don't blab to police	Don't blab to police	Car stealing
AIDS	AIDS	
Running away from home	Running away from home	
Girls' rights	Girls' rights	
Girls' health	Girls' health	
Contraception		
Legal ages		

Source: Mohr, 1986b: 22.

rigines. Some of these are: lack of respect for Aboriginal culture and way of life; lack of prior contact with Aborigines; and arbitrary treatment of Aborigines on the basis of ethnic characteristics. Widespread stereotyping often means that young Aborigines on the street have to 'justify' themselves continually – being constantly queried over what they are doing, where they are going, and so on. The systematic violation of the rights of young Aborigines was further confirmed in a recent British report. Published by the Anti-Slavery Society (Burger, 1988), the report cites instances where police in Melbourne took children to houses for beatings rather than taking them to the police station. In another example, a youth worker in Alice Springs commented that he found that up to 85 per cent of the children he had seen through the courts had been bashed by the police.

In the end, a vicious circle can develop whereby any type of police intervention is interpreted as harassment, leading to 'inappropriate' behaviour on the part of Aboriginal young people. This then leads to further punitive action being taken by the police, resulting in an even worse situation. Over a long period of time this circle will ultimately lead to great strife for the participants, and especially for Aboriginal young people, who wield little social power in comparison with the forces of 'law and order'.

The media exacerbates the tensions. In November 1986 it was reported in an Adelaide newspaper (*Sunday Mail*) that one hundred youths, mainly Aboriginal, were involved in a 'brawl' with police outside the Adelaide casino. In a letter to the *Adelaide Advertiser*, Susan Buckskin of the Northern Region Aboriginal Community refuted this charge, pointing out that only six young people were involved in the disturbance. She went on to describe relations between Aborigines and police:

> We feel the Adelaide City Council and the Police Department are consciously making life very unpleasant for the Aborigines who frequent Hindley Street and the area near the casino because of pressure brought to bear by the retailers and casino management in regard to the influence on their business. This disregards the rights of any group to use the facilities of the city centre and highlights the discriminatory practices of a few influential whites in the community.

With increased attention to Adelaide city centre at times such as the biennial Festival of Arts and yearly Grand Prix, the police presence and negative focus on young Aborigines heightens (Hindley

Street Youth Project, 1987). In response to many situations seen as involving harassment by police officers and State Transit Authority railway staff, an Aboriginal 'watch committee' was formed in 1986. Initiated by concerned parents, and members of the South Australian Campaign Against Racial Exploitation, the Streetmeet Committee maintains a regular street presence as an independent monitor of activities in the young Aborigines' patch of inner-city territory.

REGULATING THE STREET: THE DRUG OFFENSIVE

According to official statistics, young people in this country are over-represented in arrests for burglary and motor-vehicle theft. Analysis reveals that "a large majority of offences for which juveniles are arrested are trivial in nature", and that arrests for violent offences such as homicide or serious assault are far less than their proportion in the population (Mukherjee, 1986: 7, 8). If we recast our terminology from that of 'criminal justice' to that of the 'street', we find that many of the crimes committed by young people are crimes of boredom (vandalism, car theft); crimes of survival (shoplifting, burglary); crimes of depression and oppression (alcohol and drug use, violence); and crimes of sexuality (status offences). But the biggest 'crime' committed by young people today is that of *visibility*.

The law positions young people in society in such a way that the question of 'space' is of major concern to them. However, the different situations that young people find themselves in, usually through no choice of their own, mean that the overall lack of material and cultural space for young people will affect different groups of young people in markedly different ways. The different uses of what space is available in turn have implications for the construction of specific social identities for and by young people. It is ironic that the coercive arm of the state bears down most heavily on those who are least able to develop their own room to move.

The contradictions arising from the position of young people in society are currently being exacerbated by wider structural transformations in the economic sphere. With one-quarter of young people under the age of twenty-four unable to find full-time paid work, the 'street' has taken on an even greater significance as a place to gather, to spend one's free time, to 'do nothing'. This is why young people are becoming more 'visible' and are increasingly spoken of as a 'problem'. As a consequence of this, attention is now being directed to further regulation of the 'free' space that young people currently occupy. Attempts to regulate the behaviour and space of young people take a number of forms. For example, security guards patrol the shopping centres, evicting 'undesirables' and keeping a watchful eye on the non-buying patrons (Presdee, 1985).

One of the most prominent campaigns that has been aimed at young people in recent years is the Drug Offensive. That young people were the targets of the 'offensive' and bore a disproportionate burden of criminal proceedings, is indicated in 1985 police statistics for Victoria. The statistics show that young people under the age of twenty-five constitute 57.15 per cent of all those proceeded against, that young people possessing cannabis constitute 34.9 per cent of all drug offences, that young people make up 66.34 per cent of all cannabis possession offences, and that young people prosecuted either for use or possession constitute 39.35 per cent of all people prosecuted for drug offences (cited in Woodger, 1987: 98–9). The intention of the Drug Offensive is to publicise the problems associated with drug abuse, and especially with the use of illegal substances such as marijuana.

Most assuredly there are major problems in Australian society relating to addiction, and to the use and abuse of various substances. And it would appear that a sizeable proportion of young people are being drawn into drug use of some kind or another, especially with respect to alcohol, analgesics and cannabis (Commonwealth Department of Health, 1986; Eckersley, 1988). However, campaigns such as the Drug Offensive are designed in such a way that they add even more pressure to the lives of many young people without adequately dealing with the sources of the problem. Differences between drug use and abuse, and between legal and illegal substances, as well as sociological differences in patterns of use – these are issues which need to be thoroughly examined if we are to gauge the impact and orientation of campaigns like the Drug Offensive. While these concerns are beyond the scope of the present discussion, we can point to several problems in existing campaigns.

The issue of drugs is often promoted in a very specific manner which does not locate it within a larger social and economic context. More particularly, the causes and patterns of drug use are often not seriously addressed, although token recognition is sometimes provided. Such campaigns are ostensibly directed to the population as a whole, and specifically 'every young person in Australia', and as such ignore the nature of drug use among specific sectors of the youth population. Given the relationship between extensive drug use and factors such as alienation, unemployment, homelessness, and loneliness, it is obvious that much drug use and abuse stems from wider material conditions and is not simply due to a lack of information or the conspiratorial actions of drug sellers.

Drug use and abuse have certain pre-conditions; until these pre-conditions are changed the Drug Offensive will not be effective. It will, however, strike those young people who are 'down and out' and dependent upon drugs as just another attempt on the part of the 'authorities' to clamp down on them. Barred from participating in society, these young people will resent a campaign which attempts to exercise even greater control over their lives, with nothing offered in return.

Indeed, it has been suggested that the most important function of the Drug Offensive is to reinforce social authority and consensus, and not in fact to tackle the drug problem in itself. Ramsay (1986: 265), for example, points out that:

> Illegal drug users are frequently young and disillusioned and are often prepared to criticise and challenge authority. Thus they have traditionally been associated with 'problem' groups in society such as students, 'lefties', punks and gangs. This makes them a subculture of concern for the state, for while the thinking of illegal drug users is not usually revolutionary in content, the state cannot but attempt to restrain and control such non-conformism.

As a 'solution' to this challenge to authority, the Drug Offensive is currently providing an ideological justification for the extension of police powers and state surveillance capabilities.

This is being done by promoting the drug issue as a major threat to Australia, and by emphasising the notion that the state is there to protect us from it (Ramsay, 1986: 267). That the Drug Offensive is aimed at social control is apparent when we examine the breakdown of combined State and federal government spending on the campaign shown in Table 5.2. The priority given to law enforcement and public relations over treatment, rehabilitation and research places the greatest emphasis on control and directed social intervention. This control operates in two ways: by coercion, through the increased ability of the state to monitor all kinds of behaviour due to new extensive discretionary powers; and by constructing 'ideal' types of behaviour in the 'community', through appeals for the active involvement of citizens in local surveillance and vigilance work.

A central aspect of this latter form of control is the manner in which norms of behaviour and proper conduct have been drawn up for young people and adults alike. In this way an attempt is being made to construct appropriate 'community norms', supported at the level of the family, neighbourhood and state, which bolster the legitimacy of the state and the social system in general (see Ramsay, 1986: 268–9). Put differently, the over-riding concern of the Drug Offensive appears to be with the 'abuse' of law and authority, rather than with the abuse of drugs.

The fear and general moral panic generated by the Drug Offensive, in conjunction with concerns over theft intrinsic to the Neighbourhood Watch scheme, work to sustain a privatised notion of crime and crime control. The focus is on self-policing which starts at home in the form of greater regulation of family behaviour. Publicity thus is often aimed at parents and their duties to police the actions of their offspring.

An example of such publicity appeared in mid-1987, when the largest non-government welfare agency in Adelaide, the Central Mission, ran a series of newspaper advertisements against drugs. The captions accompanying photographs of young people in a variety of drug-taking poses included: "Will your daughter be introduced to more than just new friends tonight?", "Where will your son be mixing tonight?", and "Who'll be picking up your

Table 5.2: Expenditure on the Drug Offensive, 1986

Category	Expenditure ($ million)
Law enforcement (extra funding)	58.8
Public relations, media and advertising	44.1
Treatment and rehabilitation	6.0
Drug research	0.6

Source: Ramsay, 1986: 264.

daughter after you've dropped her off tonight?" (*Adelaide Advertiser*, May 1987). The reader was told that parents should "care enough" to "know what our children are doing and who they are meeting". The main thread throughout the advertising campaign was to define 'good parenting': it requires parents to say 'no' to what young people want to do, to intervene actively in their affairs, and to determine their choice of friends and 'safe' behaviour. In essence, the resources of the state and expert agencies are being used in efforts to regulate young people by regulating the family. Perceived 'deviant' activity of any kind is abstracted from concrete social and economic circumstances and is instead attributed to the failure of the family (see McIntosh, 1984). This process also implicitly transfers some of the financial costs of policing young people into the private sphere.

Even within its explicit terms of reference, however, there are other problems with the Drug Offensive. The language of the Drug Offensive itself indicates that it is to be a war against drug users and sellers. The stress here is on combating drugs, on taking coercive measures to deal with the problem. This kind of approach is complemented by related campaigns such as Operation Noah which is based upon the idea of 'dobbing in a dope pusher'. The 1987 Operation Noah was spearheaded by popular cricket player Greg Matthews who, in a series of television advertisements, urged anyone who suspected another of supplying and pushing drugs to pass along the information to police during the national 24-hour phone-in. Again, this kind of punitive approach misconstrues the issues involved, in part by emphasising law-breaking behaviour relating to drugs as being the main problem, rather than the social factors which underlie drug use and abuse.

For young people, the most problematic aspect of the campaigns against drugs has been that, in practice, such campaigns have been carried out in a way that effectively cuts off the little space in society that they have of their own. Parents are exhorted to watch their children carefully and to ensure that they act in the 'proper' way. Police officers have increased powers to engage in surveillance and to intervene in the affairs of young people. And pressures are growing for even more control over the activities of young people – in the malls, in the parks, and on the beaches.

In Adelaide, for example, the issue of public alcohol consumption rose to the fore in the latter part of 1986 and into 1987. Initially media stories concentrated on attempts to stop public, and especially underage, drinking in Rundle Mall. Since then the focus has

City Council made a decision to investigate the banning of alcohol in Victoria Square and Whitmore Square in the inner city. Such banning measures most affect Aborigines and homeless people and certainly have implications for any young people who make use of these parks.

'Teenage drunks' are now seen as a major problem facing the agencies and officials identified with the Drug Offensive. The response has taken several forms. One has been to increase the penalties for supplying liquor to minors. In South Australia, for instance, new legislation raises the fine for supplying underage drinkers from $5000 to $10 000 for licensees, and from $1000 to $2000 for bar staff. In early 1987 the Bannon Government banned the sale of Lindeman's 250-millilitre Tropicana wine-cooler packs on the basis that they contravened the State's Beverage Container Act. The impetus behind this move was the widespread concern that because of their packaging (and, one might add, sweet taste), wine-coolers too closely resembled fruit juice, and this would lead to greater alcoholic consumption by young people.

What young people can do in their spare time and the places available to do it in have been subject to attempts by the state at outright control. Significantly, an anti-drinking campaign in New South Wales was called "Stay In Control" and featured a series of advertisements that attempted to convey the message that getting drunk is a 'bad thing'. A feature article in the *Adelaide Advertiser* (3 February 1987) portrayed the 'stay in control' message in the following way:

> For boys, who are more susceptible to peer pressure, the warning is, 'If you don't want to look like a jerk, don't get drunk.' A photograph shows a youth on his knees, throwing up in a squalid, graffiti-covered lavatory.
>
> The message adds, 'Believe it or not, most guys don't like to see their mates get drunk and make fools of themselves. And most girls actually get turned off by guys who get drunk.'
>
> The message for girls is more subtle but no less effective.
>
> A picture shows a semi-clad girl dejectedly sitting on the floor beside a crumpled bed. Her clothes are strewn around her. The warning is, 'You can lose more than your memory when you get drunk.'

There are a whole range of messages being conveyed here, generally directed at telling young people to manage their affairs better if they want to make positive impressions of themselves on their peers. Noting the concerns raised by Ramsay and outlined earlier in this section, we can see a concerted attempt to forge permissible conduct for 'good' boys and 'good' girls. Boys are defined in terms of mateship and (hetero) sexual appeal; girls in terms of protection of their virginity – if they are raped, they have only themselves to blame. A strong link is made, then, between drinking as a problem and other forms of acceptable or unacceptable social conduct. In this view, young people should conform to a particular set of norms, norms that in essence reaffirm traditional sex roles and which blame victims for their predicament. Instead of distinguishing between the individual as a total human being capable of engaging in a wide and contradictory spectrum of attitudes and behaviour, and the fact that certain types of drug use are 'bad', an equation is drawn up which sees drug use as equivalent to the individual being a 'bad person' in every sort of way.

Along with an ideological push to induce people to conform to certain behavioural norms, there have also been greater efforts to crack down on underage offenders. In South Australia this has taken the form of legislation banning minors from attending places such as nightclubs and discos that have entertainment venue licences after 9 p.m. and from hotels with late-night permits after midnight. In New South Wales one tactic has been to mount "a blitz on known juvenile drinking lairs" and to use extra police at the weekend to weed out the underage offenders from Sydney night-spots (*Adelaide Advertiser*, 3 February 1987).

But it is not just the bars, hotels and clubs, and parks which are coming under increasing surveillance. The beaches are a target as well. "Operation Clean Sweep" is a scheme devised to "crack down" on "louts, litterbugs and bad language" on Adelaide's beaches (*Adelaide Advertiser*, 14 February 1987). Based at Henley Beach, police 'jeans teams' – officers dressed in jeans and T-shirts – spend their time patrolling the beaches. As they mingle with the crowds, their job is to be on the lookout for behavioural offences, particularly those relating to sexual behaviour and underage drinking.

The real prevention of drug use and abuse has in the end been relegated to secondary importance. This applies to information campaigns as well, insofar as knowledge about the dangers of substance abuse has not proven to be a deterrent in the case of 'disadvantaged' categories of young people (one need only think of the phenomenon of petrol-sniffing among Aboriginal young people: even some much-publicised deaths have not stopped it). The only way to prevent widespread and chronic drug abuse by those sectors of the youth population which have been hardest hit by the depression and which are often further subjected to systematic racist and sexist attacks is to transform the conditions of their existence.

RULES OF THE GAME

Young people will not and cannot remove themselves from the public realm, nor will they stay silent. Thus, the interplay between generation-based contradictions and situation-based contradictions – stemming from the legal position of young people and their diverse social backgrounds – will engender a circle of conflict involving the state and specific categories of young people, and indeed young people in general. For each attempt to find a space or to create new space is being matched by counterposing attempts to regulate this space, and thereby to regulate young people. This can only lead to greater social unrest, further tensions between young people and 'authority', and ever more forceful rejections of new 'rules and regulations'.

This dilemma cannot be resolved without radically changing the 'rules of the game'. The differential positioning of individual young people in society means that there will be a 'natural' propensity for some young people to engage in illegal behaviour or activity which is personally destructive in nature. This kind of development cannot be overcome unless the 'differential' is removed. This requires a substantially different view of the nature of the problem. As Pearson (1983: 238–9) indicates in his work, the question of order and consensus requires extending our vision, not narrowing its focus. Hence, "If mass unemployment should threaten consent, for example, then what is fundamentally important is not whether unemployment causes crime and riots, but that mass unemployment is an evil in itself."

Similarly, if the issue of 'space' is central to the experience of being young, and is the key area of concern in the daily playing out of contradictions, then the answer does not lie in imposing even further restrictions on the rights of young people and in introducing even more regulations covering all aspects of their lives.

CHAPTER 6

Youth services and the role of 'soft cops'

The crackdown on the activities of young people takes many forms – from direct police intervention through to publicity campaigns attempting to change or regulate their behaviour. At the grassroots level, one of the important points of social contact on a daily basis for many young people lies with youth workers. The question which this chapter addresses is that of where youth workers fit into the overall scheme of social control. It is argued that through various institutional and ideological means youth workers are being called upon to play the role of 'soft cop' in regulating the affairs of young people.

The phrase 'soft cop' refers to instances where youth workers, perhaps in spite of their intentions and wishes, either willingly engage or are forced to engage in activities which prop up the system of youth regulation. They are obliged to play a social control role, characterised by the fostering of certain ideas and practices: these obscure the structural nature of oppression and inequality; they diffuse potential political struggles against the powerful; and they mediate various forms of youth rebellion.

In presenting this general argument, prevailing beliefs in such things as goodwill, piecemeal reform and individualism are critically evaluated. In addition to a discussion of the philosophical base of much youth work, the concern is to analyse contemporary structures and practices of youth work in relation to government concerns with expenditure and programme rationalisations, and with respect to the dominant ideology of skills formation as this pertains to young people.

In an examination of this nature, sweeping generalisations are hard to avoid. 'Youth work' itself is a notoriously difficult term to define, and at a national level each State and Territory in Australia has seen different developments, with significantly different styles, approaches and institutions adopted in each case. Nevertheless, by providing a general review of youth affairs, this chapter shows that, on the whole, forms of youth work which are not linked to broader processes of social regulation are rare. In order to show some of the reasons why this is the case, the chapter looks at the history of youth work; reviews current government policies in this field; explores different perspectives on youth work; and discusses the impact of different organisational structures on the practices of youth workers.

THE ORIGINS AND EMERGENCE OF YOUTH WORK

The history of 'youth work' is in essence the history of attempts to control working-class young people through organised interventions into their lives and communities.

The latter part of the nineteenth century saw many changes in the economic and social structures of advanced capitalist nations and their colonies. Greater urbanisation, new divisions of labour centred on the developing manufacturing industries, and the concentration of capital into fewer hands, were in turn accompanied by greater social unrest, increasing class conflict and militant struggles for emancipation by particular social groups. In the midst of the turmoils engendered by the transition to a new form of production, a number of significant political and social reforms took place. While the state became an increasingly prominent force in social life, male members of the working class agitated and finally won the right to vote and take an active part in the electoral process. The worst aspects of the industrial revolution – unhealthy working conditions, low pay, poor living conditions, etc. – were the issues over which unions of workers engaged in concerted struggle at both an industrial and a political level, as witnessed by the great strikes of the 1890s in Australia and the formation of the Australian Labor Party at the turn of the century.

Working-class mobilisations and middle-class fears of rebellion and revolution led to important changes in the lives of young people. Labour laws were enacted and Education Acts passed as a means of grappling with a number of interconnected issues. While the exploitation of young people was now subject to increasing regulation, the barring of young people from the economic sphere, coupled with new skill and management demands emerging in the workplace, raised new problems. The response was to set up alternative agencies of socialisation and control, in the form of reformatories and public schools. The transition to adulthood was thus fundamentally altered, with a new stage being constructed between young children and adult workers. Over time this new period in the life cycle came to be treated as 'natural', the concept of 'adolescence' designating age-based categories of people with relatively little power of an economic, social or political kind.

Two sorts of problems arose out of the new social institutions and social relations which developed during the latter part of the 1800s. The first was the question of what young working-class people were doing in their out-of-school time; the second, what young wage-earners were doing with their wages prior to settling down into traditional patterns of marriage and family life. A third factor was the increasing number of children and young people who were obliged to eke out an existence on the streets due to disruptions in the home and their exclusion (on the basis of age and skill level) from paid work. Public venues and street corners became a meeting place for many working-class young people (especially young men), as well as a location for generating survival or additional 'income' through a variety of illegal activities. Furthermore, the negative attitudes of their elders to the ruling order, combined with the growth of working-class organisations and societies based on anti-capitalist ideas and social theories, remained important counter-weights to the new mass institutions such as schools which were intended to support bourgeois notions of order and hierarchy.

It was in this social context that 'traditional' youth organisations emerged. Church and middle-class groups saw the younger members of the working class as exhibiting a range of anti-social qualities – from lack of discipline, morality and adherence to the codes of the prevailing religious order on the one hand through to being disruptive, unruly and politically irresponsible on the other. The objectives of these organisations were to instil a sense of discipline, obedience, and patriotism in their charges. These themes also underlay the activities of those organisations which were more directly concerned with the immediate needs of the poor and the dispossessed for food and housing. Hence, both the recreational model and the welfare model of youth work were bounded by concerns to provide paternalistic guidance to the 'less privileged' in society.

It is important to recognise that, while the organisations which aimed to provide 'leisure and recreation' had their origins in concern about the social situation of young people of the working class, their programmes were often 'sold' as if they applied equally to all young people. Indeed, a key concern of some youth organisations was to counter the perceived threat of socialist ideas and sense of class consciousness among sections of the youth population. Thus, Lord Baden Powell, founder of the Boy Scouts, wrote in his 1908 handbook:

> If a strong enemy wants our rich commerce and Dominions, and sees us in Britain divided against each other, he will pounce in and capture them. For this you begin, as boys, not to think of other classes of boys to be your enemies. Remember, whether rich or poor, from castle or from slum, you are all Britons in the first place, and you've got to keep Britain up against outside enemies. [Quoted in Murdock and McCron, 1976: 193.]

The construction of 'unity' among boys and girls from different classes was to be built upon activities such as recreation, camping, militaristic types of training, and moral education (see Bessant, 1987). The values of nineteenth-century youth organisations in Australia were centred on the development of 'character' and involved instilling a Christian commitment, the work ethic, clean living, and a patriotic commitment to the established political system. A clear line was drawn between the sexes in terms of the form of youth work needed: "For boys, the issue was to reform their behaviour; for girls, the issue was to reform their morality." (Maunders, 1987: 37).

The role of these voluntary organisations in offering 'charity', 'moral guidance' and 'character-building' leisure pursuits to young people 'in need' has shaped approaches to youth work up to the present day. Describing the activities of youth organisations in the nineteenth and early twentieth century, Ewen (1983: 8) comments that their legacy has proved inappropriate in a variety of ways. Fundamentally, he argues that they set the terms for youth work as that work which revolves around recreation and welfare concerns: "It is about keeping kids off the street, or it is about socially controlling them – preferably both." This view is substantively

borne out in Maunders' (1984) history of voluntary youth organisations in Australia, a work which illustrates how youth organisations
have generally played a role which complements state activities in
the areas of policing, welfare and schooling.

In the main, youth work has been directed at young working-
class people and has been oriented toward dealing with behaviour
associated with 'larrikinism' and 'delinquency'. It has also been
concerned with ameliorating the conditions within which young
people 'find themselves', such as poverty and 'disadvantage'. Seen
as a form of welfare, and as a form of preventive social control, the
main object of youth work, historically, has been to assist young
persons 'at risk'. It has often been seen and presented in overtly
benign political terms, by the practitioners themselves and by
government sponsors.

Some of the main characteristics of 'voluntary' youth work as it
has developed over the last century and a half include: a primary
focus on boys, rather than girls; middle-class volunteers and staff,
a worker exclusivity which often extends to particular ethnic and
migrant categories as well; and a 'child-saving' orientation in
working with young people. While in recent times the state has
played a greater role in the area of youth work, particularly since
the economic decline and rising unemployment of the early 1970s,
there is still considerable participation in the field by private, often
voluntary, agencies. As we shall see, this participation will probably
increase rather than decrease in the coming years, although the
terms under which non-government agencies operate are increasingly dictated by government policy initiatives.

The transition from school to work in the lives of young people
constitutes a major stage in the shaping of their future. The
breakdown in this transition due to a changed economy and high
youth unemployment has caused new types of problems to emerge.
This in turn has led to a more prominent role for youth workers, a
role which will be considered in greater depth shortly. For now, the
views of Nava (1984: 6) regarding the overall direction of youth
work are worth considering. She argues that: "Since its inception
during the latter part of the nineteenth century and the early
twentieth century, youth work has continued to aim at exercising
some form of supervision over the leisure time of poor and working-
class youth, particularly in urban areas, and at coping with opposi-
tional culture and potential delinquency." If this is indeed the case,
it becomes important to draw attention to the central role played by

the state, both historically and in the contemporary period, in shaping the context within which this kind of youth work occurs.

STATE INTERVENTION AND YOUTH WORK

The development of something which could be said to constitute a 'youth policy' is relatively new in the Australian context. The lack of such a policy until recently should not, however, blind us to the fact that the state has long intervened in the lives of young people. Indeed, it was state action taken last century in the form of education and labour legislation which fundamentally reshaped the construction of the life cycle – with adolescence making its debut as a 'new' period in one's life.

The rationale for state intervention in the lives of young people has long been part of the concern to regulate the behaviour of members of the working class. The Hawke Government's Priority One package has likewise, in practice, represented concerns with similar issues. Indeed, the approach to youth policy of governments of either political party has been directed at the perceived 'youth problem', rather than at redressing the deep imbalances and injustices in Australian society which affect so many young people.

Government is concerned with cutting costs and with keeping the lid on possible social dissent or unrest; where do youth workers fit into this picture? Perhaps one way to approach this, at least initially, is to consider what occurred during the last period of great economic crisis – the Depression of the 1930s. As in the 1980s, the governments of the 1930s looked to the schools to keep young people off the streets, and to special training schemes as a means to entice employers to hire young people as part of the 'sacrifice' required for the 'national interest' (Holbrook and Bessant, 1986).

The 1930s and the 1980s also share some similarity in government concern over possible dissent from within regarding the direction of government policy. In particular, educational workers and especially principals were subjected in the 1930s to checks on their attitudes regarding the link between the capitalist system and unemployment, a phenomenon which has its modern counterpart in the restrictions being placed upon principals who publicly object to government plans to cut educational programmes and funding (Smithson, 1987).

The two periods of economic crisis are also interesting to compare in terms of the role of non-government organisations. For example, in Victoria during the 1930s the Charity Organisation Society was given the responsibility by the Government of determining eligibility for and the extent of relief to be given. Translated into practice, this meant that the unemployed had to work for the meagre relief that they received (Maunders, 1984). In the 1980s, there is similarly a push to 'privatise' government functions by transferring them to non-government welfare organisations which, it is assumed, can do the job better and cheaper than the government can (see Graycar, 1983; Baldock, 1983).

In the 1930s the young unemployed who were not in education or training were kept off the street by agencies such as the YMCA; in the 1980s this role has fallen to a range of agencies, both government and non-government. The most important instance of state intervention in youth affairs was the establishment of the Community Youth Support Scheme (CYSS) in 1976. CYSS projects were supposed to provide activities based on employment, community service, and hobbies and interests. From the start they were designed as a means of social control over unemployed young people.

In his discussion of CYSS, Maunders (1984: 104) acknowledges that some CYSS workers have tried to act as advocates for young people. He nevertheless goes on to comment that:

> in general CYSS has remained a particularist organisation, working with individual unemployed people, rather than having an effect on the system which produces unemployment or being able to serve youth as a section of society. It has kept unemployed youth or a section of them, off the streets.

It may be the case that CYSS projects were able to offer opportunities for free leisure and training pursuits to young people, many of whom appreciated this service. But the existence of CYSS was premised upon the lack of choices available to young people, a situation where they are precluded from commercial leisure pursuits and paid employment and so are forced on to the streets in the first place. Thus CYSS is one of a range of measures designed to reduce the visibility of young people, and thus the visibility of wider social and economic problems.

A brief glance at some of the developments in the 1930s and the 1980s shows the common approaches adopted in each era, the futility of such approaches in combating the effects of the crisis, and (what is important for our purposes) the role of youth workers in ensuring public order through intervention in the lives of young people.

Since the 1930s much has changed, but big questions still remain as to where youth work is heading and the role which governments are trying to mould for youth workers. It is useful at this stage to consider some of the characteristics of contemporary youth work agencies.

If we look at South Australia, for example, we find that youth work is carried out by a range of agencies. Some of the government agencies include: SkillShare (Commonwealth); Department for Community Welfare, neighbourhood youth workers (State); municipal councils (local); Youth Initiatives Unit (State); Second Storey (State); Supported Accommodation Assistance Programme (Commonwealth). Many of these agencies involve an interlinking of federal, State and local government in finances and administration. For instance, there are cases where all levels of government contribute financially, other instances where the federal government provides the funding and the State or local government provides the administration and personnel.

There are also a number of non-government agencies. Some of these include: Service to Youth Council (SYC); Hindley Street Youth Project; YMCA; YWCA; Salvation Army; Scouts; Guides; Central Mission; other church-based groups; Service Clubs Involvement with Youth (SCIY). Many of these agencies rely upon government grants, as well as depending on volunteer workers and public donations.

Paid workers and volunteers within these various government and non-government agencies perform a wide range of tasks and engage in many different kinds of activity. These include: streetwork; accommodation; welfare support; recreation and leisure; employment projects and training; health services; and spiritual guidance. The main 'clients' for youth work are working-class, with specific population groups receiving particular attention in some cases – e.g., women, Aborigines, gay men and women, people with disabilities, migrant young people.

In terms of government funding policy, two trends of special note will influence the direction of youth work in the years ahead. The first is the shift of government functions to non-government bodies and agencies. In Victoria, for example, new conditions attached to government funding grants in effect act as 'service contracts' which must be adhered to by non-government community organisations. Richards (1987: 46) cites the example of the Victorian Youth

Advocacy Network (YAN) as an instance where government funding was conditional on the YAN accepting certain restrictions on its
work. Not only did Richards see this as a threat to independent
community organisations such as the YAN, but also as part of a
process whereby 'service provision' is in essence privatised. Thus,
he comments that

> The bald conclusion is clear: through independent community
> organisations the government is attempting to set up a defacto
> public service – a decentralised system which does not provide
> its workers with the protection offered by membership to the
> public service unions but at the same time will be responsible
> for effecting government policy.

The second trend is related to the first and has to do with the
areas of expenditure which the government is increasing and the
ways in which this is being carried out. Many youth projects are in
danger of closing down due to lack of adequate secure funding. It
must be acknowledged that new jobs are being created in youth
affairs, but these jobs are tied into specific government objectives
which may work against the social and economic interests of young
people as a whole.

For example, in a way reminiscent of the previous discussion
of state funding of non-government organisations, strings were attached to 1987–88 government grants to local governments in the
Adelaide area. The deal in this case was that either the councils
agreed to accept a substantial grant designed to get the Community
Volunteer Programme (CVP) on the road, or they would lose
additional funding for other youth projects. The problem was
twofold: first, any funding received would be tied into other funding
programmes, thereby reducing the autonomy of local governments
to determine for themselves which programmes were worth supporting and which were not. Secondly, the CVP and similar programmes were part of the development of an infrastructure for
future 'work-for-the-dole' schemes. As well, these programmes often
provide a means to influence the behaviour of the participants in a
particularly narrow direction, one which does not uncover or
challenge the fundamental causes of people's problems and which
denies legitimacy to other social and political responses on the part
of the young.

The changes announced in the September 1987 Budget that the
three existing community-based employment and training programmes – CYSS, CVP and the Community Training Programme

(CTP) – would be integrated under the aegis of the 'SkillShare' programme reshaped the boundaries of 'legitimate' youth work across the nation. Funds for SkillShare projects are available to non-profit community organisations and local governments to sponsor 'skill formation' training programmes for long-term unemployed people of all ages and from various 'disadvantaged' groups. The sponsor bodies have to secure contributions in cash or in kind of 15 per cent in the first year and 20 per cent in the second year. The effect of the SkillShare funding guidelines has been to reduce the number of youth services and staff, and to place even greater emphasis on training. Future project funding is contingent upon the achievement of targets for employment and further education as measured according to local labour-market conditions.

For CYSS youth workers in particular, this move to integration is transforming their roles and reducing their autonomy. Not only have staff and existing projects been threatened by rationalisation, but the new integrated programme favours a vocational approach over one which provides non-vocational and support services. For example, all activities provided by the new programme are to be vetted for approval by the local CES manager. As the president of the national CYSS project association commented at the time of the announcement of SkillShare: "The effect of all these changes will mean that there will be no room for local innovation, and no room for a local community to respond to the needs of their young unemployed people. Instead, we will have a standardised 'curriculum' for all Projects." (Wells, 1987: 17).

Questions about the role of the CES regarding referrals and target groups, and voluntary and non-voluntary attendance, also are important to consider and still have to be resolved. The expansion in the number of CES Youth Access Centres, with a mandate to become a focus to co-ordinate the existing network of youth-related services and agencies on behalf of young people, seems to indicate a shift in state intervention both in the lives of young people and in the affairs of existing youth services. At this stage the general direction of change appears to be a narrowing of the definition of the functions of youth workers, tighter regulation of their activities, and closer monitoring of the use of project funding.

Where the money comes from and where it is to be spent is of immediate relevance to youth workers. The nature of the job, especially in the case of paid work, influences the attitudes and activities of each individual with respect to pursuing wider social and political objectives on the job (and perhaps outside work as well). There are a number of reasons for this, such as the necessity to toe the line if one is to retain the job and thus an income. The main concern in the next section, however, is to explore in greater depth the different perspectives which are associated with particular kinds of youth work.

PERSPECTIVES ON YOUTH WORK

In general, youth work is labelled as such because of the area of work, rather than the particular skills or perspectives of the worker. As Quixley (1985: 16) puts it: "The youth sector is not drawn together by similarity of function, but by similarity of client group." The 'unity' of the field therefore resides in the fact that youth workers occupy a particular place in the 'community', one which is distinct from that of parent or teacher, and one which primarily centres on working with young people outside the usual institutional frameworks of home, school and work.

There is no single 'practice of youth work'. Instead, there is a variety of approaches, many different kinds of motivations for entering the field, and substantially different contexts for the achievement of particular objectives. The fundamental questions to ask at this stage are 'Why is this the case?', and 'What implications does the answer to this question have for the political importance of youth work in the wider scheme of things?'.

The actual practice of youth work lends itself to diverse interpretations of the youth worker's role, and of the 'needs' of young people. Many of the 'values' and 'concepts' apparent in youth work derive from a particular orientation, be this welfare provision, recreation services, or community development. For example, provision of recreation service may be informed by notions such as 'character-building', 'competition', 'leadership', and 'leisure'; welfare service by terms such as 'benefits', 'disadvantage', 'clients' and 'services'; and community development by concepts such as 'empowerment', 'self-help', 'participation' and 'life skills'. In practice, of course, individuals may hold many different values at the same time, or apply concepts to specific activities as suits the situation.

From a structural perspective, the role of youth work is to control and direct the behaviour of young people in society. Its main function is to contain 'youth problems', rather than to challenge the basis from which these problems stem. As Carrington (1986: 48) comments: "The practice of youth work exists and is supported by the community (either directly or through government) in order to deal with the most observable 'problems' of young people, not to deal with fundamental inequalities." The differences noted above, however, indicate that at the level of practice and ideology there are multiple aims and orientations within youth work. Thus, while 'control' can be seen to constitute the broad framework for the practice of youth work, this is by no means a monolithic entity which totally excludes the possibility of alternative forms of youth work.

Even granting the different motivations and perspectives held by people active in youth affairs, it is important to recognise that due to political, bureaucratic and resource factors (as well as factors relating to the personal attributes of youth workers) the scope for 'progressive' youth work is severely limited, and indeed the meaning of 'progressive' youth work is subject to varying interpretations. For example, after describing the gains made by youth workers in Britain in securing benefits for young people such as youth facilities, excursions and camps, Nava (1984: 7) comments that this kind of 'softer practice' nevertheless "remains predicated upon a welfarist cultural-deficit model which conceptualises certain sectors of youth as in need of supervision, protection and 'life skills'; which, in short, tends to hang on to the notion of certain sectors of youth as a problem". On the other hand, in Australia (as in Britain) there has also been the development of 'political activism' in youth work, albeit a limited development to date. 'Progressive' youth work in this context sees the traditional approaches as providing only short-term relief to some of the young people affected by the changes occurring in society. In this view, "what is necessary is to form a political base within youth affairs which can begin to redress the causes of such things as homelessness, poverty and unemployment" (Pisarski, 1986: 10).

Broadly speaking, the main political division amongst youth workers appears to be between the 'liberals' and the 'radicals'. The former tend to engage in the more conservative 'softer practice', which bears some similarity to the 'child saver' movements that first emerged in the nineteenth century. The latter base their work on political objectives, objectives which are tied into wider class, gender, and ethnic struggles, rather than being defined in terms of 'young people' themselves. What concerns us here is to explain the popularity of 'liberal' views in the field and why the 'radical' views tend to hold less sway.

One way to approach these questions is to consider who the

youth workers are, and to what ends they aspire as *workers*. Although little research has been done on the social background of youth workers, available surveys (e.g., Youth Workers Network of South Australia, 1984) show that there is fairly even participation by men and women, and there is over-representation of people from middle-class backgrounds (if educational credentials are used as an indication of class). It could be argued that for these people, their position is dependent upon the maintenance of the system as it is – both in broader class terms as members of the middle class, and in occupational terms as potential paid workers in youth affairs.

While political attitudes and perspectives are not determined by class background in a straightforward or unproblematic way, nevertheless, the middle-class and essentially conservative orientation of many individuals in youth affairs manifests itself in debates surrounding 'volunteerism' and 'professionalism'.

Volunteerism

Many youth workers start out in the field through participation in a particular project or agency as a volunteer. The individual motivations for involvement may be diverse, ranging, for example, from concerns with welfare, through humanitarian or religious beliefs, to notions of fostering social change. In the context of paid youth work and the provision of specific 'services', however, volunteerism has other connotations going well beyond individual motivations. Politically, for instance, an emphasis on the involvement of volunteers runs the risk of individualising solutions to social problems and implicitly justifying the abrogation of state responsibilities for the less powerful in Australian society. Thus, insofar as volunteerism is seen as an adjunct to the social welfare system – a 'residual' category of work that nevertheless receives active political support for the part it plays in compensating for the inadequacy of government initiatives and programmes – then it can be seen as part of a conservative social and economic agenda (see Mowbray, 1982; Baldock, 1983).

Acceptance of 'volunteerism' as a principle of 'participation' and provision of services also opens the door to the acceptance of policy developments such as 'work-for-the-dole' schemes. 'Voluntary' work can be used as means of obtaining cheap labour to compensate for government cutbacks in areas such as health, education and social-welfare programmes. Ironically, then, a volunteerist perspective, based on the notion of charity and good works, assists the development of schemes that directly threaten the future availability of paid employment in youth affairs.

Organisationally, the limited number of overtly 'political' organisations in the social action sense means that volunteers are usually initiated into youth work via agencies which are fairly conservative in outlook. This conservatism takes the form of a mix of 'welfarist' approaches which have their origins in charity provision, 'individualist' approaches which treat the problems in terms of personal deficiencies (lack of education, love, training, etc.), and 'values' approaches that see the problem in terms of incorrect socialisation (lack of leadership, responsibility, spiritual guidance).

Activity in such agencies also plays its part in socialising volunteer workers into 'ways of doing things' appropriate to the agency, rather than necessarily doing things in ways which are useful and appropriate to young people themselves. Thus, youth workers learn to perpetuate the agency (e.g., through learning how to write funding submissions); to co-operate with the management committee; to adopt particular leadership models and relative positions in the agency hierarchy; to subscribe to co-operative participation models and consensus theories. All these may be useful on their own, but they are of dubious value where social change necessitates forms of conflict and confrontation which go beyond particular agencies' 'normal operating procedures'. To put it differently, volunteer training teaches workers how to be 'respectable' and 'respected' by the power brokers (government officials, funding bodies, management committees), and thus ensures that youth work itself will be 'respectable' and not traverse the lines of social conformity in any significant sense.

Finally, the middle-class backgrounds of many volunteers allow them to step into the 'helping' role, and to escape the life conditions affecting their charges. They can thus feel secure in the knowledge that they are performing a humanitarian function, without directly experiencing the pressures which could lead them to reject such a limited approach.

Professionalism

The limited nature of humanitarian approaches is also important to sustaining a belief in youth work as a budding 'profession'. The perception that the problem will not go away, and that radical solutions requiring a political activist approach are 'too extreme', open the door for a detached practice of youth work, which regards it as an occupation rather than as a political exercise. In this way, youth work is dissected into its component parts, involving certain identifiable skills and knowledge for particular kinds of tasks (e.g., group work, counselling, grant writing). By establishing the requisite training and promoting the notion that youth work requires specific skills and knowledge, youth work can, over time, become a bona fide profession. This means that people can eventually be excluded or included on the basis of qualifications and credentials.

In addition to issues of access to the field, and industrial recognition of the work in the form of wage awards and conditions of service, professionalisation also has implications for the nature of youth work itself. For instance, the relationship between young people and youth workers can be affected by the emphasis on qualifications which may lead some people to adopt patronising attitudes because, as 'experts' in the field, they know what is best for their 'clients'. Ultimately, though, the crucial impact of professionalisation in youth work lies in its evaluation of youth work as a *job*, not as something linked to fostering fundamental social change and the risks that such a process implies.

Professional training which is centred on occupational definitions of 'need', 'skill' and 'expert knowledge' means that in many cases youth workers are ill-equipped to engage in anything more than specific 'practical' tasks. Defined by others, and by themselves, as 'workers' rather than 'activists', youth workers may feel they have no time or energy to commit to 'political' struggles, even if they see them as appropriate. Furthermore, they may not feel that they have the knowledge or political skills to take a leading role in the struggle to improve existing social structures. This extends to defence of their own working conditions and philosophical integrity as well. Being in a vulnerable position when it comes to funding can inhibit one's approach to radical youth work: income and job security may be jeopardised if funding sources disapprove of the type of work being done.

The social backgrounds of youth workers (whether they are male or female, established Australian or migrant, working class or middle class, etc.), and the general milieux of youth work (ways of working, accountability structures, conceptions of the occupation, etc.), interact to produce a small-'l' liberal view of the world and the role of youth work within this world. This becomes apparent when we consider in greater depth the constraints on the actual work done by youth workers, and the confusions surrounding the central concepts which are invoked to describe the content and objectives of youth work.

THEORY AND PRACTICE IN YOUTH WORK

Youth workers are positioned as workers in a matrix of relations involving various institutions, organisations and networks. There are major constraints on what a youth worker can or cannot do in terms of paid or volunteer work in most youth work agencies. This is apparent in terms of employment within the government sector. Youth workers who work for a government department such as the Department for Community Welfare or the Department of Employment, Education and Training are subject to a myriad of bureaucratic rules and regulations. Power tends to be structured hierarchically, and the work ethos places great stress on 'careerism' and 'professionalism'. The latter notion is interpreted as requiring a certain distance from the 'client'; the work undertaken is supposed to reflect the political judgements of elected politicians as expressed in public policy, rather than the autonomous evaluation of persons with expertise in a specific area.

As a worker in the government sector one is also limited by restrictions placed upon one's specific area of work. Narrow government definitions of 'need' mean that youth work tends to focus on one facet of an individual's total problem. As George and Wilding (1976: 122) point out, the result is that "There is neither an overall approach to the individual's problem nor any real recognition that the faults lie not in the individual but the system." Insofar as 'needs' are constructed and treated separately, often by more than one government agency or department, youth work tasks are fragmented and there is less scope for dealing with a young person's overall situation.

In the case of non-government agencies the constraints can be both 'external' in nature and 'internal' to the agency. An example of the first is the case of organisations which are financially dependent upon state grants. Since their continued existence is premised upon further funding, there are necessarily great pressures to present a 'respectable' face to the public and a non-antagonistic attitude to government policy. Always looking over their shoulders at the threat of having their funding cut off, these agencies walk a tightrope: on the one hand trying to meet objectives related to grassroots demands, and on the other attempting to accommodate the political and policy imperatives of the government in power. It is notable in this regard that, as mentioned in Chapter 1, when the Fraser Government attempted to disband CYSS in 1981 a national campaign by CYSS workers and their supporters prevented this

from occurring (see Freeland, 1985). In 1988, however, the integration of programmes into SkillShare not only staved off reaction to
the real demise of CYSS, but it pitted CYSS workers against each
other in bitter rivalries for funding, as projects tried to outdo each
other in showing their adherence to government guidelines and
rhetoric about skill formation.

In the case of non-government organisations which are not solely
or overwhelmingly reliant upon government grants, the pressures to
conform to conservative models of youth work practice are of a
different character. Here the 'internal' constraints may be either
ideological or philosophical constructions of the problem (e.g.,
humanitarian emphases on providing charity to the 'needy'), or the
fact that, for these agencies to survive and grow, they need to be
able to garner public support in the form of donations. Since the
income base in this instance is intentionally broad, the fact that
business organisations and middle-class sections of the population
are among the fund-raising targets necessarily leads to a stated or
unstated 'consensus' as to the conservative role of the agency in
question. To engage in 'radical' action would lead to the withdrawal of support from the more affluent or politically powerful sections
of the community.

Regardless of the source of funding for particular youth work
agencies, most youth work focuses on providing services. Youth
workers are paid or volunteer to work with young people, to assist in
developing their self-esteem, their skills, their abilities to communi-
cate and interact with other people, to provide welfare and counselling services: in a word, to help young people 'cope' with a whole
variety of personal, social and economic problems. Indeed, certain
needs can be met (to a certain extent) on an individual basis.
However, if the focus of the day-to-day tasks of youth workers is on
meeting *individual* needs this will reduce the time and energy
devoted to actions based on general social needs.

If the above summary describes the current practices of youth
work, then we must ask how successful youth workers are in
performing this role. To answer this we could point to specific
'outcomes' with this or that young person – this person found a job,
this one got over their depression, this one managed to break a drug
habit, this one no longer ekes out an existence on the street, this one
has found secure accommodation. Overall, however, what has
really changed? For every one young person who is assisted, scores
more are 'out there' and entering the 'need' category for the first

time; perhaps to find 'salvation' through their youth worker, perhaps not.

Since youth work is circumscribed by organisational structures, funding dependencies and servicing functions within the employment or occupational sphere, the scope for political activism appears to be small. Nevertheless, some youth workers see youth work *in itself* as a form of radical action, involving as it does forsaking aspects of the middle-class economic dream in order to spend one's time and energy in the task of helping others. Additionally, the language of the field may influence how practitioners see themselves and their roles.

The language one uses creates a particular conceptual framework for analysing the nature of the 'problem' and influences the choice of tactics and strategies for dealing with it. The 'progressive' veneer of the language used in youth affairs is deceptive: in fact it can exert a conservatising influence on participants in the field who subscribe to these ideas. Here we can refer to a couple of the more common terms employed in the field in order to illustrate the ways in which particular language is used to justify certain kinds of practice.

'Participation'

The idea of public participation as a 'good thing' can be a mechanism to diffuse and co-opt potential dissent and political challenges to government policy and action. This occurs where it is closely associated with a pluralist conception of power and where it is incorporated into a co-operative framework for the resolution of conflicts (see Mowbray, 1985). This is most apparent in government concerns to increase participation by people in youth affairs on issues that concern them. Either 'young people' are treated as a generic, undifferentiated category which ignores the deep divisions of class, gender and ethnicity, or specific 'population groups' or youth work representatives are invited to participate in this or that programme. The crucial factor here is that only those organised groups which are considered 'legitimate' in the eyes of the powers-that-be are invited to 'participate' in official deliberations. This practice is bolstered by supporting, acknowledging or funding only those groups and organisations which are willing to play ball according to the guidelines laid down by the government. In these instances, then, participation is restricted to discussion and action as set out in a predetermined political agenda.

Another way in which 'participation' can operate as a conservatising force is that it can implicitly lend credence to a pluralist view of power. Such a view sees economic and political inequality as reflecting particular interest groups, rather than as something which is structurally determined and highly concentrated in society. It follows from the pluralist view of power that if participation is to take place it must include all kinds of viewpoints, and must involve all sections of the 'community'. It is assumed that each group has a right to have its interests acknowledged, and that resolution of conflict should be through consultation and negotiation as a means to balance conflicting interests. Not only does this kind of approach ignore the substantial and real power differences between different categories of people, but as well, it leads to co-optation. The emphasis thus becomes one of working through the 'proper' channels, using the 'correct procedures' and accepting the 'majority decision' of the consulted groups as a whole.

This model of participation is the one most often identified with the day-to-day practice of youth work, involving as it does constant 'consultation' with funding agencies and government bodies. Not surprisingly, most government calls for public participation conveniently sidestep the question of class. Certain 'population groups' are targeted, that is, those which are defined as being in 'need' or 'disadvantaged'. But no attention is given to the fact that the overwhelming number of young people that youth workers deal with are at the bottom of the class structure, be they migrants, women or Aborigines. This can play an important ideological role insofar as groups and organisations which explicitly base their analysis on radical political philosophies such as socialism and feminism are seen as outside the mainstream of popular discourse.

A more insidious aspect of this is the way in which 'radical' views are presented as being divisive. The argument is along the lines that since, after all, 'we are all human', if we are to strive collectively for social improvements then this is the 'common ground' from which we must start. Extending the logic of this position further, the first virtue of youth work then becomes that of participation rather than equity. On the one hand, this can lead to a situation where "community work starts with a problem of poverty, converts it to one of decision-making, and offers participation as a solution instead of substantially increased resources" (Thorpe, 1985: 20). On the other hand, the 'balanced' structure of public participation leads to action based on the lowest common denominator, in which the various interest groups represented search for issues upon which they can agree. Such 'equal' representation undercuts action on more substantive matters and fails to alter or challenge the existing unequal and oppressive structure of social relations. As Sandercock (1983: 86) succinctly puts it: "The poor want better housing, better jobs, better schools. They want results. If participation can achieve these for them then it is valuable. So far, it has not."

For youth workers who, by virtue of their job, have to play the participation game, the danger is that they will carry ideas derived from particular work practices over into all other spheres of their work. The result will be a more conservative interpretation of social change and social power, and the radical dynamic may be lost as 'lobbying' and 'negotiation' come to be seen as more important than they really are in effecting significant social and political change. 'Participation' implies that there are two equal sides in the negotiations, and that what is to be negotiated is in fact negotiable. Since structural change is not something which can be subject to negotiation, the most one can hope for is piecemeal reform – if the state of the economy will allow it.

'Empowerment'

The notion of empowerment is another favourite concept of youth affairs, although there are a number of confusions arising out of its use and misuse. In its more limited formulations, empowerment simply refers to giving young people an opportunity to gain access to new skills and facilities, and fostering a sense of confidence and self-worth in the individual. Minimally defined, it refers to a process of gaining and developing power. This is sometimes interpreted as meaning that the role of youth workers in the empowerment process is to offer 'non-directive' guidance, to let young people 'do their own thing' with sympathetic support and interpersonal skills to be called upon if the need should arise.

The problem with this conception of empowerment is that it assumes that young people do indeed 'know their own minds'. Yet, as Roberts (1983: 57) reminds us, "Young people, with no established adult identities, are typically uncertain of their abilities and interests." Furthermore, "The only stable sources of interests and self-concepts to which young people can resort are the roles prescribed by the wider society." In a capitalist, patriarchal and racist society, this can have worrisome consequences. Giving a free rein to young people in the name of empowerment can in fact distort what is meant by a 'non-judgemental' perspective in youth work by ignoring the deep divisions between specific categories of people whose interests may conflict. These differences are crucial. For example, study has shown that young men often play a 'policing' role in preserving definitions and boundaries of masculinity and femininity (see Nava, 1984). A narrowly-defined 'non-directive' approach to empowerment in this case would effectively serve to perpetuate the oppression of one category of young people under the guise of not intervening in the affairs of another category.

One problem with treating the issue of empowerment in an abstract sense is that it can ignore the real power relations that exist between youth workers and the young people they work with, and how power is actually used. This is perhaps most visible in the case of youth refuges and the like where 'rules and regulations' are a necessary part of accommodation provision. But it surfaces in other ways as well. For instance, a recent study (O'Connor, 1987) of youth workers in Queensland on the question of legal assistance found major problems in the assistance provided. In addition to survey results which indicated a marked lack of knowledge on the part of youth workers about the legal aspects of problems such as job dismissal, discrimination and social security appeals, the study found that the actions of youth workers in many instances undermined the assertion of young people's legal rights. Thus, as O'Connor (1987: 95) points out:

> In relation to young people our services are, at best, paternalistic in approach, at worst they are overtly controlling and patriarchal. Decisions in relation to the individual's health, welfare, legal or educational needs are justified in terms of a best interests perspective. A key determinant of whether a person obtains needed legal services is problem identification and referral by an informed intermediary. Yet welfare workers continue to play God by responding to their client's [legal] problems in terms of 'what's right' and of reasonableness, not rights.

This is a major allegation to make, and one which appears to contradict in concrete terms the empowerment ideal. Yet, in some ways it could perhaps reflect a situation where empowerment comes to be seen as the 'property' of the youth worker. Since it is youth workers who have the requisite 'expertise', then it is they who will define situations and the ways and means by which a young person is to be empowered. Where there is this sense of ownership, the chances are that the development of dependency by the young person on the youth worker will serve in fact to *disempower* the young person.

A major problem with the empowerment concept is that it is too often interpreted in strictly individualistic terms, being applied in practice simply as part of providing a service. Political and social problems can thus inadvertently be reduced to individual problems. This approach treats individual young people as 'victims', and thus fits into the 'soft cop' framework of youth work practice. As van Moorst (1984: 40) has commented: "most youth workers are still soft cops, because they continue to disorganise working class youth, by segregation, by age and by employment status, and by providing individualised support, rather than building group power and solidarity". This criticism is true to the extent that the provision of specific services precludes action to mobilise young people collectively on broad social and economic questions.

An individual-centred approach may, as well, fail to acknowledge important class differences in constructions of what the 'problems' are. For example, middle-class concerns with equality of opportunity and a greater emphasis upon self-esteem and assertiveness for young women can lead to situations where young working-class women wind up blaming themselves for their lack of 'success', or rejecting such techniques because they do not confront *their* realities – i.e., their 'career' choices, families, boyfriends, notions of femininity and so on (see Otto, 1982).

In a similar vein, the teaching of 'survival' or 'life' skills may run counter to the mode of survival adopted by some young working-class men. As Ewen (1983: 14) wryly observes:

> ... survival is what larrikinism, like Artful Dodgerism, is all about. In such a sub-culture things do fall off the backs of trucks (and always have), milk and bread have a habit of disappearing from doorsteps, there are a variety of ways of making a fast buck with no questions asked, the welfare system is there to be ripped off where you can get away with it. The middle-class moral ethos has attempted to intervene and counter-act these traditional survival skills as inimical to its own interests, but all it has to replace them with is client-dependency.

'Skill' in this instance tends to be constructed in terms of self-improvement, self-image and self-control. As such it is often seen as compensatory and therapeutic, involving the training of young people in new ways to 'cope' better with life's problems in a manner which feeds into a framework of competitive individualism (Cohen, 1984). Working-class cultural traditions, such as solidarity, are quietly discarded, as are alternative models that stress the collective working out of problems.

BEYOND THE 'SOFT COP' SYNDROME

Radical notions of empowerment see it in terms of social and political education, as a form of consciousness raising. While service may be provided for individuals in the first instance, empowerment means providing the skills, knowledge and resources for collective struggle. The whole point of intervention, from the point of view of political action, is to organise with young people to change the situations and structures which necessitate youth worker involvement in the first place. It is at this level that empowerment becomes meaningful, since it is seen as part of the process of social change.

In strategic terms, the emphasis in radical youth work is not on providing services as such, but on mobilising young people through service provision with the aim of either struggling for greater social justice in the form of actual social reforms, or dealing with instances of injustice and defending the social rights of young people in particular situations. In either case the struggle itself is an important part of the politicisation process insofar as it leads to a questioning and radical critique of the existing social system.

A crucial factor is that such strategies are based on action. As we have seen, young unemployed people have become more visible in Australian society and measures have been adopted to regulate their behaviour; one result of this is an increase in the number of clashes between the police and young people. The response to one such clash in the Melbourne suburb of Fitzroy is instructive. After police assaults on young people in the area in December 1984, a 'Police Watch Action Group' was formed. This group organised support for the young people involved, assisted them through the existing legal process, and engaged in a campaign involving publicity and demonstrations outside the Magistrates Court (see Woodger, 1987). This combination of tactics not only challenged the legitimacy and authority of state officials, but enabled young people and youth workers to learn through practice a range of political skills. Experience gained in these kinds of specific campaigns can then be drawn upon for struggles in other spheres of action and wider activist projects (environment, peace, women's liberation, socialism, etc.), as well as for activity on issues such as unemployment and housing.

Another example of youth work practice which is not fixed to a social control agenda is provided by the example of StreetLink, an Adelaide youth project mainly dealing with 'street kids'. The people at StreetLink have worked through a number of the shortcomings of 'traditional' youth work approaches. By 1987, they had developed a form of intervention which countered the notion that the problem lay with 'the intrinsic faults of young people'. As part of this process, they criticised four related approaches: these were 'rescue' (do things for young people); 'control' (give them a firm push); 'empathy' (provide sympathy and understanding); and 'environment' (a change in surroundings will change the client). Each of these approaches implied a 'save and rescue' type of attitude, and in practice had led to burn-out, conflict, a depowering of youth worker and young person, or a constant search for a more 'appropriate' environment.

The alternative model developed by StreetLink was based upon different assumptions. These included: the recognition that young people have the capacity to make choices and that they are responsible for their actions; there is a need to increase the number of choices; one cannot impose change; people's qualities are defined in relationships with other people; and that to understand why people act in a certain way it is useful to look at the restraints which are stopping them from acting in other ways. The notion of 'change' is viewed as an integrated process involving the individual (and their attitudes and ways of life), and social structures (and the barriers, restraints, and power differences pertaining to these). Acting as a team, and eschewing a case-work approach, members of StreetLink attempt to get young 'street kids' involved in what they want, in terms of their immediate personal circumstances. But, as well, StreetLink staff attempt to lead by example in organising campaigns on issues they feel are important. 'Youth issues' are constructed as broader social issues reflecting the state of society as a whole. The members of StreetLink themselves organise political campaigns on a range of issues, and attempt not to advocate on behalf of individual young people or groups of young people but instead to provide them with knowledge and explanations about things such as bureaucratic processes and social issues; as a result, young people make their own choices and in some instances decide to join in the political campaigns.

The ultimate 'success' of youth work from this perspective is not gauged by the number of 'clients' assisted, but by how far there is to go before youth workers are no longer needed. In this vision of societal goals, one of the aims of youth work is to attack the cause, to do away with the need for someone to 'pick up the pieces', to 'keep them off the street', to provide 'handouts to the needy', to soothe the bruised bodies and psyches of the young.

The regulation of the behaviour of young people by youth workers is to a certain extent a consequence of the fact that youth workers' behaviour is also regulated. This takes the form of overt political controls by the agencies within which they work. It also is manifest at the level of ideas, where certain stock phrases and loosely defined concepts can cover a multitude of sins. The relative lack of power of youth workers means that on their own, and regarding their function as service provision, they can achieve very little for young people beyond superficial improvements in the life conditions of a small proportion of those in need. Insofar as the conditions generating the need are not tackled, the revolving-door syndrome so characteristic of youth service will continue for some time, and the role of youth workers as defined and shaped by the state will increasingly be questioned by young people themselves.

CHAPTER 7

Conclusion: Control, space and rebellion

The current trend in youth policy is for a more coercive role for the state in its interventions in the lives of young people. From an initial emphasis on job creation and employment as expressed through the Wages Pause Programme and the Community Employment Programme, the late 1980s have seen a shift in government focus: first toward individual 'deficit' programmes such as the Australian Traineeship Scheme; and more recently toward outright 'regulatory' measures which place the burden of and blame for unemployment on the young by means of 'activity' tests.

The imposition of authority, discipline and passivity on young people through a range of bureaucratic and ideological measures in education, training, the law, and community-based centres and programmes, has been matched by the exclusion of young people from 'politics' in general. This exclusion is both a simple one – their needs and opinions are ignored in parliamentary elections and policy formulation – and one in which youth dissent is channelled in predetermined avenues of 'participation' through government-funded youth bodies or the use of phone-ins and surveys.

As well as direct control, it is with the moulding of specific types of character traits that the powerful are especially concerned. The influence of agents of social control such as schools, training programmes, police and youth workers, however, will be mediated by an individual's social background. Attempts to reform or reshape the behaviour and attitudes of young people involve complex layers of conformity and non-conformity and variable 'definitions of the situation' by the people involved. The profound changes which have occurred in the juvenile labour market and the entrenched nature of high youth unemployment have created a deep sense of insecurity, uncertainty and identity crisis among many of the young people most affected by the economic downturn. The anger, boredom, frustration and alienation of a growing number of young people has manifested itself in several ways. This chapter discusses the variety of individual and collective, organised and unorganised, attempts by young people to cope with or change their world.

THE POLITICS OF YOUTH

Offering to 'bring Australia together', the Labor Party succeeded in convincing many people in the lead up to the March 1983 federal elections that it had an economic policy which would be fairer in principle than that of Fraser's coalition of Liberal and National Party. Under the rubric of 'reconciliation' and 'reconstruction', new Labor leader Bob Hawke offered the hope that all sections of the Australian community could work together, sacrifice together, and together pull Australia out of the depths of recession. In an ALP policy speech in February 1987, he announced that "we shall ask all sections of the Australian community to show the common restraint and share the common burden for the common national purpose". The emphasis has been on co-operation, consensus and concili-ation, rather than the conflict and coercion of the Fraser era.

The conditions under which the Labor Government was elected ensured that two major factors were to operate during its tenure in office. The first was the 'sacred' nature of the Accord between the Labor Party and the Australian Council of Trade Unions (ACTU) which was to be held intact at any cost, regardless of any break with traditional labour policies (see page 45). The second factor was the increasing prominence of 'outside' social forces in public debate and mass mobilisations on specific issues, especially with the decline in influence of Left forces within the ALP and the unions as a direct result of the Accord. Thus, the environmental movement, spear-headed by such groups as the Tasmanian Wilderness Society, and the peace movement, headed by People for Nuclear Disarmament, were to become the most 'popular' and visible expressions of grassroots activism.

Meanwhile, poverty, homelessness and unemployment were

afflicting greater numbers of young people, yet little was being done for them. The Hawke Government had not shown much inclination to be sympathetic to their problems, and 'politics' was seen as a case of negotiation between the Government, the ACTU, business leaders, and industrial courts – all of which were perceived to have little to do with the concerns of young people. When the December 1984 elections were called, many young people were cynical about whether the outcome of the vote could make any difference in their lives.

But this election did make a difference. For the Labor Party was to receive a rude shock to its electoral strategies and ambitions – in the form of the Nuclear Disarmament Party. In the very short time from its establishment to election day, the NDP amazed political pundits and pollsters by achieving significant success at the polls. To the chagrin of the Labor Party in particular, the NDP managed to garner some 6 per cent of the vote.

Much of this vote came from young people under the age of twenty-five, including many people who were voting for the first time. Many people under voting age also actively took part in the election campaign, spreading the word and helping to distribute election materials. The fact that Peter Garrett, lead singer of the rock band Midnight Oil, was standing as an NDP candidate did much to publicise the new party's cause. His connection with a band which had an enormous following, and whose songs dealt with current social issues, was certain to have an impact when young voters were presented with a chance to demonstrate their support. The reasons given for the success of the NDP vary, depending on the commentator – from disenchantment with the rightward direction of the Australian Labor Party to fervent hopes that the new party would bring home the importance of 'peace' issues to traditional politicians. What could not be ignored, however, was the electoral impact that single-issue parties could have on Australian politics, and the important role young people could play in this process.

The year 1985 was the International Youth Year. As with other projects of this nature, IYY was used to channel monies into high-profile ventures and advertising. The 'International Year' bandwagon usually means that issues are raised, concerns expressed, limited funds released, commitments made, and – in the end – momentum reduced, as the next 'International Year' is suddenly upon us. The rise of the NDP in late 1984, however, provides an important backdrop to the strategies and policies adopted by the Labor Party during IYY; namely, the introduction of the Priority One package. Young people were seen as important: not just because it was International Youth Year; not just because they were experiencing real problems of unemployment and homelessness; but because they had shown themselves to be a force to be reckoned with in parliamentary politics.

As events since that time have shown, however, the Hawke Labor Government has shown considerable reserve when it comes to systematically tackling the substantive issues affecting young people. The attitude of the Government was captured by John Dawkins when he was the Minister assisting the Minister for Youth Affairs (i.e., the Prime Minister). For Dawkins, it was important to keep the hopes of young people up, even if their problems could not be dealt with overnight. As he put it: "It is disturbing to see young people pessimistic, but hopefully idealism and the belief that they can sustain a peaceful world will give them a more optimistic view of themselves and the future. It is their entitlement to have idealism and optimism." (quoted in Martinkus, 1986: 25).

In practice, the main features of current government policy have been an emphasis on 'busyness' and 'control'. The Government has gone out of its way to encourage young people to stay in school, to enter into training of some kind, or to stick with their existing jobs no matter how unsatisfactory they may be. The Government has backed away, however, from any sort of major policy commitment to creating employment for young people, or providing them with income security and the things this implies such as access to accommodation, independence, consumer power and so on.

At a rhetorical level Government Ministers have acknowledged the collapse of the teenage labour market and spoken of the need for young people to gain skills which will make them employable. Little mention is ever made of the structural transformations occurring in the economy which will prevent employment opportunities ever again opening up at an adequate rate under the existing economic system. The focus on 'training' nevertheless serves three useful purposes: it blames the victim for being unemployed; it depoliticises the issue of unemployment (thereby setting up punitive and accusatory responses focusing on 'dole-bludging', dole 'rip-offs', lack of 'family' responsibilities, etc.); and it transforms the concept of 'education' into a technical, instrumental exercise rather than a broader liberal conception of skills and knowledge.

Increasingly, the concern has been with social control and financial efficacy, rather than with questions of inequality and social justice. This control is exercised by means of a range of mechanisms: economic (manipulation of welfare provisions); ideological (emphasis on the 'family' as the main support for individuals); and directly coercive (law-and-order campaigns and vigorous regulation of public space). With the emphasis on making young people take up the narrowly defined 'options' offered to them, and the power to stop benefit payments if young people decide not to exercise these 'choices', attention has been directed at those 'lazy' young people and 'cheats' who are 'irresponsible' and who do not know a 'good thing' when they see it.

The Government and the Opposition in effect share common positions on various policy questions, and especially in the area of youth affairs. Policy differences which are discernible are of degree, not of kind. Each side is adamant that the way to tackle the 'problem' is to make things even more difficult for those people forced to rely upon state benefits. One consequence of this is that appeals for the youth vote are becoming more rhetorical, rather than making substantive proposals.

Bob Hawke began the trend by stepping on stage at rock concerts, appearing on *Countdown* and encouraging 'young Australia' to have its say via talkback radio shows as part of the selling of Priority One. The Liberal response, as outlined in a leaked strategy paper, was to "talk the language of young people, by mentioning rock singers, popular films and sport, whenever addressing them". The paper further urges that: "If there is a popular movie, try to draw some lessons from it or use a particular popular phrase (e.g., 'Make my day' from Clint Eastwood)" and "If Bruce Springsteen is all the rage, then at least make reference to him somewhere in a discussion." (*Canberra Times*, 2 December 1986). Meanwhile, the polls consistently find young people cynical and ill-disposed toward all politicians. Nevertheless, while politicians themselves have been less than successful in gaining the confidence and respect of young people, and young working-class people have become increasingly alienated from active political participation, the message of politicians and of government publicity campaigns has had a significant impact on their attitudes.

Potential youth resistance to government measures – either in the form of organised political action or in alternative uses of public spaces and social institutions – has been contained in various ways. One of these is through particular constructions of the 'problem' which serve to displace attention from the collective nature of their plight. The translation of social problems into individual ones is crucial, and has significant ramifications for the self-concept of individual young people.

The media, for example, have been actively pursuing issues such as unemployment and the state of young people in ways which, through images of young people as 'threats', 'victims' and 'parasites', target young working-class people as a major source of woe in Australian society (see pages 105–10). The opinions and perspectives of politicians, businesspeople and welfare workers have been interwoven into media stories in such a way as to provide a relatively coherent, if occasionally contradictory, picture of 'young people in the 1980s'. Regardless of the specific intentions of media journalists and editors, the particular way in which this picture has been constructed has clearly been connected to the efforts of the state to shape the perceptions, attitudes and behaviours of young people in a specific direction, in line with notions of self-discipline and self-blame.

The success of such media campaigns in moulding youth attitudes and beliefs in line with a more conservative and 'self-reliant' world outlook would, at least on the surface, appear to be evident in recent opinion polls (see Eckersley, 1988). For instance, a survey by Australian National Opinion Polls (1987: 8) in 1986 found that young people were more likely to attribute youth unemployment to 'youth apathy' and a lack of skills than they were in 1984. The survey results showed that "Young people attribute the cause of unemployment mainly to their own attitudes, lack of motivation ('the dole is too easy to get') and lack of skills." The poll suggested that young people's attitudes reflect the media portrayals of the issue, as influenced by government policy.

Similar types of attitudes were also apparent in a survey of young people involved in a training scheme in the South Australian town of Whyalla (White, 1989). A question on the main problems facing young people, for example, elicited responses which were extraordinarily critical of the young unemployed:

> They get pissed too much and think they're shit hot yet they can't do fuckall. No motivation to get up and go. A bunch of no hopers.

> No will to get work. They'd rather rage, and drive fast cars, no ambition.

> Frustration, unemployment, poverty, crime, etc., but I consider that that is mostly brought about by their own sheer idiocy in 90 per cent of the cases.

I couldn't care less. Young people are just as much in control of their own lives. I've had to fight for what I own, so why shouldn't they.

It would seem, then, that the thrust to 'blame the victim' in much of the media treatment of youth issues has had a marked impact on the perceptions of many young people. While such coverage may have influenced attitudes, when it comes to behaviour the situation is quite different. This is because at this level young people often do not have much choice in the kinds of things they can or cannot do.

The image of young people is one thing; their real experience of dependency and constraint is another thing altogether. Lack of opportunity as producers, less power as consumers, challenges to traditional ways of asserting masculinity and femininity, fewer options for leisure and recreation, and feelings of less autonomy and control over their lives, contribute to varied responses by young people to their changed social state.

INDIVIDUAL RESPONSES AND SUBCULTURAL SOLUTIONS

The response of young people to their position in society and their lack of power (economic, political, social) varies considerably in practice. At the unorganised and informal level, the response ranges from 'magical' solutions offered by becoming a member of a 'spectacular' subculture; opting-out strategies such as suicide, retreat into a self-contained shell, and the taking of drugs and alchohol; engaging in crime; for young women, having a baby; through to taking on the mantle of religious-based 'salvation'. The trend to extreme and personal 'solutions' to the situations within which young people find themselves is evidenced, for example, in the fact that the recorded number of suicides of people aged between fifteen and nineteen more than doubled over the period 1966 to 1986 (Eckersley, 1988).

How a young person sees the world and their part in the world depends on the specific social context into which they are born. In particular, their attitudes and behaviour will be conditioned by factors such as family background and the cultural milieu within which they are brought up. The experiences of working-class females and males, for example, have been linked to cultural elements such as solidarity within the workplace and the neighbourhood, an importance attached to 'lived knowledge' which unites ideas and practical skills, informality in social networks, and finding fulfillment in one's personal capacity for labour (Dwyer et al., 1984). Different life experiences and behavioural patterns, then, are closely associated with the class and ethnic background of the young person (Walker, 1987, 1988; Johnson, 1984). Constructions of 'masculinity' and 'femininity' themselves involve markedly different experiences, social expectations and life chances for men and women and likewise vary according to class and ethnicity (Donaldson, 1987; Willis, 1979; Thomas, 1980; Griffin, 1985a).

One can point to a range of problems which are shared by 'all young people', for example questions relating to sex and sexuality, expressions of autonomy, money, work, and leisure (see Wilson and Wyn, 1987; Youth Affairs Council of Australia, 1983). But the experience of being young in each case is conditioned by the position of individuals as members of a class, a gender and an ethnic group. The diversity of cultural influences 'available' to young people is in turn influenced by the limits of and pressures on their daily lives.

For instance, given the structural and cultural restrictions placed upon the 'choices' available to young working-class men, both in terms of job opportunities and spare-time activities, attempts are often made at a subcultural level 'magically' to resolve the dilemmas facing them (Hall and Jefferson, 1976; Hebdige, 1979; Brake, 1985). This might be done through the construction of a specific symbolic identity – such as identification as part of a local 'gang' which stresses and exaggerates the importance of Greekness, Aboriginality, the disco scene, or ocker mannerisms – by deviation from the dominant styles of dress and conventional behaviour. All these are examples of collective responses to problems associated with working-class experiences. Of central importance to young working-class men is the idea of winning space for themselves: "cultural space in the neighbourhood and institutions, real time for leisure and recreation, actual room on the street or street-corner. They serve to mark out and appropriate 'territory' in the localities." (Clarke et al., 1976). If we go beyond 'spectacular' subcultures and locally-based friendship networks to consider working-class males as a whole, it can be said that the conception and realisation of space is experienced in fundamentally different ways by different classes and ethnic groups.

For young women, the notion of space is once again specific to their particular circumstances – their position in structurally and culturally defined locations. In this instance the domestic sphere is central, as are cultural roles pertaining to females. With few exceptions (see Otto, 1982), young women do not form their own subcultures, at least not in the sense in which working-class males do in the 'public domain'. Young women tend to play a subordinate role within a male subculture, to engage in subcultures organised around time and activities at school, or to spend time with a small number of intimate friends, often using the bedroom as a private sanctuary (Thomas, 1980; Brake, 1985; Griffin, 1985a). The 'magical' solution exhibited by some male subcultures to problems of space and identity are mediated in this instance by patriarchal ideologies and practices.

This is reflected, for example, in a recent study by Carrington (1989) of girls' toilet graffiti. The study shows that the 'retreat to the public toilet' represents both a manifestation of the highly circumscribed and regulated behaviour of girls in the public sphere *and* the creative use of toilet space as a means of social expression, refuge and freedom from surveillance. Thus, the basis for action and the use of space and time by young men and young women is related to the extension of existing opportunities, opportunities which are themselves shaped by material circumstances (money, public facilities) and ideological constructions of appropriate behaviour (notions of 'femininity' and 'masculinity').

Youth responses to the crisis often take sublimated political forms, partly because of the complexities of social background and different opportunity structures and lifestyles. They are compounded by physically isolating factors and by the lack of political education offered in Australia's major institutions. Many young people have no secure base from which an organised political response to their situation may be possible. For instance, there are over 280 crisis youth centres in Australia. But these are too few to accommodate the thousands of young homeless, and furthermore, the shelter which is offered tends to be short-term, thus fostering the development of a perpetually transient population of individual homeless young people. The increasing regulation of public space, and the lack of sufficient places to congregate make it difficult for young people to get together in an atmosphere conducive to the development of political consciousness.

The lack of relevant 'political' education is evident in the number of Australian residents who fail to register to vote, most of whom are under the age of twenty-five. As an electoral office report prepared after the 1983 federal election (Australian Electoral Office, 1983) observed, the majority of this group reach eighteen years of age "without any feelings towards or knowledge of our political system and what it means to live in a democracy". Lack of knowledge is only part of the problem. 'Politics' turns young people off both because they lack input into decision-making and because governments have failed to deliver the goods for young people.

This, in turn, raises a dilemma in that, as Moore (1986: 50) puts it:

> Political involvement has failed to capture the hearts and minds of a new generation of young people who are suffering hardships of a severity not seen since the Depression. Many young people feel (quite justifiably) that politics is an alienating, boring irrelevance. On the other hand, young people of the mid 1980s are in dire need of a social critique capable of explaining their position and suggesting solutions.

Where such social critiques have been provided, especially under certain favourable conditions, then young people have indeed responded. This certainly was the case with respect to the rapid rise in popularity of the Nuclear Disarmament Party. As we saw in the last section, having rock singer Peter Garrett stand as an NDP candidate did much to win youth support for the new party.

It needs to be emphasised, however, that the politicisation of young people which seemed to occur during the 1984 federal election happened under 'exceptional circumstances'. Furthermore, music-industry interventions in social and political issues (whether by Peter Garrett, or the 'Live Aid' campaign) tends to be transitory in nature. When the 'event' is finished, so too is much of the initial enthusiasm for a specific project. In the meantime the hegemonic power of 'mainstream' pop culture continues to marginalise 'politics', to present 'traditional' alternatives and options to young people, and generally to mystify the nature of real social relations.

The fragmented nature of youth responses is particularly evident in the case of phenomena such as rioting, street fighting and aggression which are beginning to feature more prominently in Australian society. What individuals and groups of young people decide to do is not necessarily defined by the participants themselves as being 'political' in nature, although their actions nevertheless imply a particular relationship to the dominant patterns of economic and social life. From a broad subcultural perspective, young people can be classified in terms of belonging to networks and groups which are 'respectable', 'delinquent', 'culturally rebellious' or 'politically militant' (see Brake, 1985). In the context of a push for 'law and order' that has been backed by governments of all political persuasions, it is the 'delinquent' subcultures which have attracted the most scrutiny and sensational treatment by the mass media.

A further 'criminalisation' of young people's behaviour is one outcome of state measures designed to deal with media-defined delinquent groups. In 1988, for example, the newly installed Liberal Government in New South Wales substantially increased the police force and introduced a Summary Offences Act as a means to "wage war on hooliganism". Dealing with 'offensive' conduct or language, the Act bodes ill for particular groups of young people. Research has shown, for instance, that provisions such as those contained in the Act have been disproportionately used against Aborigines in towns in north-west New South Wales (Brown, 1988). The use of such legal powers by the police against marginalised groups of young people will simply not work as a means of reining in aspects of their public behaviour. On the contrary, such measures inevit- ably reinforce the subcultural identity of the targeted young people and contribute to further conflict in the local community. In a discussion of the relationship between young Aborigines and law and order campaigns in western New South Wales, Dillon (1987: 253) makes the comment that:

> By calling certain forms of behaviour 'criminal' the incidence of criminality will automatically be increased. Criminalising victimless behaviour will in turn further alienate 'offenders' from law enforcement agencies and the social order being 'protected' by those agencies, thus increasing the potential for unambiguously criminal behaviour such as violence to persons or property.

The origins of much conflict between specific subcultural groups and the police lies in both the antagonistic nature of relations between police and young people, and in the inequalities and depressed material circumstances of the young people. Media stor- ies about the 'law-and-order crisis', accompanied by political action oriented toward 'crime prevention' as the preferred policy response, will heighten rather than reduce the prevalence of 'delinquent' subcultural activities.

This can also be seen in the case of Sydney graffiti groups. In this instance constant media attention over a period of several years has both affirmed their identity, and helped to amplify this identification for the young people involved. Persistent media stories on graffiti have in fact reinforced the notoriety of such activity. One result of this has been the burgeoning of graffiti groups, which thrive on the media attention given to their work. Media coverage itself may actually contribute to the bonding of individuals around a central activity that simultaneously acts as a key to subcultural identification.

The process of amplification and response can in turn engender a further dynamic in the relationship between young people, the media, and the forces of law and order. The murder of a young Sydney woman in September 1988 sparked a flurry of media stories on the dangerousness of the 'graffiti gangs'. Five teenagers and a young man in his twenties were charged with the crime. Newspapers made much of the fact that the young people had 'no fixed address' and were members of a Sydney railway graffiti gang. Subsequent articles and reports emphasised that the activities of this particular group of young people were by no means atypical. Thus, a feature article in the *Weekend Australian* (17–18 September 1988) was spiced with descriptions such as "Graffiti gurus bash and loot for money"; "Most steal for 'existence' and sleep anywhere they can. When they do go on the rampage, they combine three activities – 'popping, searching and rolling', that is, taking pills, breaking and entering and assaulting"; and "The majority have homes but choose not to go to them." In this sort of 'moral panic' reportage the reasons for this kind of street activity (i.e., graffiti) tend to be glossed over, as are the wider socio-economic processes which provide the context for a substantial growth in the number of young people doing graffiti. Media reportage on graffiti work has provided the impetus for some young people to assert themselves by engaging in such activity. In the end, gross generalisations about the dangerousness of some young people are used to support calls for further restrictions on the activities of other young people, and especially those who have been most marginalised by the economic crisis.

The activities of young people at a subcultural level, while reflecting the experiences and consciousness of their generation, at the same time mirror the wider social divisions in society. At an individual level, however, different young people have different degrees of commitment to their peer networks and subcultural practices. Hebdige (1979: 122) observes, for example, that:

> It can represent a major dimension in people's lives – an axis erected in the face of the family around which a secret and

immaculate identity can be made to cohere – or it can be a slight distraction, a bit of light relief from the monotonous but none the less paramount realities of school, home and work. It can be used as a means of escape, of total detachment from the surrounding terrain, or as a way of fitting back in to it and settling down after a week-end or evening spent letting off steam.

We must acknowledge the complexity of the position of young people in a broader matrix of social relations, including particular subcultures. But to focus on the individual young person and their personal solution to existential dilemmas tends to restrict discussion to a specific situation, and avoid an analysis of attempts by young people to intervene, in a self-consciously political fashion, on specific economic and social issues. It is to these attempts that we now turn.

YOUTH ORGANISATIONS AND SOCIAL CHANGE

Youth subcultures tend to centre on small groups in defined localities. The Australian experience is that subcultures rarely attempt to mobilise wider numbers of young people in a conscious effort to change (or reaffirm) the existing social structure. Analytically, one might be able to show the similarities between different groups of young people from a range of localities and backgrounds who are involved in particular types of behaviour: rule-breaking (in relation to particular codes of 'style'), anti-school ('resistance') and law-breaking ('delinquency'). But there is not necessarily an organisational connection between these groups; the similarity in response is due to common experiences of wider institutional structures and relations. It is not generally due to a shared consciousness of purpose or to co-ordination of actions.

In organised political activity, young people in Australia generally orient towards three types of collective practice. These include membership of organisations for young people (the boundaries of which are determined by government definitions of 'youth affairs'); student organisations; and a variety of activist youth organisations.

Youth affairs

The Youth Affairs Council of Australia (YACA) is the peak non-government 'official' youth organisation in Australia. It has counterparts in most of the States and Territories, such as the Youth Affairs Council of South Australia. Up to 1988 YACA was comprised of representatives from various member forums, including the National Youth Council of Australia (NYCA), the Conference of Australian Youth Organisations (CAYO), the Nationwide Workers With Youth Forum (NWWYF), and the National Forum of State Youth Affairs Councils (NFSYAC).

Commonly referred to as organisations which provide an 'independent voice for young people', youth affairs councils are funded by government. Their main tasks are in developing policy and communicating a 'youth perspective' to appropriate government departments. Paid staff in these organisations are sometimes seen as 'youth professionals' or 'youth bureaucrats'. This is partly a consequence of the limitations built into the functions of such bodies.

The guidelines under which youth affairs councils operate stipulate that they are to concern themselves with 'young people'. This broad designation is of course extremely problematic given the diversity of interests and the different positions of young people in the social structure. Furthermore, it is not entirely clear what the 'representational' base of these organisations consists of. For instance, although governments sometimes look to youth affairs councils for feedback on particular policies and programmes, it is difficult to see how the views adopted by these councils necessarily reflect what is felt among young people themselves. Put differently, the small numbers of people who are actively involved in member organisations, coupled with the generally middle-class nature of such organisations, renders suspect the notion that these councils are 'representative', in either a direct quantitative sense or in terms of the specific interests of particular categories of young people.

Youth affairs councils tend to be oriented towards 'communication' rather than 'action'. Their main role is to 'consult' with governments on youth issues and policies. Where criticisms or suggestions are offered there is no guarantee that these will be taken into account in government deliberations. Lacking a numerically strong lobby base, regarded as superfluous rather than essential, and dependent upon government funding for their operation, these councils have little leverage in their dealings with government. In those instances where there might be the possibility of running a campaign which threatens the government – whether through leaflets, meetings or demonstrations – the governments may as a final recourse cut off funding for these bodies.

In addition, the dependence of youth affairs councils on funding opens them up to manipulation by governments. This was apparent at the first Youth Affairs Assembly held in February 1986 in Melbourne. Organised by the YACA, the conference was meant to assess the situation of young people in Australia and to provide direction for future strategies and action on youth issues. In the event, the most memorable outcome of the conference was the attendance of Bob Hawke. The presence of the Prime Minister distracted attention from the main agenda items as the media showed up in force to spread the word about his Government's new 'initiatives' with respect to young people. Meanwhile, young people who wished to protest against various aspects of Labor's youth programme were either not allowed into the meeting hall (partly due to the $60 registration fee) or were not permitted questions during the opening session which featured the Prime Minister. After a couple of staged 'photos with young people', the Prime Minister made his exit and left the conference participants to 'consult' among themselves.

As a political avenue for young people, then, youth affairs councils appear to be very limited in what they have to offer, although they can play an important subsidiary role in assisting a range of issue-based groups.

The other areas of youth affairs which receive government endorsement and 'official' recognition are those organisations run for young people. Although basically comprised of young people, these organisations involved structured activities developed *for* young people by 'adults', rather than springing from the practices of young people themselves. The main concern here is with those groups which, although they may receive some government funding and support, are not themselves government agencies. Generally speaking, these groups can be divided into those which are primarily concerned with 'leadership' training, those concerned with recreation and leisure pursuits, those arising out of a concern with migrant or ethnic identity and culture, and those which have a religious orientation. Often the activities of these organisations overlap. A list of some of the organisations active in South Australia illustrates the nature of these bodies.

Leadership training: Australian Red Cross Society; Girl Guides Association; Girls Friendly Society; Rotaract; Scout Association of Australia; Salvation Army; Young Men's Christian Association (YMCA); Young Women's Christian Association (YWCA).

> Recreation and leisure: Carclew Youth Performing Arts Centre; Cirkidz Youth Circus Project; Community Youth Clubs Association; Regency Park Centre Recreation Programme; Unley Youth Theatre; YWCA; YMCA.
>
> Migrant and ethnic groups: Aboriginal Community Centre; Greek Orthodox Archdiocese State Youth Committee; Indo-China Refugee Association; Polish Youth Association in Australia; Serbian Australian Cultural Society.
>
> Religious groups: Anglican Youth; Bible Society of Australia; Church of Christ; Down Under (Uniting Church); Lutheran Council of South Australia; Salvation Army; Scripture Union.

While for presentation purposes these groups have been lumped together, nevertheless major differences exist between them in terms of perspective, intention and activities. The Girls Friendly Society, for example, has objectives which are conservative in nature and which reaffirm 'traditional' values. Its main purpose is "to give glory to God by bringing girls and women into the full life and fellowship of the Church, and by helping them to know, love and serve Jesus Christ". This is to be accomplished by programmes which are based on "worship, study, work and play; including camping, arts, crafts, cooking, working with the aged, and personal development" (Association of Youth Organisations, 1986: 24). By way of contrast, the stated aims of the Young Women's Christian Association are more liberal in nature:

> Strengthened by the Christian Faith enriched by the world wide membership of women and girls, we seek to provide opportunities for women and girls to develop their full potential, express our concern for the whole community in responsible action, and strive to achieve peace, justice and freedom of all people. [Association of Youth Organisations, 1986: 60.]

The major distinguishing characteristics of these groups are: they focus on structured activities of some kind; they are not explicitly 'political' in orientation; they perform a 'service' role; and they aim to change particular behavioural and attitudinal aspects of the *individual*, rather than existing social structures.

The student movement

Probably the most visible expression of 'youth politics' in the late 1980s has come from the secondary and tertiary education sectors.

In the case of secondary-school students, the push to get young people into educational institutions or training programmes, and the raised expectations surrounding the relationship between more education and better employment opportunities, has meant that the issue of general educational conditions has recently come to the fore. Strikes by school students occurred in a number of centres during 1988 (*Resistance* Magazine, Autumn, 1988). In Perth, students at several schools went on strike in February over shortages of teachers and classrooms, chaotic timetables and in support of students turned away from classes due to overcrowding. In Hobart, the Elizabeth College Pressure Group was formed early in the year to protest against overcrowding, inadequate teaching resources and poor school facilities. The biggest demonstrations of student discontent, however, have occurred in Sydney. In June secondary students attended protest meetings and 5000 marched in order to vent their anger at the State Government for its stand on the maintenance and staffing of disadvantaged schools, changes proposed for the Higher School Certificate examination, and proposals relating to the punishment of student 'offenders'. On 1 July, at least 15,000 students went on strike in New South Wales. Further strike actions called for by the School Students' Union were also strongly supported by students across the State. The advent of such actions indicates the growing disenchantment of students with a system that not only severely limits their rights but which also fails to provide a suitable environment for meeting raised expectations regarding the importance of education in obtaining a place in the labour market.

In tertiary education, the 1984 collapse of the Australian Union of Students (AUS) was followed in succeeding years by a series of media commentaries which spoke of the conservatism of students on campus and the moribund character of student activism. However, the introduction of a $250 'administrative fee' by the Hawke Government, further funding cuts to tertiary education, and the support given to privatisation in the education sphere, rapidly changed this political landscape.

In March 1987 students all over Australia took part in mass demonstrations against the new tertiary education fee. Rallies, marches and sit-ins were organised in all State capitals. In several centres students were attacked by police or university security staff as they carried out their protests, with arrests taking place in Sydney and Brisbane. Across the country anti-fees campaigns were quickly organised to fight against the Labor Government's new fees policy. Although opponents of the fees were branded 'rich Liberal Party supporters' by the then Minister for Education, Susan Ryan, it was apparent that the campaign was organised by the more radical forces on campus, and that it enjoyed widespread student support.

The militancy of students over the specific issue of fees created a crisis of legitimacy for the Hawke Labor Government, especially since the Whitlam Labor Government had abolished tertiary education fees and fostered strategies to make post-school education more accessible to a range of 'disadvantaged' groups. The Government was conscious of the potential power of the 'youth vote' after the rise of the NDP in 1984, and subsequently took steps to dampen down the growing unrest on campus. In addition to naming the fee an 'administrative' fee, rather than a tuition fee, and labelling protestors as being 'Liberals', other measures were organised from within the student movement itself to head off future confrontations.

The most significant of these lay in the intervention by members of the National Organisation of Labor Students (NOLS). In opposition to the National Free Education Coalition, there was a concerted push throughout 1987 to form a new national union of students to replace the defunct AUS. While in theory such an organisation could constitute a step forward in student efforts to combat the austerity measures perpetrated by the Commonwealth Government, in practice it was often used to sidetrack the efforts of activist students away from the immediate issue of fees. The emphasis was on the narrow and bureaucratically conceived goal of organising the student movement around a new national union, rather than on building upon existing campaigns as a means to draw more students into the political process.

In May 1987, delegates from various State student unions met in Canberra to discuss the formation of the new national union. Campuses in South Australia and the Australian Capital Territory had no voting rights, and neither did major campuses in Sydney, Melbourne and Perth. The majority of delegates at the conference were members of NOLS, an organisation of the Australian Labor Party. Significantly, many of the ALP-dominated student unions had done very little to mobilise and involve students in the anti-fees campaign, while campuses with large campaigns had been manoeuvred out of the negotiations for a national union or had rejected the legitimacy of the NOLS leadership. After an October conference the process gained further momentum and by December the new National Union of Students (NUS) was formed.

The first executive and full-time office bearers of the new union reflected the dominance of the Labor Party, with the Left Alliance faction and Independents filling most other leadership positions, and the Liberals effectively marginalised. While calling for a national student strike in March 1988, a strike readily supported by activist anti-fee campaigners, the NUS also put much time and resources into lobbying politicians. But the failure of the attempt to influence decisions on fees and educational issues at the ALP National Conference in Hobart that year, and the prominent media coverage of campus Labor Club presidents who supported the introduction of the graduate tax, show that there are political divisions within its ranks that the NUS will have to grapple with if it is to be an effective pressure group. The failure of a NUS bid to bring a High Court challenge against the graduate tax in 1989 indicates that the development of relevant and effective strategies by the student union is needed as well.

This brief examination of student politics illustrates how, when young people collectively strive to make their voices heard, wider political forces quickly attempt to intervene in the process. This is particularly apparent in instances involving the traditional recruiting grounds of the major political parties, and where the young people involved tend to have the resources which enable them to articulate and act on their demands due to institutional factors (e.g., student union budgets and facilities) and social characteristics (e.g., the middle-class backgrounds of student leaders).

Outside the student arena, there are a number of groups and organisations which are attempting to mobilise specific categories of young people around a range of social and economic concerns.

Activist organisations

These groups are clearly and explicitly 'political' in their orientation, and their activities focus on attempts to modify, support or change existing social and economic conditions in Australia. They tend to be run by and for young people themselves, although they may be linked to 'parent' organisations of some kind, whether these are a national or State coalition or a national political party. In some cases they may be linked to or share the political perspectives of international movements and organisations (see Kultygin, 1987).

For example, organisations in South Australia of this nature include: Adelaide Young Christian Workers Movement; Australian Young Labor Association; Tangent (young gays); Resistance

(young socialists); Young Socialist League; Young Liberal Movement of Australia; Youth Housing Network; Youth Information
Group; Campaign for a Fair Deal for Young People; Sanity (youth
peace group).

Most of these organisations and groups are concerned with issues
of 'rights' (variously defined) and are tied into wider social and
political movements. They are also action-oriented, as well as in
some cases providing services to young people. The aims of the
Young Christian Workers Movement, for instance, include:

> educate, represent and be of service to young working and
> unemployed people, on the situation and concerns they face
> within their lives, e.g., life at work, family relationships,
> leisure time, homelessness, unemployment. A movement run
> by young working and unemployed young people responding
> to these situations through a process of 'see, judge and taking
> action'. [Association of Youth Organisations, 1986: 5.]

Similarly, Resistance is a socialist youth organisation which aims to

> provide an avenue for young people to be active in and discuss
> movements and issues which affect people today. Resistance
> stands for an end to war, poverty and unemployment and
> supports things like women's rights, students' rights, solidar-
> ity with liberation struggles around the world and socialism.
> [Association of Youth Organisations, 1986: 40.]

The political perspectives of these various groups and organisations
range from being on the Right of the political spectrum (Young
Liberal Movement), to social democratic (Young Labor), and
socialist and feminist objectives (Resistance).

At a regional or local level, organisations such as the Coalition
Against Poverty and Unemployment (CAPU) in Melbourne, the
Wollongong Out-of Workers (WOW), and Working-Class Youth in
Sydney, have been involved in campaigns on the lack of jobs and
meaningful education for working-class young people, the inadequacy of income support, and police harassment. Rather than
simply reactive campaigns, much of the work of these organisations
is devoted to raising the political consciousness of young people and
to offering alternative perspectives on ways in which to restructure
existing economic and social relations.

At a national level, the most active radical challenge to traditional politics and government policies has come from organisations
such as Resistance. This organisation, for example, has played a key

role in such things as the campaign against tertiary education fees and in protest campaigns against proposals for the introduction of 'work-for-the-dole', as well as having a high profile in Third World solidarity movements and the peace movement. Coalitions such as the Campaign for a Fair Deal for Young People in Adelaide, the National Youth Coalition on Housing and the National Union of Unemployed People have also engaged in efforts to change or modify government policy or practice. At this stage, the many groups and coalitions fighting for reform have had only limited success. This is due to a range of factors: the 'top-down' approach of some campaigns where the impetus comes from paid workers in various non-government organisations; the difficulties of connecting with unemployed people in their local neighbourhoods; a chronic lack of money and resources; the problems of being seen simply as a lobby group and as such not posing any real alternative to the existing political parties or structures.

The wide array of groups and organisations which target young people as their audience may make it harder for young people as a social category to know which way to turn politically. Coming on top of the divisions which separate young people (class, sex, ethnicity), and the relative dearth of political education, the sheer proliferation of competing 'choices' open to them means that, in many cases, they take no collective action to change their world.

The public position and status of young people as victims and pariahs in society means that their participation in organised political activity tends to take two general forms. These stem from the search by young people for stability, meaning and security in their lives; their desire to escape close control by the state; and the fact that, as with ascribed characteristics such as sex, class and ethnicity, unemployment is increasingly something one cannot 'grow out of', regardless of the supposed benefits of government training and education programmes. For these people the problem does not lie with the fact of being young. The problem is that, for this particular generation, we are seeing the formation of a permanent underclass that is being denied both meaningful work and the benefits of consumer society.

The first response can be summed up in the phrase 'the politics of fear'. The frustrations, fears and anger of young people produce aggressive attacks on groups seen as responsible for the present social and economic crisis. Women, blacks, and migrants, especially recent Asian migrants, have been singled out for blame, as have Left political organisations. The buildings and walls of the major

Australian cities, for example, are covered with racist grafitti ('Asians Out'), and in Adelaide Left bookshops have been vandalised, including the firebombing of the Communist Party People's Bookshop in 1987. Neo-fascist organisations such as National Action have actively tried to reach young people by leafleting working-class suburbs and are taking a high profile in public debates over immigration and unemployment – so far with only limited success.

Fundamentalist Christian organisations have similarly been busy in appealing to young people to find 'salvation' through the paths identified by them as the true way. The message of salvation is couched in terms of the individual, and the problems of the world are simplified in explanations which see their cause in black-and-white moral terms and conspiratorial theories. The hallmark of many such organisations is virulent anti-feminism and anti-communism, each being branded as a source of evil and a leading cause of the collapse of Western society.

The second response can be labelled 'the politics of the possible'. Here the concern is to mobilise people against the very 'rules of the game' and to forge an alternative kind of social order. Comprised of socialists, environmentalists, feminists, rank-and-file union activists, and those working for peace and Aboriginal justice, these groups involve people of all ages in a struggle against the forces of reaction, oppression and conservatism. The problems experienced by young people are seen in terms of wider political and economic frameworks, rather than as solely generational. Organisationally, while young people may be encouraged to discuss matters and plan their own courses of action, strategies which specifically target young people only in terms of 'youth' issues are recognised as too limited in scope.

The emotional and practical appeal of each kind of group – whether on the Right or the Left – lies in the fact that the 'enemy' is clearly identified and the action taken is immediate, concrete and militant in character. Feeding off the insecurities of young people, extreme rightwing organisations offer them ready scapegoats, simple explanations and the chance to do something about the situation themselves. While young people are highly conscious of the division between 'them' and 'us', the notion of 'the system' is often too abstract or overwhelming, and can lead to feelings of personal powerlessness and a sense of futility. Groups such as National Action offer something concrete and tangible, even though such organisations are "primarily united against something, rather than for something" (Kultygin, 1987: 110).

Various progressive social movements gain the support and participation of young people partly because they focus on 'single issues'. The specificity of the environment movement, as evidenced in the 1983 campaign against the building of the Franklin River Dam in Tasmania, provides young people with an identifiable object and readily discernible results. The process of fighting for particular ends in turn carries with it other benefits, such as heightened self-esteem, personal value and the feeling of being part of a wider community. The 'enemy' in this instance is usually clearly identified, whether it be the government, particular businesses, or other specific groups. For young people to change the conditions of their existence in any fundamental way, however, more will be required than either narrowly conceived 'youth' responses or participation in 'single-issue' social movements. Since the crisis affecting young people has its origins in the contradictions of the capitalist economic system, activity must eventually be oriented toward changing the conditions which give rise to such crises.

For young people, angry and disoriented as a result of the impact of current social and economic trends, the political vision is finely balanced, the choices coalescing into two major alternatives – the politics of hate, fear and insecurity associated with a system in decline; or the politics of possibility, creative alternative lifestyles and social justice associated with the creation of a different kind of system. For out of the chaos of the moment, out of the collapse of the existing economic system, must arise a new form of social order. What form this takes is the key question of our age, and, ultimately, it is young people who will have a crucial role in determining which way Australia as a nation will go.

Conclusion

This book has demonstrated that the 'space' occupied by young people in Australia has been subject to ever greater state control in recent years. Under the banners of 'skill formation' and 'law and order', government policies have been directed at curbing the autonomous activities of young working-class men and women and enforcing particular kinds of conforming behaviour. Any attempts by young people to win for themselves more freedom of movement and action have been met with concerted efforts to tighten control.

One plank in government policy has been to regulate and police the activities of young people in the public sphere. This is well illustrated for example in the Western Australian Government's Crime Prevention Plan, which includes provisions to strengthen the police force; to toughen penalties for juvenile crime; to encourage changes to the lifestyle, family and schooling patterns which are leading young people to commit crime; and to control the leisure time of the young (Western Australian Government, 1988). The other plank in government policy has been to force young people into institutional settings where they can be more easily managed. This is evident in Commonwealth and State government efforts to get young people to remain in or enter some type of education or training.

While for the purposes of exposition this book has considered issues of education and training separately from issues of crime and law, there is in fact considerable overlap. Although each sphere of activity is characterised by particular kinds of control mechanisms, there is, as well, a disturbing trend toward the use of 'law-and-order' measures in the school itself. For example, the Crime Prevention Plan mentioned above also includes a tenfold increase in the Police Truancy Patrol in order to reintegrate truants into the school system. Clearly the fact that more young people are staying at school for longer periods of time (for reasons of money and employment) will generate considerable conflicts and tensions in an over-loaded and underresourced State school system.

This has led to concerns not only with the phenomenon of truancy, but also with 'discipline' within the schools. In the case of New South Wales, the response has been to introduce an even more punitive approach to schooling. According to the Deputy Premier, Wal Murray, the problem of school discipline should be managed with a firm hand (in Prior, 1988: 19). Commenting on the idea of making the use of obscene language punishable by a gaol sentence, he has said that:

> Kicking these kids out of school is no solution, no punishment for them. Most of them would love it. They can then make nuisances of themselves elsewhere, bludge on the community full-time, instead of part-time. It is no solution to move them to other schools, either. That's just spreading the trouble. Sending them to gaol sounds extreme, I agree, and some form of 'soft' institutionalisation obviously would be better, but the main thing is that they don't stay around to infect the rest of their class and their school.

Thus, the feeling on the part of some students that school is a prison could become a reality. In September 1988 a sixteen-year-old Sydney school student was charged by police under the new Summary Offences Act – for swearing in class. The student faced a possible gaol sentence of up to three months.

Earlier in 1988 a teacher in Tasmania successfully sued a fifteen-year-old female student for assault, with the Burnie Court of Requests ordering the young woman to pay $125 damages to her teacher. The press report of the incident provides frightening testimony of what 'education' means to some students (*Adelaide Advertiser*, 18 May 1988):

> The assault occurred in November, 1986, during a lunchtime confrontation with the pupil, who had indicated she would not stay back for a detention imposed for misbehaviour in class earlier that day. Mr. Brazel told the court he stood in the doorway to stop the girl leaving the class, but she tried to barge past him. He said that when that move failed, she ran to the other side of the room, built up speed and made another charge. Mr. Brazel told the court the girl charged at him four times before striking out in frustration with both fists to his chest. She then escaped through an open window.

If young people are rebellious, if they are apathetic, if they are attempting to shut out the outside world, if they are committing crimes, if they are engaging in the politics of fear or of possibility, they are doing so for specific reasons. The search for a space of their own is a response on the part of working-class young people to a society in crisis, one that has forsaken social principles of justice, equality and humanity for the benefit of the wealthy and powerful. Ultimately, the problems associated with the 'broken transitions of youth' cannot be reduced to lack of discipline or skill, or the impact of technology; they stem from and are a reflection of social structures that privilege the powerful while consigning the less powerful to poverty, alienation and the ignominious drudgery of hand-to-mouth existence. Out of the contradictions of contemporary Australian society – the enormous disparities in wealth and income, the movement toward more authoritarian forms of social control, the restrictions on outlets for creative human endeavour – young people will be faced with many choices about the kind of society they will be living in. The shape of the future is determined by the practices of the present.

References

Aarons, L. *Here Come The Uglies; The New Right*. Sydney: Red Pen
  Publications, 1987

Adrian, C. "Urban Service Allocation and Distribution: An
  Institutional Approach", in P. Williams (ed.), *Conflict and
  Development – Urban Studies Yearbook 2*. Sydney: George Allen and
  Unwin, 1984

Alder, C. "Theories of Female Delinquency" in A. Borowski and
  J. Murray (eds), *Juvenile Delinquency in Australia*. North Ryde:
  Metheun, 1985

"'Unemployed Women Have Got It Heaps Worse': Exploring the
  implications of female youth unemployment", *Australian and New
  Zealand Journal of Criminology*, No. 19: 210–24, 1986

Angus, L. *Schooling for Social Order: democracy, equality and social
  mobility in education*. Geelong: Deakin University Press, 1986

ANOP Research Services *A Survey of Community Attitudes to Issues
  Affecting Young People ANOP, 1986*. Canberra: Australian
  Government Publishing Service, 1987

Apple, M. *Ideology and Curriculum*. London: Routledge and Kegan
  Paul, 1979
  (ed.) *Cultural and Economic Reproduction in Education*. London:
  Routledge and Kegan Paul, 1982

Ashley, S. *Towards Juvenile Justice . . . Police–Youth Relations in South
  Australia: a background report*. Adelaide: Youth Affairs Council of
  South Australia, 1983

Association of Youth Organisations (South Australia) *100 000 Young*

Australians Can't Be Wrong (a directory of organisations in South Australia). Adelaide: Youth Affairs Council of South Australia, 1986

Auld, J., N. Dorn and N. South "Heroin Now: Bringing it all back home", *Youth and Policy*, No. 9: 1–7, 1984
"Irregular Work, Irregular Pleasures: Heroin in the 1980s", in R. Mathews and J. Young (eds), *Confronting Crime*. London: Sage, 1986

Australian Council of Trade Unions–Trade Development Council *Australia Reconstructed: ACTU–TDC Mission to Western Europe*. Canberra: Australian Government Publishing Service, 1987

Australian Education Council Task Force *Report of the Australian Education Council Task Force on Education and Technology: Education and Technology*. Melbourne: Australian Education Council, 1985

Australian Electoral Office *A Qualitative Analysis of Attitudes towards Enrolment and Voting*. Canberra: Australian Electoral Office, 1983

Australian Institute of Criminology "Putting the Brakes on Car Theft", AIC *Reporter*, Vol. 8, No. 2: 10–11, 1987

Australian Manufacturing Council *Skills in Manufacturing Industry: Future Directions*, 1988

Baldock, C. "Volunteer Work As Work: Some theoretical considerations", in C. Baldock and B. Cass (eds), *Women, Social Welfare and the State*. Sydney: George Allen and Unwin, 1983

Bessant, B. (ed.) *Mother State and Her Little Ones: Children and Youth in Australia 1860s–1930s*. Melbourne: Phillip Institute of Technology Press, 1987

Blackburn, J. et al. *Ministerial Review of Post-Compulsory Schooling*. Melbourne: Victorian Government Discussion Paper, 1984

Boer, B., and V. Gleeson *The Law of Education*. Melbourne: Butterworths, 1982

Boson, M. "Priority One?", *Australian Society*, June: 25–8, 1986

Bourdieu, P. "Systems of education and systems of thought", in Dale, Esland and MacDonald (eds), *Schooling and Capitalism*. London: Routlege and Kegan Paul in association with the Open University, 1976a
"The school as a conservative force: scholastic and cultural inequalities", in Dale, Esland and MacDonald (eds), *Schooling and Capitalism*. London: Routledge and Kegan Paul in association with the Open University, 1976b
"Cultural Reproduction and Social Reproduction", in Halsey and Karabel (eds), *Power and Ideology in Education*. London: Oxford Press, 1977

Bradbury, B., P. Garde and J. Vipond "Youth Unemployment and Intergenerational Immobility", *The Journal of Industrial Relations*, June: 191–210, 1986

Bradbury, B., D. Encel, J. James and J. Vipond *Poverty and the Workforce*. Sydney: Social Welfare Research Centre, 1988

Brake, M. *Comparative Youth Culture*. London: Routledge and Kegan Paul, 1985

Brown, D. "Post-election blues: Law and Order in NSW Inc.", *Legal Service Bulletin*, Vol. 13, No. 3: 99–104, 1988

Browne, P. "1981–1986: Poverty on the Rise", *Australian Society*, April: 34–5, 1987

Buckskin, S. "Casino Riot", letter to *Adelaide Advertiser*, 21 November, 1986

Burger, J. *Aborigines Today: Land and Justice*. London: Anti-Slavery Society 1988

Burns, R. "Why Should I Join The Union?", *Australian Society*, July: 54–5, 1986

Buswell, C. "Employment Processes and Youth Training", in S. Walker and L. Barton (eds), *Youth, Unemployment and Schooling*. Milton Keynes: Open University Press, 1986

Carrington, K. "Girls and Graffiti", *Cultural Studies*, Vol. 3, No.1: 89–100, 1989

Carrington, T. Address to the Annual General Meeting of the Developmental Youth Services Association of New South Wales, in *Journal of the Developmental Youth Services Association*, Sydney, Spring: 45–50, 1986

Cass, B. *Income Support for the Unemployed in Australia: Towards a more active system*. Social Security Review Issues Paper No. 4. Canberra: Australian Government Publishing Service, 1988

Children's Interest Bureau, South Australia *When Can I? Children, Young People and the Law in S.A.*. Adelaide: Children's Interest Bureau, 1985

Clarke, J., S. Hall, T. Jefferson and B. Roberts "Subcultures, Cultures and Classes", in S. Hall and T. Jefferson (eds), *Resistance Through Rituals: Youth subcultures in post-war Britain*. London: Hutchinson, 1976

Coghill, K. (ed.) *The New Right's Australian Fantasy*. Melbourne: McPhee Gribble/Penguin, 1987

Cohen, P. "Against the New Vocationalism", in Bates et al. (eds), *Schooling for the Dole? The New Vocationalism*. London: Macmillan, 1984

Commission For The Future *In Future*. Melbourne: Commission for the Future, 1986–88

Commonwealth of Australia *Priority One and the 1986–87 Budget*.
    Canberra: Australian Government Publishing Service, 1986
    Skills for Australia (produced by the Department of Employment,
    Education and Training, and the Department of Employment
    Services and Youth Affairs). Canberra: Australian Government
    Publishing Service, 1987

Commonwealth Department of Health *Statistics on Drug Abuse in
    Australia*. Canberra: Australian Government Publishing Service,
    1986

Commonwealth Schools Commission *In the National Interest:
    Secondary education and youth policy in Australia*. Canberra:
    Australian Government Publishing Service, 1987

Community Employment Program *CEP The Second Year: 1984–85*.
    Canberra: Department of Employment and Industrial Relations,
    1985

Connell, R. *Which Way Is Up? Essays on Class, Sex and Culture*. Sydney:
    George Allen and Unwin, 1983

Connell, R., and T. Irving *Class Structure in Australian History*.
    Melbourne: Longman Cheshire, 1980

Corrigan, P. *Schooling the Smash Street Kids*. London: Macmillan
    Press, 1979

Cunneen, C. "Working Class Boys and 'Crime': Theorising
    the class/gender mix", in P. Patton and R. Poole (eds),
    War/Masculinity. Sydney: Intervention Publications, 1985

Davey, I. "Growing Up in South Australia", in E. Richards (ed.),
    The Flinders History of South Australia: Social Life. Adelaide:
    Wakefield Press, 1986

Davidson, P. "Work for the Dole", Australian Social Welfare
    Union *Newsletter*, No. 1, September: 16, 1986

Davis, M. "The Political Economy of Late-Imperial America",
    New Left Review, No. 143: 6–38, 1984

Dawkins, J. *A Changing Workforce*. Canberra: Australian
    Government Publishing Service, 1988a
    Strengthening Australian Schools. Canberra: Australian Government
    Publishing Service, 1988b

Department for Community Welfare, South Australia *Mall Talk:
    A study of young people who congregate in Rundle Mall*. Adelaide:
    Department for Community Welfare, 1985

Dillon, H. " 'Law and order' politics in the 'wild west' ", *Legal Service
    Bulletin*, Vol. 12, No. 6: 252–4, 1987

Donaldson, M. "Labouring Men: Love, Sex and Strife", *Australian and New Zealand Journal of Sociology*, Vol. 23, No. 2: 165–84, 1987

Dorn, N., and N. South "Of Males and Markets: A critical review of 'Youth Culture' theory", Research Paper 1, Centre for Occupational and Community Research, Middlesex Polytechnic, 1983

Dwyer, P., B. Wilson and R. Woock *Confronting School and Work: youth and class cultures in Australia*. Sydney: George Allen and Unwin, 1984

Dyson, S., and T. Szirom (eds) *Leaving School: It's Harder for Girls*. Melbourne: YWCA, 1983

Eckersley, R. *Casualties of Change: The Predicament of Youth in Australia*. Melbourne: Commission for the Future, 1988

Economic Planning Advisory Council "Human Capital and Productivity Growth", Council Papers No. 15. Canberra: Australian Government Publishing Service, 1986

Employment, Education and Training, Department of. Press releases on September 15 Budget, 1987

Ely, J. *Reality and Rhetoric: An alternative history of Australian education*. Sydney: Alternative Publishing Cooperative in association with the New South Wales Teachers' Federation, 1978

Ewen, J. *Youth in Australia: A new role and a new deal for the 80's*. Melbourne: Phillip Institute of Technology Press, 1983

Farrar, A. "Equity? It depends what you mean", *Australian Society*, March: 21–2, 44–5, 1987a
"The carrot-and-stick strategy", *Australian Society*, October: 26–8 1987b
"Labor Gets Back To Basics", *Australian Society*, March: 39–40, 1988a
"Social Security Review maps out new unemployment benefit system", Australian Social Welfare *Impact*, Vol. 18, No. 1: 3, 1988b

Fine, B., R. Kinsey, J. Lea, S. Picciotto and J. Young (eds) *Capitalism and the Rule of Law: From Deviancy Theory to Marxism*. London: Hutchinson, 1979

Finn, D. "The Youth Training Scheme – a new deal?", *Youth and Policy*, Vol. 1, No. 4: 16–24, 1983
Training Without Jobs: New Deals and Broken Promises. London: Macmillan Education, 1987

Fonovic, A. "Teenagers' Image", letter to *Adelaide Advertiser*, 20 March, 1987

Fopp, R. "Unemployment, Youth Homelessness and the Allocation of Family Responsibility", *Australian Journal of Social Issues*,

Vol. 17, No. 4: 304–15, 1982

Freeland, J. "The CYSS Campaign: An example of collective action against cuts in services", in R. Thorpe and J. Petruchenia with L. Hughes (eds), *Community Work or Social Change? An Australian Perspective*. London: Routledge and Kegan Paul, 1985
"Reasserting the Right to Work", Australian Social Welfare *Impact*, Vol. 16, No. 4: 6–8, 1986
"Welfare and jobs connection", Australian Social Welfare *Impact*, Vol. 17, No. 4: 6–8, 1987

Freeland, J., and R. Sharp "The Williams Report on education, training and employment: the decline and fall of Karmelot", *Intervention*, No. 14: 54–79, 1981

Frith, S. *The Sociology of Youth*. Ormskirk: Causeway Press, 1984

Gamble, H. "The Status Offender", in A. Borowski and J. Murray (eds), *Juvenile Delinquency in Australia*. North Ryde: Methuen, 1985

Game, A., and R. Pringle "The Making of the Australian Family", *Intervention*, No. 12: 63–83, 1979
Gender At Work. Sydney: George Allen and Unwin, 1983

George, V., and P. Wilding *Ideology and Social Welfare*. London: Routledge and Kegan Paul, 1976

Gershuny, J. *Social Innovation and the Division of Labour*. Oxford University Press, 1983

Gleeson, D. "Further Education, Free Enterprise and the Curriculum", in S. Walker and L. Barton (eds), *Youth, Unemployment and Schooling*. Milton Keynes: Open University Press, 1986

Gorz, A. *Farewell To The Working Class: an essay on post-industrial socialism*. London: Pluto Press, 1982
Paths To Paradise: on the liberation from work. London: Pluto Press, 1985

Gray, I. "Civil Liberties and Young People", *Youth Studies Bulletin*, Vol. 6, No. 3: 30–2, 1987

Graycar, A. (ed.) *Retreat From The Welfare State*. Sydney: George Allen and Unwin, 1983

Griffin, C. *Typical Girls? Young women from school to the job market*. London: Routledge and Kegan Paul, 1985a
"Turning the Tables: Feminist analysis of youth unemployment", *Youth and Policy*, No. 14: 6–11, 1985b

Hall, S., C. Critcher, T. Jefferson, J. Clarke and B. Roberts *Policing the Crisis: Mugging, the State, and Law and Order*. London: Macmillan, 1978

Hall, S., and T. Jefferson (eds) *Resistance Through Rituals: Youth subcultures in post-war Britain.* London: Hutchinson, 1976

Hancock, L., and M. Chesney-Lind "Juvenile Justice Legislation and Gender Discrimination", in A. Borowski and J. Murray (eds), *Juvenile Delinquency in Australia.* North Ryde: Methuen, 1985

Harman, C. *Explaining the Crisis: A Marxist re-appraisal.* London: Bookmarks, 1984

Harvey, K. "Homelessness Among Young Women", in S. Dyson and T. Szirom (eds), *Leaving School: It's Harder For Girls.* Melbourne: YWCA, 1983

Hawkins, G. *Resistances To School.* Sydney: Inner City Education Centre, 1982

Hebdige, D. *Subculture: The Meaning of Style.* London: Methuen, 1979

Higgins, D. "Social Security Review: Young People's Needs", *Equity: A Bulletin of Income Security and Taxation Issues,* Vol. 2, No. 4: 3, 1988

Hindley Street Youth Project *Annual Report.* Adelaide: Hindley Street Youth Project, 1986

Annual Report. Adelaide: Hindley Street Youth Project, 1987

Holbrook, A., and B. Bessant "Responses to youth unemployment in the 1930s and the 1980s". Paper presented at the Conference of the Australia and New Zealand History of Education Society, Adelaide, August, 1986

Hunt, F. J. "The Control of Schooling", *Education and Society,* Vol. 3, No. 2 – Vol. 4, No. 1: 1–15, 1986

Jamrozik, A. "Winners and Losers in the Welfare State: Recent trends and pointers to the future", in P. Saunders and A. Jamrozik (eds), *Social Welfare in the Late 1980s: Reform, Progress or Retreat?.* Sydney: Social Welfare Research Centre, 1987

"Young People, The Family and Social Class: Issues for Research and Social Policy", *Youth Studies Bulletin,* Vol. 7, No. 1: 26–32, 1988

Johnson, L. "The Uses of the Media: An interpretation of the significance of the mass media in the lives of young people", *Discourse: The Australian Journal of Educational Studies,* Vol. 4, No. 2: 18–31, 1984

Johnston, K. "A Discourse for All Seasons? An ideological analysis of the Schools Commission Reports, 1973 to 1981", *Discourse: The Australian Journal of Educational Studies,* Vol. 2, No. 1: 17–32, 1983

Jones, B. *Sleepers Wake! Technology and the Future of Work.* Melbourne: Oxford University Press, 1982

Speech given to Annual Conference of the South Australian Institute of Teachers. Reported in S.A. *Teachers Journal,* 6 August:

15, 1986a

"Living By Our Wits", *In Future*, Vol. 1: 9–14, 1986b

"Barry Jones on why we face a whole new ball game", *Weekend Australian*, 7–8 June: 22–3, 1986c

Karmel, P. et al. Report of the Interim Committee of the Schools Commission: *Schools in Australia*. Canberra: Australian Government Publishing Service, 1973

Karmel, P. et al. *Report of the Review Committee: Quality of Education in Australia*. Canberra: Australian Government Publishing Service, 1985

Keating, P. *Budget Speech 1987–88* (September). Canberra: Australian Government Publishing Service, 1987
Budget Speech 1988–89 (August). Canberra: Australian Government Publishing Service, 1988

Keeves et al. *Final Report of the Committee of Enquiry into Education in South Australia: Education and Change in South Australia*. Adelaide: Government Printer, 1982

Kirby, P. "The Passing of a Golden Age", *In Future*, No. 3: 12–14, 1986

Kirby P. et al. *Report of the Committee of Inquiry into Labour Market Programs*. Canberra: Australian Government Publishing Service, 1985

Kissane, K. "The Education Dilemma", *National Times*, February 28 to March 6: 39–40, 1986

Kultygin, V. *Youth and Politics*. Moscow: Progress Publishers, 1987

Lamble, R. "Car Theft in New South Wales – the size of the problem", *The Insurance Record*, July: 267–9, 1987

Lea, J., and J. Young *What is to be Done about Law and Order?*. Harmondsworth: Penguin, 1984

Legge, K. "$300 000 to promote youth scheme", *National Times On Sunday*, 26 October: 5, 1986

Lever-Tracy, C. "The Flexibility Debate: Part time work", *Labour and Industry*, Vol. 1, No. 2: 210–41, 1988

Levin, H., and R. Rumberger "The Low-Skill Future of High Tech", *Technology Review*, August–September: 19–21, 1983

Loney, M. *The Politics of Greed: The New Right and the Welfare State*. London: Pluto Press, 1986

Maas, F. "The Dangers of Turning 16", *Australian Society*, July: 43–4, 1987a
"The Abolition of Junior Unemployment Benefit – Who should bear the cost?", *Youth Studies Bulletin*, Vol. 6, No. 3: 14–16, 1987b

Mandel, E. *Late Capitalism*. London: New Left Books, 1975

Manwaring, T., and N. Sigler (eds) *Breaking the Nation: A guide to Thatcher's Britain*. London: Pluto Press and New Socialist, 1985

Marginson, S. "The Report of the Quality of Education Review Committee 1985", *ATF Research Notes*, No. 8. Melbourne: Australian Teachers Federation, 1985
"Education Cuts in the 1986–87 Federal Budget", *ATF Background Notes*, No. 55. Melbourne: Australian Teachers Federation, 1986a
"Are Students Human Capital? The Free Market Theory of Education", *ATF Research Notes*, No 15. Melbourne: Australian Teachers Federation, 1986b
"Free Market Education", *ATF Research Notes*, No. 18. Melbourne: Australian Teachers Federation, 1986c
"The May Mini-Budget: Whatever happened to Priority One?", *ATF Background Notes*, No. 64. Melbourne: Australian Teachers Federation, 1987

Martinkus, A. "The Man Behind the Policies" (interview with John Dawkins), *Australian Society*, June: 24–5, 1986

Mattera, P. *Off The Books: The rise of the underground economy*. London: Pluto, 1985

Maunders, D. *Keeping Them Off The Street: a history of voluntary youth organisations in Australia 1850–1980*. Melbourne: Phillip Institute of Technology Press, 1984
"Providing Profitable and Instructive Amusement: Values underlying the development of youth organisations in Victoria", in B. Bessant (ed.), *Mother State and Her Little Ones: Children and Youth in Australia 1860s–1930s*. Melbourne: Phillip Institute of Technology Press, 1987

McCallum, D. "Passing Through the Eye of an HSC Needle", *Education Links*, No. 29: 5–7, 1986

McDivett, I. "Housing and Young People's Outreach: An adjunct to shelters", *Youth Studies Bulletin*, Vol. 5, No. 2: 36–8, 1986

McIntosh, M. "The Family, Regulation and the Public Sphere", in G. McLennan, D. Held and S. Hall (eds), *State and Society in Contemporary Britain*. Cambridge: Polity Press, 1984

McKay, J. "Leisure and Social Inequality in Australia", *Australia and New Zealand Journal of Sociology*, Vol. 22, No. 3: 343–67, 1986

McRobbie, A., and J. Garber "Girls and Subcultures", in S. Hall and T. Jefferson (eds), *Resistance Through Rituals*. London: Hutchinson, 1976

McRobbie, A., and M. Nava (eds) *Gender and Generation*. London: Macmillan, 1984

Miller, P. *Long Division: State Schooling in South Australian Society.*
    Adelaide: Wakefield Press, 1986
Mohr, R. *Distribution and Patterns of Use.* Sydney: Streetwize Comics
    Evaluation Project, Phase 1, 1986a
    *"That's What's Really Happening": Young People's Access and
    Responses to Streetwize Comics.* Sydney: Streetwize Comics
    Evaluation Project, Phase 2, 1986b
Moore, T. "Pop and Politics", *Australian Society*, July: 50–1, 1986
Mowbray, M. "Localism and Austerity". Paper presented at the
    Conference of the Sociological Association of Australia and New
    Zealand, August, Sydney, 1982
    "The Medicinal Properties of Localism: a historical
    perspective", in R. Thorpe and J. Petruchenia with L. Hughes
    (eds), *Community Work or Social Change? An Australian Perspective.*
    London: Routledge and Kegan Paul, 1985
Mukherjee, S. "Youth Crime in Australia: Conclusions", *Youth
    Studies Bulletin*, Vol. 5, No. 2: 2–8, 1986
Muncie, J. *"The Trouble With Kids Today": Crime in post-war Britain.*
    London: Hutchinson, 1984
Murdock, G., and R. McCron "Consciousness of Class and
    Consciousness of Generation", in S. Hall and T. Jefferson (eds),
    Resistance Through Rituals. London: Hutchinson, 1976
Naffin, N. "Women and Crime" in D. Chappell and P. Wilson
    (eds), *The Australian Criminal Justice System – the mid 1980s.* Sydney:
    Butterworths, 1986
National Labour Consultative Council *Labour Market Flexibility in the
    Australian Setting.* Canberra: Australian Government Publishing
    Service, 1987
Nava, M. "Youth Work Provision, Social Order and the Question
    of Girls", in A. McRobbie and M. Nava (eds), *Gender and
    Generation* London: Macmillan, 1984
Neave, R. "Young Women and Juvenile Offences", *Australian
    Society*, June: 31–3, 1986
New Internationalist Theme: "Life Sentence: The Politics of
    Housework", March, 1988
Northern Adelaide Development Board "Northern Adelaide 2000
    . . . the way ahead". Salisbury: Northern Adelaide Development
    Board, 1987a
    "Report of Activities 1984–86". Salisbury: Northern Adelaide
    Development Board, 1987b
Oakley, M. "Development and Decentralisation of an Urban
    Complex: a study of Adelaide and Elizabeth", unpublished

thesis, Advanced Diploma of Teaching, Salisbury Campus, South Australian College of Advanced Education, 1973

O'Connor, I. "Legal Education for Social Welfare Workers: Has it made a difference?" *Legal Service Bulletin*, Vol. 12, No. 3: 93–6, 1987

O'Connor, I., and C. Tilbury "Enhancing Youth Access to Legal Services", *Youth Studies Bulletin*, Vol. 6, No. 3: 22–9, 1987

O'Connor, P. *Refuge Handbook*. Canberra: Southside Youth Refuge, 1985

O'Donnell, C. *The Basis of the Bargain: Gender, Schooling and Jobs.* Sydney; George Allen and Unwin, 1984

Office of Crime Statistics, South Australia *Crime and Justice in South Australia*. Adelaide: Attorney General's Department, 1986

O'Malley, P. *Law, Capitalism and Democracy*. Sydney: George Allen and Unwin, 1983

Organisation for Economic Co-operation and Development (OECD) *Review of Youth Policies in Australia*. Paris: OECD, 1984

Otto, D. "Common Ground? Young women, subcultures and feminism", *Scarlet Woman*, No. 15: 3–8, 1982

Pearson, G. *Hooligan: A History of Respectable Fears*. London: Macmillan, 1983

Pearson, P. *Twilight Robbery: Low-paid workers in Britain today*. London: Pluto Press, 1985

Pisarski, A. "Why Train Youth Workers?", *Journal of the Developmental Youth Services Association*, Sydney, Spring, 1986

Pocock, B., and K. Windsor "Quality, not Quantity", *Australian Society*, April: 38–9, 1988

Poole, M. "Adolescent Leisure Activities: Social class, sex and ethnic differences", *Australian Journal of Social Issues*, Vol. 21, No. 1: 42–56, 1986

Powell, S. "Child Care on the Cheap", *Australian Society*, July: 18–21, 1987

Presdee, M. "Invisible Girls: A study of unemployed working-class young women". Paper presented at the Tenth World Congress of Sociology, Mexico City, Mexico, 1982

"Youth Unemployment and Young Women", *Radical Education Dossier*, No. 23: 4–7, 1984

"Agony or Ecstasy: Broken transitions and the new social state of working-class youth in Australia", Occasional Papers No. 1, South Australian Centre for Youth Studies, Magill Campus, South Australian College of Advanced Education, 1985

"Class, Culture and Crime and the New Social State of

Australian Youth". Paper presented at the Australian
Criminology Institute Bi-Annual Conference, Canberra, 1987

Presdee, M., and R. White "Australian Youth Policies in the '80s",
Youth and Policy, No. 21: 1–6, 1987

Preston, B. "Assessing Testing and PIs", *The Australian Teacher*, No.
20: 15, 1988

Prior, T. "The Nationals' Big Wal lays down the law for
'schoolyard punks'", *Adelaide Advertiser*, 21 June: 19, 1988

Quixley, S. "The relative merits of in-service and pre-service youth
sector training", *Youth Worker Training Handbook*. Adelaide: Youth
Affairs Council of South Australia, 1985

Ramsay, R. "The Drug Offensive: a critical appraisal", *Legal Service
Bulletin*, Vol. 11, No. 6: 264–9, 1986

Raskall, P. "Wealth: Who's Got It? Who Needs It?", *Australian
Society*, May: 21–4, 1987

Richards, C. "Community Groups: Autonomy at risk", *Australian
Society*, July: 46, 1987

Roberts, K. *Youth and Leisure*. London: George Allen and Unwin,
1983

Robins, D., and P. Cohen *Knuckle Sandwich: Growing up in the
working-class city*. Harmondsworth: Pelican, 1978

Rumberger, Russell "An Exchange: The Economic Decline of
College Graduates: Fact or Fallacy", *The Journal of Human
Resources*, Vol. xv, No. 1: 99–112, 1980
"The Job Market for College Graduates, 1960–90", *Journal of
Higher Education*, Vol. 55, No. 4: 433–54, 1984

Ryan, B. "Accountability in Australian Education", *Discourse: The
Australian Journal of Educational Studies*, Vol. 2, No. 2: 21–40, 1982
"Revising the Agenda for a Democratic Curriculum", *Australian
Journal of Education*, Vol. 30, No. 1: 66–84, 1986

Ryan, S. "Future relies on developing skills", *Australian*, 20 August:
21, 1986

Salagaras, S. *Facing the Challenge: a research project into the educational
needs of 15–19-year-olds in Whyalla*. Vol. 2. Whyalla: Western Area
Education Department of South Australia 1985

Sandercock, L. *Cities For Sale: Property, politics and urban planning in
Australia*. Melbourne University Press, 1977
"Who Gets What Out of Public Participation?", in
L. Sandercock and M. Berry, *Urban Political Economy: The
Australian Case*. Sydney: George Allen and Unwin, 1983

Smart, C. *Women, Crime and Criminology: A Feminist Critique*. London:
Routledge and Kegan Paul, 1976

Smithson, A. "Freedom to Criticise: a dilemma for teacher as professional and employee", *Education Links*, No. 31: 16–21, 1987

South Australian Council of Social Service *Poverty in South Australia: a caring State strategy*. Adelaide: South Australian Council of Social Service, 1987

South Australian Education and Technology Task Force *Making Things Work: learning for competence and enterprise*. Report of the Education and Technology Task Force to the Minister for Technology. Adelaide: Ministry of Technology, 1986

South Australian Police *Annual Report 1985–86*. Adelaide: Police Department, 1987

South Australian Youth Incomes Task Force *Report*. Adelaide: Youth Bureau, 1988

Staden, F. "Ignorance is Bliss?", *Youth Studies Bulletin*, Vol. 6, No. 3: 33–7, 1987

Stilwell, F. *The Accord . . . And Beyond: The political economy of the Labor Government*. Sydney: Pluto Press, 1986

Stratman, P. "Legal Issues Particularly Affecting Young Women", in S. Dyson and T. Szirom (eds), *Leaving School: It's Harder For Girls*. Melbourne: YWCA, 1983

Streewize Comics Produced by Redfern Legal Centre Publishing in conjunction with Marrickville Legal Centre and the Legal Aid Commission of New South Wales, 1985–88

Summers, A. *Damned Whores and God's Police: The colonization of women in Australia*. Ringwood: Penguin, 1975

Sweet, R. *The Youth Labour Market: A twenty-year perspective*. Canberra: Curriculum Development Centre (World of Work Monograph Series), 1987

Sydney Independent Study Group "Making Futures for Young People", special double issue of *Education Links*, No. 26, 1985

Thomas, C. "Girls and Counter School Culture", *Melbourne Working Papers*, University of Melbourne, 1980

Thorpe, R. "Community Work and Ideology: An Australian perspective", in R. Thorpe and J. Petruchenia with L. Hughes (eds), *Community Work or Social Change? An Australian Perspective* London: Routledge and Kegan Paul, 1985

Van Moorst, H. "Working with Youth: a political process", in *Beyond The Backyard*, National Workers With Youth Conference Report. Melbourne: Nationwide Workers With Youth Forum, 1984

Wajcman, J., and S. Rosewarne "The 'feminisation' of work", *Australian Society*, September: 15–17, 1986

Wakim, J. "Working with the Streetwise", Progress Report. Adelaide: Service to Youth Council, 1986
Compiler of book of poems by 'street kids', *FTW*. Adelaide: Service to Youth Council, 1987

Walker, J. *School, Work and the Problems of Young People*. Canberra: Curriculum Development Centre (World of Work Monograph Series), 1987
Louts and Legends: Male youth culture in an inner city school. Sydney: Allen and Unwin, 1988

Wallace, C. "From Girls and Boys to Women and Men: the social reproduction of gender roles in the transition from school to (un)employment", in S. Walker and L. Barton (eds), *Youth, Unemployment and Schooling*. Milton Keynes: Open University Press, 1986

Weis, L. "High School Girls in a De-Industrializing Economy", in L. Weis (ed.), *Class, Race and Gender in U.S. Schools*. Albany: SUNY Press, 1987

Wells, G. "Comment" (on the demise of CYSS), Australian Social Welfare *Impact*, Vol. 18 No. 3: 17, 1988

Western Australian Government *Working Together To Beat Crime: The Western Australian Government's Crime Prevention Plan*. Perth: Government Printers, 1988

Westhorp, G. "Lessons from Overseas", a background paper on 'youth guarantee' types of schemes. Adelaide: Youth Affairs Council of South Australia, 1987

Wexler, P., T. Whitson and E. Moskowitz "Schooling by Default: The Changing Social Functions of Public Schooling", *Interchange*, Vol. 12, No. 2–3: 133–50, 1981

White, D. "The New Consolidation of Schooling in Australia", *Discourse: The Australian Journal of Educational Studies*, Vol. 9, No. 1: 72–80, 1988

White, R. "Education and Work in the Technological Age", *Discourse: The Australian Journal of Educational Studies*, Vol. 6, No. 1: 52–68, 1985a
"Australian Teachers and the Impact of Computerization", in Lawn (ed.), *The Politics of Teacher Unionism*. London: Croom Helm, 1985b
Law, Capitalism and the Right to Work. Toronto: Garamond Press, 1986a
"The New South Wales Teachers' Federation: Educational Change and Industrial Strategy", in Spaull (ed.), *Australian Teacher Unionism in the Eighties*. Melbourne: Australian Council for

Educational Research, 1986b
"Getting 'Streetwize' About Legal Rights", *Legal Service Bulletin*,
Vol. 12, No. 3: 90–3, 1987
"Progressive Teachers in Whyalla: School Dynamics in an Age
of Uncertainty", paper prepared for the ATF Research Papers
series. Melbourne: Australian Teachers Federation, 1988
"Students, Vocationalism and Progressive Education",
Discourse: The Australian Journal of Educational Studies, Vol. 10,
No. 1, 1989
Willcox, J. "Elizabeth tops the State in welfare subsidy stakes",
Adelaide Advertiser, 16 April, 1987
Williams et al. *Report of the Committee of Inquiry into Education and
Training: Education, Training and Employment*. Vols 1 and 2.
Canberra: Australian Government Publishing Service, 1979
Willis, P. *Learning to Labour: How working-class kids get working-class
jobs*. Westmead: Saxon House, 1977
"Shop-floor culture, masculinity and the wage form", in Clarke,
Critcher and Johnson (eds), *Working Class Culture: Studies in history
and theory*. London: Hutchinson, 1979
"Youth Unemployment 1: A New Social State", *New Society*,
29 March: 475–7, 1984a
"Youth Unemployment 2: Ways of Living", *New Society*, 5 April:
13–15, 1984b
Wilson, B., and J. Wyn *Shaping Futures: Youth Action For Livelihood*.
Sydney: George Allen and Unwin, 1987
Wilson, P., and J. Arnold *Street Kids: Australia's Alienated Youth*.
Melbourne: Collins Dove, 1986
Wilson, P., and A. Scandia "Questions for the Royal Commission",
Australian Society, September: 31–3, 1987
Windschuttle, K. "High Tech and Jobs", *Australian Society*,
November: 11–13, 1984
"Workfare and full employment", *Australian Society*, December:
17–19, 1986
Winship, J. "'A Girl Needs To Get Street-wise': Magazines for the
1980s", *Feminist Review*, No. 21: 25–46, 1985
Woodger, A. "Youth Advocacy: A Victorian experiment", *Legal
Service Bulletin*, Vol. 12, No. 3: 97–9, 1987
Wrennall, L. "The Turbo Kids", *Youth Studies Bulletin*, Vol. 5, No. 2:
4–8, 1986
Youth Affairs Council of Australia *Creating Tomorrow Today*.
Melbourne: Youth Affairs Council of Australia, 1983
"Law, Social Justice and Young People", Law Issues Paper.

Melbourne: Youth Affairs Council of Australia, 1988

Youth Affairs Council of South Australia "Towards a South Australian Youth Offer: Strategies in the non-government sector". Adelaide: Youth Affairs Council of South Australia, 1987

Youth Worker "The Traineeship Scheme", July: 21–3. Adelaide: Youth Affairs Council of South Australia, 1986

Youth Workers Network of South Australia *Survey Report*. Adelaide: Youth Affairs Council of South Australia, 1984

Index

For EU product safety concerns, contact us at Calle de José Abascal, 56–1°, 28003 Madrid, Spain or eugpsr@cambridge.org.

www.ingramcontent.com/pod-product-compliance
Ingram Content Group UK Ltd.
Pitfield, Milton Keynes, MK11 3LW, UK
UKHW010041140625
459647UK00012BA/1518